MARKET DAY IN PROVENCE

FIELDWORK ENCOUNTERS AND DISCOVERIES

A series edited by Robert Emerson and Jack Katz

Market Day
in Provence

Michèle de La Pradelle

Translated by Amy Jacobs

THE UNIVERSITY OF CHICAGO PRESS · CHICAGO & LONDON

The late Michèle de La Pradelle was directeur d'études at the Ecole des Hautes Etudes en Sciences Sociales and the author of *Paris Luxe* (1975) and *Urbanisation et enjeux quotidiens* (1985).

Amy Jacobs has translated a number of books, including *An Anthropology for Contemporaneous Worlds*, by Marc Augé (1999).

THE UNIVERSITY OF CHICAGO PRESS, Chicago 60637
THE UNIVERSITY OF CHICAGO PRESS, LTD., London
© 2006 by THE UNIVERSITY OF CHICAGO
All rights reserved. Published 2006
Printed in the United States of America

15 14 13 12 11 10 09 08 07 06   1 2 3 4 5

ISBN: 0-226-14184-5 (cloth)

Originally published in French as *Les vendredis de Carpentras: Faire son marché, en Provence ou ailleurs*, © Librairie Arthème Fayard, 1996

Library of Congress Cataloging-in-Publication Data

La Pradelle, Michèle de.
    [Vendredis de Carpentras. English.]
    Market day in Provence / Michèle de La Pradelle ; translated by Amy Jacobs.
        p.   cm.—(Fieldwork encounters and discoveries)
    Translation of: Les vendredis de Carpentras: faire son marché, en Provence ou ailleurs.
    Includes bibliographical references and index.
    ISBN 0-226-14184-5 (cloth)
    1. Markets—France—Carpentras—Social aspects.
    2. Fairs—France—Carpentras—Social aspects.   3. Carpentras (France)—Commerce—Social aspects.   4. Carpentras (France)—Economic conditions.   I. Title.   II. Series.
        HF5474.9C37713 2006
        381'.1'094492—dc22
                                                        2005014063

This book is printed on acid-free paper.

TO J.B.

Contents

Foreword to the American Edition

The writing of this brief foreword as 2005 begins is a bittersweet task. Michèle de La Pradelle died in the last days of 2004 of a rapidly developing cancer. She had already structured a rich legacy in the creative sensibilities of devoted students, but her leaving abruptly interrupts the trajectory of a meticulously cultivated career. This is a moment to celebrate continuity in a partial rebirth. Readers will quickly discover how well this book preserves the unique delicacy of her investigations. Michèle de La Pradelle wrote with such a thorough fusion of mind and materials that her spirit is here made palpably accessible to a new world of readers. The calm patience of her curiosity is itself an inspiration. In chapter after chapter, she turns our gaze back to the Provençal market to appreciate yet another nuance of its seemingly indefatigable social life.

Part of the distinctive quality of mind evident in this book is Professor de La Pradelle's easy way of crossing boundaries that usually keep others unaware of the existence of essentially harmonious, foreign voices. Without a pause, she serves the interests in Provençal life of a mixed readership of cooks, tourists, journalists, novelists, and a variety of social scientists studying markets, culture, and interaction in public. Thanks to Amy Jacobs's fluid translation, there is no disfigurement of the elegantly written French text, innocent of pedantic mannerisms, which was a winner of the Prix Louis Castex of the Académie Française, as it metamorphoses into a colorful second life in English. While written within anthropological traditions, this close investigation of the traditional Friday market at Carpentras injects an elusive truth into academic battles over the sociological nature of ethnicity. Professor de La Pradelle was vividly aware of how the past practically constitutes the grounds for current realities, but she was also constantly alert to the anchoring of current routines in historical myth. In this book-long meditation, the micro, the meso, and the macro find their most adept conciliator. The reader's eye never leaves the interaction details of the market's mise-en-scène, even while our guide reveals the vast institutional supports working just offstage. The text's focus on the nuances of behavior in the market gradually draws out an emotionally profound portrait of national identity from what others might render as insignificant if slightly histrionic routines of public commercial life.

At the risk of using a cruder language than any Michèle de La Pradelle would have used, I would point to three revelations in her book. One is the dependence of characteristic small moments in the local market scene—ways of inspecting, bargaining, presenting, and taking postures toward goods, customers, vendors, and bystanders—on "backstage" operations that must be kept out of immediate awareness for the market to work. These include the biographies that lead people to become vendors, the ways that vendors get what they sell, the strategic shaping of just how they sell, the machinations of the volunteer-agent who allocates spaces to vendors, and the racial and economic stratification of vendors relative to each other and to the owners of storefront shops. In Michèle de La Pradelle's broad investigative reach, sociologists will recognize the familiar ambition of ethnographers to document how each moment of social life, no matter how creative, spontaneous, and idiosyncratic it may seem, is the product of a vast collective act, the fitting together of lines of activity by myriad people acting in times and places so separated that most of them remain lifelong strangers to each other. Anthropologists might stress the transformation in the nature of goods and people as they make their way to a vendor's stall. Michèle de La Pradelle seamlessly traces both themes, in the process making clear the depths of institutional strategy and symbolic magic that underlie seemingly prosaic and transparent acts of buying and selling on Carpentras's public streets.

A second revelation is of a sort much more familiar to continental European sociological thinking than to Anglo-American social researchers. The book is structured around a tripartite comparison. At the center is the open stall market that for centuries has materialized on Fridays on the streets of Carpentras, a town in southern France not far from Avignon. On one side of this "farmers' market" is the scene at Auchan, one of France's "*hypermarchés.*" *Hypermarchés* are bigger than U.S. supermarkets. In exterior appearance they look like our "big box" warehouse stores, but they sell a comprehensive range of consumer goods—groceries from canned goods to fresh fish, cheap clothing, expensive wine, serious hardware, and so on—in retail-oriented quantities arranged on shelves and cut to order at service counters. On the other side is the truffle market that operates in Carpentras outside of tourist pathways in the late fall and early winter. What makes the analysis rare is not the "compare and contrast" of patterns or structures, but the negations and mimicked connections with other settings that shape the market experience in Carpentras. The claim is not only analytical, it is phenomenological. Like an American student of behavior in public places, this French researcher portrays the situationally manifested realities of Carpentras, but she knows that, because the people there also have absorbed the lore about the truffle market and regularly go to stores like Auchan, the experience of any market scene will always be formed through a contrast with what is understood to go on in those elsewheres. Part of the unusual challenge she takes on is to convey the significance to the Friday market in Carpentras of what is experienced as not happening there. The Carpentras market exists as a distinct kind of social experience in large part by claiming to be like the truffle market, which mostly it is not, and by claiming not to be like Auchan, which in many ways it is. If the market at Carpentras is to work, customers there must at all times take for granted that they are not at Auchan and that the scenes around them bear some continuity with the much less accessible truffle market, which in fact does not depend for its existence on its image as a traditional market or on tourists. The truffle market is so richly negative in its routines—fleeting in time, the personnel invisible to outsiders, transactions hidden in hushed small group scenes and idiosyncratic expressive conventions—that it does not have to profess not to be something else in order to be itself. But the Carpentras Friday market must pull off a double negation, making clear that it is not Auchan, and doing this without any apparent effort.

That the Carpentras Friday market creates a seemingly unique place without committing any indictable fraud, even after Professor de La Pradelle has exposed all its sleights of hand, indicates the third and most surprising revelation in the book. Many sociological ethnographers can recount their shock at being attacked when they have brought their manuscripts "back to the field." But despite showing a behind-the-scenes that is studiously obscured on the market's front stage, this book was not only widely acclaimed in France but also specifically embraced by its subjects. Some critics were unhappy that a notorious episode from 1990, the anti-Semitic desecration of a recently interred body in Carpentras's centuries-old Jewish cemetery by skinheads, and the ugly realities behind it, were not mentioned. But the fact that the everyday cultural drama of the Provençal market covers over ethnic conflict is not incidental to its charms.

On the contrary. The Provençal life that Carpentras represents is a cherished part of the vast project of sustaining a national French identity. Revered in family memory, honored with visits that are vacation rituals, memorialized in every cultural medium from popular song to best-seller novel to iconic cinema setting, the Provençal market is a central institutional support for an ethnic identity that the French construct as transcending time, urban/rural place, and differences in social status. As Michèle de La Pradelle emphasizes, the market is a place that gives material meaning to community, creating an equality among all who can pay for a tomato, regardless of their differences in social position elsewhere in life. We are used to thinking of the market in capitalism as the source of hardened, harshly divisive inequalities, but (in an irony that may not be coincidental) in its everyday micro-interactions, a public street market selling groceries and low-cost dry goods is the most egalitarian and gently communalistic site in social life.

Current social research bristles with a combination of fascination and discomfort over definitions of ethnicity and national identity. Many academics point to the destructive political manipulations in which ethnic identity, nationalism, and racial ideology are promoted, in the process throwing radical doubt on whether there is a foundation to the claims and anything to be honored. Many movements in academic life run in the opposite direction, demanding respect for the historically denied rights of subjugated minorities and resisting assimilation to the point of flirting with claims that a given ethnic identity carries a distinct sacred/spiritual character. Michèle de La Pradelle here shows us a third, more comprehensive and compelling way to understand the social construction of ethnic identity, which she neither debunks nor treats as immanent.

The communal identity claim that is sustained by the Carpentras Friday market is at once sensual and mystical in its appeal. The market's stalls reek with claims about roots. There is the "*terroir*" or soil that supposedly gives a unique flavor to its products. There are the market's location and conventions, which are recognized as grounded in practices dating back millennia. Family outings to the market are understood to grow from the base of intergenerational memories. And there is the insatiable appetite to celebrate the truffle: the quintessential product in the iconography of provincial markets, the truffle is a fungus that grows in enigmatic ways, hidden under the earth, on the roots of a subset of oak trees, and allegedly discoverable only with the aid of special hunting pigs and dogs.

But even more important for understanding the construction of national ethnic identity is the author's clarity on the relative transparency of the drama of collective roots. With the exception of some foreign tourists, virtually everyone knows discrediting facts about the collective drama (that this vendor just moved down from Paris, that those meats were bought from the same wholesaler who supplies the supermarkets, that the prices are no bargain, and so on), and yet it all still works. It is not sufficient to say that everyone agrees to suspend disbelief; that simply begs the question: Why should they? If the Provençal market is theater, its theatrical qualities are not to be used by the analyst only in the style of a Goffmanian metaphor, as a heuristic device. The Carpentras Friday market is compelling theater because it works as a vast participatory dramatization; its genius is as a kind of method acting for the masses. This study enables us to see that the power of culture to confer group identity lies not, in some mystical way, in its substantive contents, nor is it simply derivative from its political manipulations. The appeal of ethnic culture is in its value as an excuse for the process of creating culture, just as, for masses of mundane believers, religion is an indispensable excuse for sustaining faith, just as sex is often a convenient excuse for making love. If the play's the thing, it's not the folio but the playing that is the inspiration. *Market Day in Provence* guides the reader to see the transparency of the historical and substantive claims of ethnicity, in the end revealing that what motivates ethnic culture are the seductive impersonations it makes possible.

Jack Katz

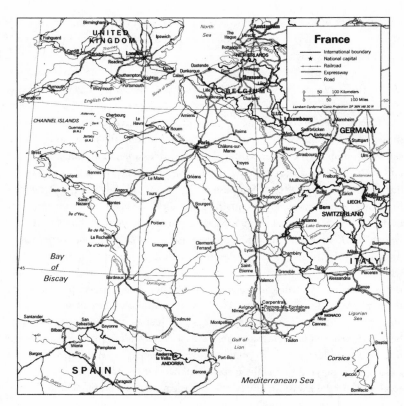

France

Carpentras, the old city

Introduction

Market society has no need of its street or stallholder markets. It has developed other forms of distribution that better satisfy its demand for rational efficiency and profit. And yet such markets persist (though there are fewer of them in some places than others). France's "new cities" clamor for them; planners see them as a way of preventing suburbs from becoming dormitory communities; and in the ill-defined "conurbations" of the West Coast of North America there is a passion for these new "agoras," which provide them at last with a center if not a past. In the early 1980s this paradox was surprising enough to the French government, then launching a vast research study of commercial urban development, that they appealed to an anthropologist to explain why this seemingly anachronistic institution, whose economic advantages were at the very least problematic, was enduring and indeed thriving.[1]

I

In truth, the question already implied a certain type of response, and the fact that the government had turned to an ethnologist reflected a well-established supposition. The change that my study was supposed to confirm was that markets had gradually been emptied of their "economic" content and were now of exclusively "cultural" significance. Though such markets had once occupied a crucial place in regional economies (went this interpretation), they no longer did so. What was being perpetuated was the institution's "animation" and "entertainment" function. The markets themselves played a marginal role in distribution networks, but the modern public loved these powerful moments of local life, which gave them a taste of types of social interaction, sociability, that had more or less vanished. In the cold world of market rationality, markets offered a little extra soul. They thus belonged on the "symbolic" side of things, assumed to be ethnology's turf.

I understand better now the discomfort this caused me then. We live in an "economism"-saturated world, economism being the illusion that the abstractions necessary for constructing economic knowledge are themselves reality. The "truth" of every exchange or trade situation is imagined to inhere in its economic aspect; "the economic" is thought of as defining the deep structure of these realities, while social relations among actors in them are presumed to be no more than a façade, if not entirely superfluous. The tendency is to make markets, the institutional spaces in which buyers and sellers meet and engage in transactions, into mere manifestations or epiphenomena of The Market, the abstract set of transactions occurring around a given category of goods (strawberries or steel, for example), a geographical area (the European Common Market), or, more generally, the laws of the market economy. It is as if once the economic functioning of a market had been explained, there were nothing more to describe.

Economism thus defined, and often remaining implicit, is the reason that only markets in exotic or archaic societies—societies assumed not to know the joys of the market economy—seem possible objects of anthropological analysis. The more widespread Market domination is, the less markets seem to have a consistency of their own that would make them worthwhile objects of study.

This understanding is reinforced by our most powerful theoretical representations of how societies evolve economically. Karl Polanyi and the school of economic anthropology he inspired established a radical opposition between modern society, where the self-regulating Market reigns, and traditional societies, where goods exchange is always "embedded" in the social relations of persons and groups (kinship, status hierarchy, domination, and so on).[2] One effect of this understanding was to free us up to look at "others" without the blinkers of market-economy categories. But given that our own society was understood to be governed entirely by Market determinism upon its emergence from the "great transformation," another effect was that *our* marketplaces, in contrast to those of Indians or Berbers, ceased being relevant objects of anthropological study.[3] In an all-encompassing market economy it does not seem legitimate to isolate a particular moment in the institutional arrangement of exchange, or to consider the physical places in which exchange is practiced as relatively autonomous microsocial spaces. Because market transactions in modern societies seem to involve nothing more than an anonymous mechanism, those transactions are believed not to lend themselves to anthropological analysis, which by definition focuses on actors, their identities, the play of their interrelations, and the meanings they deal in and manipulate.

And yet the fact that goods exchange no longer takes place among relatives, clans, chieftains and their subjects does not mean it ceases to be a social relation, to involve decidedly social relations. Instead, those relations are expressed in a different mode, which I purport to describe here. In fact, purely economic analysis of exchange always involves a reasoned construction of social reality rather than simple empirical observation. To focus on the value exchanged on markets, while dismissing as secondary the ephemeral society that takes shape around a market stall or counter, is to engage in an abstraction of the same nature (though perhaps slightly more legitimate) as considering the potlatch to be nothing more than a system of interest-bearing loans.

The same logic dictates that everywhere in modern society that the monetary value of transactions is low, economic explanation is insufficient, and this means that the market, picturesque micro-event with no significant effect on the balance of payments or the firmness of the franc, becomes a social space once again and thereby a fitting object for ethnology. It seems to me, however, that the tiny Monday morning market at Saint-Didier [Provence], the open-outcry wholesale fish market at Concarneau [Brittany],[4] the famed Hôtel Drouot auction house in Paris, and the Wall Street stock exchange can all equally be the focus of anthropological study. We need to overcome a kind of unreflecting resistance that leads us to believe that wherever economic stakes are high, social relations are diluted or effaced, and wherever they are limited, sociality blossoms and thrives as an end in itself.

It is nonetheless far from self-evident how to produce a properly ethnological description of a market exchange situation in our society—as I realized almost as soon as I set foot in the marketplace, or marketplaces, of Carpentras. It was not easy of a Friday morning in the Place du Palais, and even less so plumb in the midst of the trucks lined up on the cement surface of the *marché-gare*, former rail station where growers sell produce wholesale, to get the right perspective, that distanced but attentive view of social relations that never reifies economic life, from which Polanyi and his students looked at "others' " markets. First, my training had not prepared me for this. I knew considerably more about the itinerary of "Kula" objects in the Trobriand Islands than the trajectory of hothouse tomatoes from grower to housewife's basket, more about the subtleties of the gift or matrimonial alliance arrangements than the circuit of an itinerant stallholder.

Above all, as I observed and described actors' behavior, how could I keep from thinking in terms of the "great divide" between the economic and all the rest, i.e., the "social" or "cultural," between the serious and the superfluous, when the actors themselves had internalized that vision of things and spontaneously shaped their discourse in terms of those categories? When I tried to get the grower-sellers gathered at the counter of the *marché-gare* café at six in the morning around the first *petit blanc* of the day[5] to explain to me the ambiguous relations between them and the shipper-buyers, good-humored at some moments, at others tense and conflictual, they kept pointing me back to the hard law of the Market and the benefits of competition. Conversely, when I interviewed customers here and there among stallholder display tables on the Rue de la République, asking them about the morning's market purchases, my object of study seemed to shrink down to the market as celebration of a local tradition and respondents' declared delight in the convivial social interaction they can engage in there.

I was sorely tempted to divide my material into transactions carried out by actors reduced to their role of buyer or seller, and encounters, conversation, and the many ways the citizens of Carpentras make their market the city's primary locus of local sociability. Geographers were the first to provide minute descriptions of street markets and regional market networks and how they fit into wider-range distribution circuits. In this their works were precious to me. Moreover, they have been of crucial importance to the few existing ethnological studies of markets.[6] But geographers' monographs never seem to go beyond adding a "sociocultural dimension" to study of the market's "economic role," explaining, for example, that wherever commerce "is no longer an indispensable basic activity, it becomes a matter of initiation, entertainment, or a relay."[7] For geographers, markets are places where information, local news, rumors, and in some cases propaganda circulate, together with commodities. In sum, above and beyond their economic function, markets have an "animation" or "entertainment" function that geographers, concerned to provide an exhaustive analysis of the phenomenon, are careful to take into account.

Other thinkers and other references led me to the same impasse. I was working at the time with Michel de Certeau. His way of describing "the art of doing" and "user practices" as subtle and ever-available means of subverting accepted norms was then renewing the flagging genre known as "analysis of everyday life." If I used de Certeau's terms, I could think of the market as an institutional frame within which to identify the thousand and one ways people have of getting around exchange rules, playing cat and mouse with them, "poaching" within and by means of the dominant cultural economy,[8] appropriating codes and spaces "so as to compose hitherto unknown formalities."[9] This kind of approach would allow me to bring to light the tactics used in everyday life— "the nocturnal ground of social activity," as de Certeau once put it—that a certain sociologism tended to obscure. But the danger in doing that was that I might reinstate the distinction between the market perceived as a more or less functional cog in the national distribution system and the social and cultural uses people make of it.

The whole problem is due to the unanalyzed or repressed economism that prohibits people from thinking—or makes them forget—that market exchange is itself a social relation of a certain type. Whether people are negotiating the price of truffles, artworks, or tomatoes, goods-value exchange defines a situation where, during a given stretch of time, in a particular place, and for that particular activity, the actors recognize each other as equivalent partners no matter how unequal they may otherwise be in terms of power or status. All such partners accept the rules of the game, the first of which is that none may claim any kind of advantage or privilege external to the exchange situation. Of course, each "player" has his or her hand (the quality of the merchandise or the art of displaying it to advantage, buying power, acted indifference, and so on), but each is also just as worthy as any other. In this ephemeral society of buyers and sellers, all are alike and recognized as such. People have no names or qualities, at least in principle.

Wherever transfer of goods is mainly a matter of reciprocity rules used by partners to affirm, confirm, or claim an identity or status, the market situation remains exceptional or marginal. But the fact that market exchange occurs between anonymous or impersonal partners in no way implies that it is not also a social relation. We tend to imagine that once the exchange relation has been freed of kinship or hierarchy constraints, it enters into a world of pure economic science where disembodied rational agents are each motivated by margin calculations and all are influenced by the "invisible hand." This is why it seems that anthropological description of market exchange can only involve identifying whatever interferes with the "normal" functioning of such exchange, i.e., functioning in compliance with economists' models. I am referring here to what can happen when "traditional" relations interfere in "modern" exchange, e.g., symbolically or affectively aberrant uses of market value and money. We easily forget that neutralization of actors' identities is the properly social condition for market exchange. As such, it has nothing to do with the abstracting move of making the market an object of economic understanding and knowledge. Not knowing the buyer I have in front of me or acting "as if " I did not is one possible way of treating the other. This fully social behavior must not be confused with the intellectual procedure whereby real actors are replaced by economic agents.

Societies do not wake up one fine day and discover the market economy as if it were Euclidean geometry or thermodynamics. They are either endowed or not with the institutional and historical conditions that allow for the instating of a particular mode of social relations: market exchange. For this mode to appear, it is enough for the partners to find themselves in a situation where the game is governed by the rule of anonymity. Once persons have been effaced—for Weber the market is the "most impersonal relationship of practical life into which humans can enter with one another"[10]—commodities raise their head. Marshall Sahlins was surely right to imagine market exchange as a possible though extreme figure in the series of "primitive exchange" forms; namely that of "negative reciprocity," a type of relation where any sort of "sharp practice" goes, because partners' identities are either temporarily bracketed off or deliberately ignored.[11] This type of relation is unlikely to occur within a network of kinship relations, neighbors, or allies, where the purpose of circulating goods is precisely to signal to the other who one is or claims to be. Marx noted that genuine market exchange presupposed partners unknown to each other and thus tended to develop at community boundaries.[12] Likewise, if there is never a moment when the prince and the powerful stop coming first, then the game is rigged from the start. This is why Montesquieu insisted that the law prohibit nobles from engaging in commerce: "Merchants with such rank would set up all sorts of monopolies. Commerce is the profession of equal people, and the poorest despotic states are those whose prince is a merchant."[13] Conscious of this requirement, the kings of Imerina forbid their relatives to perturb the markets with claims to special privileges. As Françoise Raison explains, the point was to "make the market a place of horizontal relations . . . among isolated individuals defined wholly by their quality of anonymous seller or buyer." [14]

Market exchange thus presupposes—and thereby induces—a social space of nonsaturated identities. The effacing of statuses and qualities that is the market's negative condition institutes a specific field of social relations. When individuals enter a market, they leave their identities at the door, presenting themselves as mere "bearers" of the economic relation. In market exchange, as Marx put it, "persons exist for one another merely as representatives . . . of commodities." [15] *Homo economicus* (or *mercantilis*) is by definition anybody; he has no clan, no cast, no nation, or at least this is the rule by which he is engendered. But Marx saw this as nothing more than the mechanism that maintains the fetishistic illusion particular to bourgeois society—relations between people disappear, to be replaced by social relations among things—whereas entering into relation behind a mask in fact makes possible another kind of relation, one that breaks with the rules governing daily-life activities and the forms of domination that structure society as a whole. My hypothesis here is that the equivalence of trading partners, a formal equivalence of course but also fully acted out, together with the anonymity that partners adopt for the length of the transaction, always engenders a specific type of social space. That space is of course ephemeral, confined within highly specific temporal and spatial limits; it is perhaps almost a fiction. But it is worth describing for itself. It is my object and that is my objective here.

I was far from having such a clear understanding of things on the frosty May morning in 1980 when I arrived in Carpentras. It was afterward, upon thinking about what I had observed and what people had explained to me of the different markets in the city, but also bolstered by my experience of other exchange situations, that I gradually developed a plan for anthropologically studying market exchange. I had been sent to study an institution, the *marché forain* (itinerant stallholder street market), that seemed to constitute a miraculously preserved tradition on the fringes of modern forms of mass marketing. I had been sent by people who assumed that ethnology's particular vocation was to study local survivals and microcultures. But by virtue of the "field" so defined, I found myself face to face with an anthropological object—market exchange as social relation—that proved relatively novel and actually quite contemporary, in that under cover of Provençal exoticism and ancestral heritage, the logic of behavior on this market, the perpetual play around anonymity that is its operative principle, was in fact thoroughly modern.

2

It was not yet 6 a.m. when the high-speed night train from Paris arrived in Avignon. There has not been a direct train from Paris to Carpentras for a long time, and the first bus for the city left only two hours later. The Avignon bus station, which during the summer theater festival is full of colorful crowds every hour of the day and night, looked modest and provincial that cold spring morning. Only one café was open in the sleeping city, serving a handful of benumbed customers.

The bus goes along the Avignon ramparts, then whizzes past warehouses, auto repair shops, supermarkets, and apartment complexes. Rows of thuja soon announce the countryside, though the area remains rather undefined, with villas, flower gardens, gas stations, used car lots, and furniture stores eating into the farmland. To the untutored traveler, the bus stops in this landmarkless space seem arbitrary. And the passengers, often elderly or immigrants from the look of them, all carrying voluminous shopping bags, do not appear clearly either city or country dwellers. The bus arrives at Pontet, where many get off on Saturdays: this is the stop for the Auchan supermarket and mall, where people from Carpentras come to spend weekend afternoons and go shopping.

The next twenty-kilometer stretch of highway is very slow going. Carpentras inhabitants often prefer to bypass it, taking a slightly longer route through the small town of Pernes, attracted, too, by the landscape out that way. Long hedges of tall reeds and cypress trees trace a neat checkerboard of 30- or 40-square-meter fields full of trim crops. The strict ordering of the place, the flatness of it, the water flowing everywhere through canals and *filioles* [water furrows], the meticulous care with which the land is tended are a surprise for the traveler more accustomed to the Provence of Jean Giono or Cézanne.

After Monteux, the billboards multiply; supermarkets with vast adjoining parking lots reappear; settlement becomes denser, the roadway narrows, the white pyramid of Mont Ventoux looms onto and blocks the horizon—we are entering Carpentras. The city is built on a vast plateau that slopes gently to the south and drops off sharply in all other directions. This is where the Rhone valley begins, and the foothills of the Alps. After Mont Ventoux come the Gigondas mountains; further south the Vaucluse mountains; and beyond the

Coulon valley, the Lubéron mountain range. To the south and west is the monotonous Comtat plain, the geometric spaces of its irrigated farmlands stretching as far as the eye can see. The area's wealth is recent. Extensive irrigation works entirely transformed the natural conditions of the nineteenth century. The main canal passes along the city's edge. Beyond it stretches a landscape of fruit trees—cherries around Saint-Didier, apricots around Suzette—while the hillsides on the other side, near Beaumes-de-Venise and Caromb, are more or less given over to vineyards, though this is also where "truffle oaks" like to grow.

Carpentras today is made up of two distinct zones: the old city, which is what people mean when they say "the city," and its immediate surroundings, designated by the same place-name. There are no longer any thick walls delimiting the city center—the ramparts were destroyed in the nineteenth century, with the exception of the Porte d'Orange. But the city remains sharply divided. Wide boulevards lined with tall trees form an unbroken green enclosure around the center. Within: a dense, homogeneous maze of houses on narrow, ochre-colored streets; without: an *extra muros* space where a few disparate constructions dot gardens and fields for growing *primeurs* (early fruits and vegetables).

Once exclusively farmland, the immediate outskirts of the city are today overrun with warehouses for packing and shipping produce, storage facilities, commercial-use buildings, apartment buildings, and freestanding houses. But beneath the apparent disorder, the space is sharply differentiated; the architectural hodge-podge in this rough, discontinuous country landscape is in fact governed by a strict ordering principle. The plain to the north of the Auzon river with its landmark aqueduct, dominated by the pebbly slopes of Mont Ventoux and the "Dentelles" of Montmirail, is known to be cold and windy. Here stand side by side the two most dilapidated public housing projects, Les Amandiers and Les Eléphants.

The area to the west near the freeway entrance to Avignon was developed earlier. Behind the stone walls facing the calm, pretty streets of the neighborhood on the other side of the Boulevard Albin-Durand, one can make out vast nineteenth-century houses on solid foundations. Further along, the scene changes to an anarchic proliferation of apartment buildings and tract housing. To the south, on lands traditionally used to grow fruit and vegetables, is the site of the first *marché-gare*, set up by the municipality in 1963. It was soon closed down and the area declared a future industrial zone. In the 1980s, however, that project was not the success its creators had hoped for. Even after following the

9

many signs to it, you never feel you have arrived. Beyond the fringe of heterogeneous constructions on the city's edge, beyond the former *marché-gare*, where a few crates of *primeurs* are all that are handled now, beyond the immense public housing development of Pous-du-Plan, there are a few packaging and crate manufacturers, a few construction material warehouses and wholesale centers, but they look quite lost in these fields striped with protective plastic tunnels for growing *primeurs*. Cypress trees have been pulled up in some places and the earth overturned, but there has been no follow-up. Elsewhere a cement surface has been laid and left, calling to mind an abandoned parking lot.

East of the city, the suburbs seem to spread against their will. Construction in the area below the Allée des Platanes is relatively modest: scattered among the pines are an Intermarché supermarket and a few apartment buildings named "residences" (Résidence du Comtat, du Ventoux). In the direction of the Vaucluse mountains the relief sharpens. Here the view is of an unbroken landscape of vineyards and orchards. Some city dwellers still spend Sundays in their family *cabanon* amid these vineyards.[16] On the hillside of La Lègue, once laced with olive-tree-lined strolling paths, the local bourgeoisie have recently built vast, comfortable villas. Their terraces look out on a compact mass of pink-tiled roofs, the old city, from which protrude the belfry and the steeples of Saint-Siffrein cathedral and the Observance.

3

Why was I studying the Carpentras market and not the picturesque covered market of Limoges, or the relatively urban market on Avenue Joliot-Curie in Sarcelles?[17] I have no particular links to the Carpentras area, no cabanon on the slopes of Mont Ventoux. I could answer with a tedious account of a series of contingencies—but in truth I do not remember who once described the vitality of the Carpentras market to me with such enthusiasm—or prosaically announce that it was a choice made by default. Or I might acquit myself thus: to feel fully receptive, I preferred a "field" far from Paris, and for the sake of convenience, a medium-sized city. I might also mention a few swiftly dispelled illusions about the mildness of the Provençal climate.

But from my point of view here, that of an anthropologist studying market exchange, the fact is that any market would have done. Indeed, if the hypothesis of this work is on the mark, it should be verifiable everywhere. The Carpentras market is therefore only an example, and it would lose this virtue if it had not been chosen fairly arbitrarily. It might be thought that in selecting Carpentras I had a culturalist bias, that I would understand what I observed on this market as the effect of a particularly warm, convivial variety of sociability, the Provençal variety. This is not the case. In my view any market situation, mutatis mutandis, generates a specific field of social relations—a statement no truer for the South of France than the North.

This understanding does not affect the perfect uniqueness of the Carpentras market, however. That market generates its own field of social relations, different from the one in Apt or Vaison-la-Romaine, for instance. In order for the case of Carpentras to function as an example, it had to be described in its full singularity. Therein lies the paradox of the anthropological approach: however general the object, the study necessarily involves a detailed account of the particular reality at hand. It must both take into account the identity of the observed society, the fact that it is different from any other, and make that society function as an example. The Samo, however Samo they may be, must be able to stand as a conclusive case of "semicomplex systems," and the Nuer, as Nuer as they are, must also work as a model of "segmentary" political structure.

My interviews with Carpentras inhabitants thus inevitably implied a malentendu, this being one possible form of the "distance" both presupposed and induced by any anthropological proceeding. It goes without saying that for the inhabitants of Carpentras their market is unique. The finest market of all, they explained to me—and their pride is nothing new. "Carpentrassians," wrote a Carpentras potter of the early nineteenth century in a poem in Provençal of which I here offer the gist, "may glory in the fact that nowhere else in France or Europe can such merchandise be found or such trading done."[18]

Their market is also the oldest, they believe. Indeed, they like to think it has existed since time immemorial. Situated midway between the Rhone valley lowlands and the foothills of the Alps, sheltered from the impetuous *mistral* wind, how could Carpentras not have attracted surrounding populations since time began, as its Celto-Ligurian name, Carpentoracte, "high city passed through," seems to indicate? Its destiny as a marketplace may likewise be read, so they say, in the name Forum Neronis[19] that the city bore during the Roman period, after Tiberius Nero, an obscure lieutenant in Caesar's army, triumphed (easily) over the local tribe of Meminians—though the existence of a market (near Saint-Siffrein) is attested only from the fourteenth century.[20]

Carpentras thinks of itself first and foremost as a trading city, and the market is therefore an essential reference in self-definition and celebration of local identity. Carpentrassians think of Friday mornings as a way of collectively commemorating the original vocation of the place. The market is the soul of the city—yet another reason it has no equal.

Conscious and proud as they are, the city's inhabitants were not at all surprised by my interest in their market. They saw my painstaking study of it as homage to its exceptionalness: why expend such effort on a place if it were not truly original? The fact that Carpentras was for me merely an example, the idea that my choice could have been arbitrary, was not locally acceptable or even conceivable. The question "Why Carpentras?" rather than Limoges or Sarcelles is simply not asked in Carpentras. Affirming one's identity precludes thinking of oneself as a case among others. People told themselves I was just writing another monograph, aimed like all the others at promoting the image of their city by celebrating the merits of its market. It is true that in my way I have helped make it "a market like none other," as it now has "its own" doctoral dissertation, unlike Apt or Vaison, where chance might just as well have led me. [21]

Despite its reputation for being the cultural poor cousin of its brilliant rival Avignon, Carpentras in the 1980s boasted dynamic intellectual activity in the field of local history; studies by local scholars were being published by the Editions du Nombre d'Or and the review *Rencontres*, put out by the Association Carpentrassienne de Diffusion Culturelle. Among the first-ranking local experts was Doctor Brun, much more interested in his historiographical researches than in his profession, dentistry, which he practiced in the office inherited from his father-in-law.

Clearly the scholars were going to have to think of me as a new member of their little set. Indeed, the curiosity manifested by my questions seemed to them continuous with their labor of memory, and they were pleased to initiate a stranger into their common history. They knew that I too spent long hours poring over the archives in the elegant *hôtel particulier* that houses the Bibliothèque Inguimbertine, core and centerpiece of the Comtadine patrimony, whose directors—among them Georges Bataille (though I have some difficulty imagining him as a local-culture clerk) [22]—have so enthusiastically assembled period furniture and local painters' work for the city's various museums.

I too, of course, occasionally allowed myself to be taken in by this enjoyable game. The more familiar I became with the city and its market, the more I felt a party to my interlocutors' pride. But whatever impression I may have given and however pleasant I found the diverse manifestations of local narcissism, I

12

was interested not so much in the content of popular or scholarly knowledge of the place as in why this was so important to these people, what was at stake in it for them. Theirs was indigenous ethnography, aimed not only at celebrating or transmitting but also at producing a local microculture. The Friday market was one of that culture's major rites. But I was not there to participate in their enterprise, to give it the official stamp of "scholarly" ethnography, and I certainly was not there to portray the market and its city as a closed little world by listing features, traditions, or customs that distinguished it from all others.

The often passionate interest in the market I encountered among Carpentrassians and inhabitants of the surrounding area had to be understood as an essential part of how the market functioned. I could hardly describe the field of social relations generated by the market without taking into account the decisive role the market played in defining and perpetuating local identity. The fact that for the inhabitants the market was a "monument" as unique as the famous "ball with rats" on the pediment of the Porte Juive [Jewish gate][23] or the venerated relic of Saint Mors in the church of Saint-Siffrein[24] helped make it a truly public place, and therefore one that could not be reduced to its distribution function. If I failed to perceive the forms of collective identification that were both the condition and the real point of the behavior I observed, I would fail to grasp the event of the market, the meaning of what happened around the stalls on Friday mornings.

Buying one's turnips in front of one of France's oldest synagogues, one's cap at Barnabé's in front of the Roman victory arch described by Prosper Mérimée[25] (this is also where the summer festival is held), and one's fresh peas beneath the belfry of the counts of Toulouse—these are not matters of indifference, especially since there is always a local scholar ready to explain how the city owes its prosperity to the privilege granted its market in 1155. The market would not be what it is without the imagery that goes with it and the imagery it has elicited. "Old, indolent lady of Provence, Carpentras nods and dreams," wrote André de Richaud in 1927. "She remembers her youth, the Jews locked away in their obscure quarter, gallant, bergamot-scented bishops extending the purple *berlingot* of their amethyst ring to the lips of the Comtat's *grandes dames*, and the sight of young Petrarch playing on the cathedral steps, hair blown back by the wind . . ."[26]

Dreaming is the order of the day here on Friday mornings. A particularist spirit that has hardly any occasion to show itself these days comes back to life around the market. Thanks to the popes, the Comtat Venaissin, plumb in

13

the middle of Provence, long enjoyed the privilege of being officially outside French territory.[27] People use history to distinguish Carpentras from its neighbors, though this does not stop them from presenting the city to the outside observer as "typically Provençal." Its present prosperity is thus a pretext for recalling the brilliant court of the Holy See six centuries ago. It matters little—dreams are not bound by history—that the pope held court here for no more than a few months and never returned after the disastrous conclave of 1314.[28]

And it gets one nowhere to object that there is little connection between the splendors of bygone days and the prodigious display of victuals in today's city's streets. You are reminded that Pope Clement V, of fragile health, chose to leave Avignon for the Comtat, [29] which he called "the garden of my delights," an expression that in the minds of Carpentras market regulars is less likely to evoke Hieronymus Bosch than the vast, sumptuous selection of fruits and vegetables at Boyac's Jardins du Comtat in the Place de la Mairie. Relating how the rector appointed by the pope to manage the Comtat fought with the city bishop over who would get the best fish just in from the Mediterranean or the streams of the Sorgue, each staking his claim the instant the market opened, is a way of giving some "historical" substance to the fishmongers' stalls at the Porte d'Orange, the last vestige of the city walls. These anecdotes are on everyone's lips, even in this region, the *patrie* of Daladier, where the Parti Radical is traditionally strong.[30] They all work to inscribe the town's market somewhere in the heart of Christendom.

4

Whatever the pride inspired in Carpentrassians by the Friday stallholder market, symbol par excellence of local identity, the city owes its role as regional capital to what is known here as the *marché-gare*, the wholesale produce market held on and identified with a vast cement surface on the edge of the city lit by glaring streetlights. Nothing picturesque about the *marché-gare* and nothing to set one dreaming.

This market corresponds to quite a different history, but one that is also heroic and therefore also often recounted. An epic story, worthy of the American Wild West, of how in the space of a century the peasant people of the place, ruined by phylloxera and the sudden obsolescence of the madder plant,[31] transformed an expanse of scrubland (*garrigues*) into a meticulously tended garden. They say they turned the red-pebble soil of the southern part of the city into gold. The memory of this more recent adventure, in which relatively new generations shaped the landscape and established the current way of life, is just as important in collective Comtat heritage as more distant historical references.

In fact, given the numerous trading and shipping activities that go on here, Carpentras may be said to live off its wholesale market. The *marché-gare* operates daily from April through October. (On winter Fridays it is replaced by an extensive but rather sorry-looking wood and grapevine market, where producers stand behind rows of sticks that all look alike. I confess I rather neglected that component.) But though it is a center of Carpentras trading activity, this kingdom of tomatoes, melons, and the famous "Carpentras strawberry" was ultimately moved to the periphery of the city, first to Les Platanes, a wide space running along the eastern edge; then, in 1963, a few kilometers further out into the ill-defined zone of warehouses, storage facilities, and plastic-covered plantings described above. The relegation of the wholesale market to a location outside the city is a spatial reflection of the distinction between the roles of the two markets. At one, national-level professional buyers purchase agricultural products from grower-sellers; at the other, the same products are redistributed, supplied, to inhabitant-consumers. In the first case products become commodities through wholesale price determination; in the second they cease to be commodities in order to be consumed. These two antithetical economic functions were once closely intertwined in a single urban marketplace.

A person going to the Carpentras market on a Friday morning in the first decade of the twentieth century moved from retail sellers in one street to specialized trade stalls in the next. City inhabitants were allowed, within limits, to purchase provisions at the latter. Today only a few hard-to-recognize vestiges of this market subsist, with one exception—the truffle market. This highly particular market is held each winter Friday off to the side of the general activity yet only a stone's throw from the secondhand clothing dealers and low-priced jeans stalls in the Place de la Mairie. Despite appearances, it is the largest market of its kind in France.

The street market, then, which people like to imagine as having operated for centuries, is in reality, in its present form, quite a modern phenomenon, the result of moving commercial trading activities to distinct places such as the *marché-gare* and into specialized networks. Though one can still buy one's thyme or chives there, the bulk of these crops is now processed by the Ducros herb and spice company and shipped to supermarkets throughout Europe. The traditional look of the market, which explains much of its success, is thus due to

15

an amputation: everything related to modern forms of trade of the sort adapted to producing for a far-flung international clientele has been moved out. Only truffles, a luxury item and a tightly circumscribed market, small quantities circulating among few hands, have escaped exile. The truffle market remains a place where country people can come and sell what they have gathered in a market where almost all other sellers today are professional retailers. It is a precious, archaic, "authentic" touch, to which Carpentras "Fridays" owe a significant part of their renown.

Carpentras is thus a complex marketplace, a combination of complementary functions carried out in different spaces at different times. The street market is only one component among others. But the three worlds composing the Carpentras market are decidedly distinct, as I learned very early on. I did often encounter the same actors in the different markets. Consider Chardon, a wine-grower from Caromb, whose assistance was crucial in initiating me into the mechanisms of the *marché-gare*. In the summer he was at that market regularly, selling his *chasselas* or *muscat-de-Hambourg* table grapes, while on winter Fridays he was very likely to take a stroll through the wood and grapevine market before going to join his wife at the street market in the Place de la Mairie. Likewise, as soon as the *trufficulteurs* had pocketed their truffle money, they almost never resisted the pleasure of checking out the vast display of fishing and hunting equipment at the entrance to the street market. And yet the further I progressed in my analysis, the clearer it became that from one marketplace to the next, the same actors were acting in different "plays." The rules were not the same for the three games; they defined the contours of three heterogeneous spaces. In terms of economic geography, my three markets today are three distinct components of one market. It was only in the vast single market of bygone days, which I managed to reconstitute thanks to the archives in the Bibliothèque Inguimbertine, that the three were truly united.

To demonstrate that in moving from one market to another one changes social spaces, it should be enough to show the different position I occupied in each of them. In the joyous bustle and disorder of the streets of the old city on Fridays, in the dense crowd moving slowly among the stalls, the extreme diversity of actors is apparent at a glance: tourists, city residents, farmers from the surrounding countryside, others. Lost in this disparate, anonymous mass, where people come as much to *bader* [gander] as to shop, I am utterly unremarkable and there is nothing unusual about my presence. For people who don't know me, I am only one customer among many in a place that great numbers

of foreigners choose to visit. For the many inhabitants who know I live here—
I rented a small apartment in the Rue Saint Jean, next to the *souspréfecture*—I
easily pass for a woman who has adopted and been adopted by the place; there
are many such living in the villages on the slopes of Mont Ventoux and the Vaucluse plateau, and they never miss the Carpentras market. Even my insistent,
wide-ranging curiosity, though it cannot be confused with the well-meaning,
naive questions of passing tourists, does not appear entirely out of keeping: I
am there every Friday, and this is my way of joining in the show, participating,
willingly and knowingly, in the staging of it.

But not far from the crowds and congestion in the Rue de la République a
completely different event is taking place, almost as an aside. This market, the
truffle market, seems a small, closed world. In a clearly delimited area, sheltered
from inquisitive eyes and in accordance with strict protocol, a few *rabassiers*,[32]
together with a few truffle brokers and processors and a few informed amateurs, trade in this unique edible.

At the street market, I am continuously implicated in the scenes I observe.
In addition to the information I collect, I can use my experience as actor, the
"competence" as customer I have acquired at the permanent stalls of the Rue
de Bretagne and at the Place d'Aligre market in Paris. In sum, I can engage
in "self-analysis," as Marc Augé counsels.[33] But at the truffle market I have no
such means at my disposal. I am entirely external to the little club of truffle
people, and I need an introduction. I met a few of them during the summer I
spent studying the *marché-gare*. Standing between rows of crates bursting with
peaches and apricots, up against the hard law of the Market, producers would
say to me, "This winter you'll see—the truffle market is a different matter!" In
early November I began reminding my interlocutors of this promise and ultimately gained access to the place, officially open to all but in practice restricted
to the initiated. I was indeed a foreigner there, but one whom they enjoyed
teaching the rudiments of their art and sharing their enthusiasm with. Like the
hunt, the truffle is a genuine object of passion, and a pretext for interminable
tale telling. The mystery of it, vague and secret, hovers over the stage on which
it is exchanged.

Once again, this is an entirely different world from the disenchanted one of
the *marché-gare*. There trucks line up at sunrise on an eighteen-hectare platform
in special parking lanes marked by type of product, and everything is organized
strictly the same way every day—an orderliness that evokes the cold rationality
of a business. Beneath everyone's apparent affability, the atmosphere is heavy

with pent-up, controlled tension. In this professional gathering place where everyone has a specific procedure to perform and knows exactly whom he is dealing with, I am once again immediately perceived as an outside observer— whose presence is especially untoward in what is an essentially male world. But once the procedure is over and the grower-sellers are engaged in animated conversation at the nearby truck-stop café over an *andouillette* [pork and veal chitterling sausage] and fries and a small, round glass of côtes du Rhone red wine, they are not loath to call on me to testify to the poor price melons went at ("Just wouldn't go up today!") or tomatoes ("Italy and Spain are flooding us!") not to mention the red spiders "eating up the crops."

However different they may be, each of the three markets I observed successively in various seasons confirmed my hypothesis in its own way. Because exchange brings temporarily equal partners together in the same game, this activity in all three cases gives rise to a specific space where ties to ordinary social life and the relations of inequality that govern it have been broken— in three distinct ways. Carpentras was proving a "field" itself susceptible of comparative internal analysis.

At the *marché-gare* the stakes are serious. In the confrontation organized here between producers and buyers, the prosperity and very survival of the former depend on the price determined with the latter. After the siren has sounded, buyers step into the long lanes where producers stand next to trucks overflowing with melons or tomatoes awaiting what fortune will bring. They are anxious to see if the buyers are "moving in quickly" or if, on the contrary, they're "roaming." If buyers are "nervous," haggling will be intense and the producers will have to struggle to keep prices from falling. "They" pass by or stop next to one or another truck, size up the quality of the merchandise at a glance, throw out a figure. Sometimes, particularly in slump periods, producers will call out to buyers—"So you'll take them?"—but it is out of the question to make a sales pitch. The transaction lasts only seconds. Seller accepts with a nod, or refuses and demands a higher price, though if buyer turns away seller is probably ready to pull him back by the sleeve, so great is the dread of having to "bring the goods back home."

Once I had become familiar with the *marché-gare* I took the liberty of pointing out to Belin, a young, modern-spirited farmer who "does" melon near Pernes, and Pons, specialized in strawberries but also an inveterate *rabassier*, that this trading procedure is time-consuming and not really in their interest. "But it gives everyone a chance," they answered. Nothing is fixed in advance, one can win as well as lose: "It's the best solution, because it ensures equality and fairness." This explains their unwavering attachment to the institution, which is also "natural" and "has existed since time began." "We've built cathedrals out of cement," said one, "but this is still the market of olden days, archaic, from the time of the Gauls!"

In reality, the game of supply and demand is skewed here by the combined effect of a number of factors: the parallel practice of selling produce directly to noncommercial customers, competition from neighboring markets, unequal access to economic information, and so on. The shippers generally win out over the duration of a "campaign" [season a given fruit or vegetable is sold], as the growers in their way know full well: "They're the masters." Still, every morning the game begins again from scratch. He who has "no luck" today might just have some tomorrow. It is surely this form of distributive justice, ensured by face-to-face confrontation between buyers and sellers, as well as the pleasure that "colleagues" take in getting together every day in a space remote from the domestic world and farming constraints, that make the shippers' domination acceptable.

When transactions get under way at the truffle market slightly before 9 a.m., the atmosphere is radically different. There is no perceptible tension between the *rabassiers*, who have set the week's "harvest" at their feet, and the truffle brokers and processors there to buy it. Trading takes place in silence—no haggling, no nerves—and is over in a few minutes. Demand is always greater than supply, and the economic stakes for sellers are much lower than at the *marché-gare*—you can't make a living selling truffles. The confrontation between equal trading partners here is more a matter of an immutable, customary ceremonial. It would not do for truffles to be traded like *marmande* (beefsteak) tomatoes or "big green" [table grapes]. The partners are there not to do business, it seems, but rather as connoisseurs whose purpose is to ensure that the *rabasse* journeys from the arid slopes of Mont Ventoux to the supercivilized world of luxury item shops like Fauchon and Lamazère under the best possible conditions.

Specific social fields develop around exchange at both the *marché-gare* and the truffle market, but they involve professionals only, sellers who have temporarily left behind the domestic and village framework of agricultural labor, and buyers for whom trading is the main activity. Though the modes are different, in both cases the partners' formal equality engenders a relative solidarity between actors who are nonetheless rivals. Since selling at the *marché-gare* involves a direct one-to-one relation with the shipper (as opposed to a collective auction procedure, for example), competition among producers is masked. No one attributes his misfortune to the good fortune of his neighbor, and the shipper appears to be an indispensable mediator, the guarantor of equal opportunity. He is of course the main beneficiary of the operation, but with the consent of all. As for the truffle market, the very object of the exchange is a rare, wild-growing edible whose secrets are known only to the experts. As such it engenders a small world of initiates, *rabassiers* and traders, all engaged, however unequal their economic power, in a fraternal celebration of the same cult.

At the street market, the general principle of equality operates in an entirely different way, opening up a public space rather than organizing a "closed circle" or pit where supply and demand face off among professionals. There are no prices to be determined here, and the general tone is of an entertainment, though some are there to spend and others to earn. In the streets and squares of the city, around an itinerant stallholder's stand or in the cluster of people listening to a street hawker, every customer, however powerful or humble, is worth every other. Professional sellers run the game of equality with everyone's accord and participation. The market is a fictive world. Since people "hide their power in their pocket," in Marx words, they can act as if everyone were equal. This is obviously no miraculously preserved haven of equality, but ordinary relations of hierarchy or domination, while neither forgotten nor denied, here take on the syntactic form imposed by trading game rules. For a few hours and within very specific limits, the classic liberal representation of society as a pacified world in which free and equal individual wills coexist seems realized, for the pleasure of all and in an atmosphere of generalized good humor.

The street market is not a coming together of experts but a collective ceremony in which each person is both actor and spectator. Each has temporarily left at home his or her status or quality to play at being nothing more than a Comtadine going to market, and everyone treats each other as a fellow citizen. In the name of this shared identity and under cover of anonymity, it is possible to transgress ordinary custom and practice, in a kind of generalized interacquaintanceship as joyous as it is make-believe. The attraction exercised by such markets no doubt explains why market society is pleased to sustain them without really needing them.

PART ONE

The Market Stage

1. City Tour

In my memory, Carpentras is a sunrise city; it shows its truest face at dawn.[1]
The streets and squares of the city center are sound asleep, or look to be, when
the small, rickety vans packed to the gills with fruits and vegetables come rock-
ing along the boulevards. The city sleeps on, but at the edges it is already
furtively astir.

The morning agitation is most intense on Fridays, when it penetrates the old
city. Well before six, heavy trucks arrive at the city gates, illuminating the Place
du Théâtre with their headlights. Some stop there: truck doors bang shut; unloading begins immediately. Others move cautiously with a muted roar into the
thick, shuttered silence of the Rue de la République. A few head up the steeper,
less practicable Rue Vigne, rattling my windowpanes. Slowly, obstinately, they
push along the narrow streets to their usual spots. The widest arrive first—
later the streets will be so crowded they could not get in that far—and these
sellers take longest laying out their wares. Vendors set up by decreasing order
of truck size. After the big mobile shops come vans, then cars with or without
trailers.

Stallholders park as soon as they arrive at their spots. Mobile shops are
parked directly on the right of way, while sellers who use their vehicles only to
stock merchandise park some distance back. If the street is too narrow, they unload and go park elsewhere. Trestle tables, boards, stall structures, and canopies
are positioned quickly. The movements are precise, and talk is reduced to a
minimum. Perdiguier, who sells shoes, needs over an hour to set up on his thirty

meters of tables, whereas egg and goat cheese vendors, who often display their wares on simple folding tables, are not in such a hurry. The traditional stall is getting stiff competition these days from the mobile shop with sales counter. But even these are often extended by means of tables and trestles.

The first to arrive are already piling up colorful bolts of cotton and silk, hanging lace curtains, carefully aligning men's caps. Nearby, a *charcutier* is hanging sausages and mortadella rolls from the uprights of his truck. At the pretty produce shop named Jardins du Comtat (Place de la Mairie), on the outdoor display tables set up on market day, employees are building pyramids of tomatoes, aligning melons, piling up lettuce heads. In winter the work is done in the half-light with benumbed fingers. It becomes harder to circulate around seven, when supply-side agitation is at its peak. The last vehicles negotiate their way among the trestle tables. The contrast is sharp now between the empty side streets just touched with sunlight and the long, shimmering ribbon of activity that winds through the heart of the old city.

Place du Théâtre—that is, the northeastern side of the *place* officially called Aristide-Briand, but that name does not seem to be used—is an essential pole of the street market. Situated at the intersection of highways to Avignon, Pernes, and Saint-Didier, this square is sometimes called Place Notre-Dame in memory of the eponymous gate destroyed along with the city walls in the 1800s. It is nearly impossible not to pass through, as it adjoins the main north-south thoroughfare into the city center, the Rue de la République, and is the starting point for the outer boulevards running east and west. This is where the old merchant city meets the lush irrigated *primeur* farmland. Carpentras's vocation to be a combined agricultural and commercial center is highly visible here. Elegant, imposing buildings line the square. The *hôtel-Dieu* (hospital) commissioned by Bishop d'Inguimbert, with its long, tall-windowed façade topped by flambeau urns in pure eighteenth-century style, attests to the glorious past of the Comtat capital, while hotels and banks are evidence of the city's current dynamism.[2]

The Place du Théâtre maintains its privileged position on Fridays. It is one of the main loci of the market and the means of reaching the rest of it. This is where vehicles and buses let people off coming in from the country. The size of the square, its renowned merchants, most of whom are traditional stallholders from well-known families, and the diversity of available products explain why it is bustling with customers as early as 8 a.m. There are at least thirty stands of all sizes here.

This is also where the truffle market is held every week in the winter. Though at a slight distance from the rest of the activity and relatively inaccessible to strangers, it is nonetheless a focus of general attention, as reference point—stallholders unload "in front of the truffles," "just behind the truffles"—and the place where habitués discuss what price the black diamond will bring today or comment on the presence of this or that local hero of the truffle world, thereby keeping a sort of chronicle of the weekly event.

Near the hospital, a set of wide, shallow stairs, vestige of the Dominican monastery, descends toward the intersection at the edge of the square. This is where *fripes* (secondhand clothes) are sold. Dresses, shirts, pants, and blouses are heaped onto bare boards laid over low trestles, a tangle of different fabrics and sizes, men's and women's jumbled together. By 9 a.m. a colorful, heterogeneous crowd—ordinary Comtadines, immigrant workers, passing tourists—are elbowing into the bays and turning over the merchandise in tireless search of a bargain. A shirt is extracted from somewhere near the bottom of a pile; the customer lifts it up for examination in full sunlight before asking the price. On top of the steps, two or three secondhand luxury clothing dealers set up. These clothes are on hangers on long racks: immaculate starch-stiff white shirts, tiny price tags—one hardly dares touch. In display cases set on damask-covered folding tables, a few objects from another time: antique pocket watches ornamented with brilliants and lids featuring enamel-painted portraits and scenes, glittering paste belt buckles, tortoiseshell pill boxes . . .

The center of the square is occupied by *la confection*. About fifteen stands offer quite ordinary clothing: canvas and corduroy pants, jeans, heavy knit sweaters, plaid shirts, batches of socks. In summer, garlands of bright-colored T-shirts attached to awning poles twist in the sun, giving the whole place a festive air. Some stands are specialized in men's, others in women's. The labyrinth also features baby clothes and lingerie. In front of the Crédit Lyonnais, Perdiguier *père* and *fils* sell shoes from their mobile shop: sturdy ones for walking and working in the country, "city" shoes of comfortable appearance, carpet slippers that never wear out, and so on. At the edge of the market space, there is another big mobile shop, this one a hardware and cleaning products "bazaar," a sort of downsized, itinerant BHV basement.[3]

During the hunting season, a big stall in line with the Rue de la République sells cartridges, game bags, boots, hats, knives, and other gear. This is where truffle excavators customarily spend a part of their morning's earnings. Next to it the small "Maisons Provençales" truck often sets up, with models of local villas similar to the full-sized ones on view on the way into the city: pink rough-cast walls, a covered terrace for meals. Information and sales brochures available here.

Often enough, the voice of a hawker pitching his product may be heard above the general hubbub. The Place du Théâtre is a favorite spot for *posticheurs* touting and demonstrating the merits of a miracle stain remover or ever-so-easy-to-operate food processor.[4] A small crowd regularly gathers around, scattering when the spiel is over. In summer, "pizza trucks," *beignet* sellers, long rows of all-purpose cooking pots, and diverse clay receptacles set out on canvas cloths on the ground take their places among the usual stands.

The market continues from the square into the Rue de la République, penetrating the old city. The city center is a tight weave of streets, buildings joined and pressed close together. Into the narrow spaces left free by this configuration the market flows, infiltrating the labyrinth of narrow tortuous streets, many of which give onto unexpected public squares. At first glance, it seems to invade everything, insinuate itself into the smallest interstices. But a more attentive look reveals that it is organized along two axes, one running north-south between the Porte d'Orange and the Porte Notre-Dame, another east-west between the Porte de Mazan and the Rue de l'Evêché. It is only after entering the heart of the city, between the episcopal palace and the town hall, that the market flows unhindered into nearly all available space. In fact, its trajectory follows the streets on which the main storefront shops are located.

In the Rue de la République as elsewhere, the tightness of the space requires stallholders to set up in the roadway and sometimes on the sidewalk. The stalls are not in an unbroken line, as they are in Paris, and stallholders are careful to allow pedestrian access to fixed boutiques, though some stalls do somewhat block display windows. Here there are no mobile shops, except in an occasional recess or where the street widens. The sedentary shops in the Rue de la République sell prestigious goods: perfume, jewelry, sweets, clothing, cameras, and the like. They are among the city's finest and best-known. The thirty or so market stalls here are generally of modest size, and with the exception of a shoe stand, are small businesses run by a single person or couple. They are not always the same from one Friday to the next; this is one part of the market where stallholders are likely to be "occasionals." The products on sale are extremely varied. Next to a "Paris articles" stand (the term generally refers to notions), a man engraves name and address plates; baby clothes may be purchased next to a Bible stand; tools next to used books. But the stands fall roughly into two categories: "crafts" and "organic" products (lavender sachets and other fragrance diffusers, wooden toys, leather bags and belts), sold primarily by stallholders without a permanent spot; and clothing, "fittings for the body" in administrative language, a term that encompasses hosiery and notions, and fittings for the home, all sold mostly by regulars.

The intersection of the Rue de la République and the Rue du Vieil-Hôpital is one of the liveliest spots in the market. This is where the city's most renowned *posticheur*, Jacky Thevet, exercises his talents. A native of the region who lives in Avignon, Thevet has been coming regularly for twenty-five years. There is enough space here for a stall open on all four sides, enough space for a crowd to gather round. And Thevet always gets his crowd, a mix of potential customers and amused onlookers often there just for the show. His script is always the same, and the regulars in the audience eagerly await their favorite bits, as at a concert. The idea is simple. He chooses a couple, usually country people or immigrants, and makes his pitch to the woman, presumably an expert in his subject and likely to hold the purse strings. His dishcloths were woven in the Vosges, his blankets are made of merino wool, his sheets won't fade at 60°C. Because the wife "knows about such things" she can have eight dishcloths for the price of six, four blankets for the price of three—he counts them out ostentatiously, leaping from corner to corner of his stall with each new item, unfolding each piece of linen, exhibiting it on all sides, then briskly folding it up again and piling it onto the arms of the dumbfounded husband, who ultimately disappears behind a mountain of napkins, collapses under sheets and bedspreads, to general laughter and merriment.

Further on, the Rue de la République intersects the Rue du Collège and the Rue Moricelly to form the Place Sainte-Marthe. The houses here are imposing, richly decorated. The *place* holds ten or so small stands: a honey producer, a goat cheese maker, sellers of novelty and imitation jewelry, candy, underwear, faïence, and earthenware.

At the threshold of the Rue Moricelly the market stops. The city's most elegant buildings are on this street. Despite the damage Carpentras suffered in the nineteenth century, its architecture remains fairly uniform and is not without grace. Most houses on this street are two and three stories high with a supplementary half story, "the attic," characterized by a horizontal line of square openings. This is where mulberry leaves were left to dry when many of the city's inhabitants kept silkworms and were engaged in some farming activity. The pulleys used for bringing up the leaves may still be seen on several façades.

The prestige of this street cannot be fully explained by its architectural qualities. People speak admiringly of the *hôtels particuliers* (private mansions) of the Pazzis and the Isnards, whose ancestors won renown in the time of the popes; they speak of the magnificent wrought-iron balustrades of their staircases. The old Comtadine families living in this street are evoked with veneration—an elderly demoiselle, for example, of whom one may catch a glimpse in her garden overgrown with wisteria and lilac, moving amid stone statues enlaced with fig-tree branches. The street is named after one of the local "benefactors," a baker's son and freemason who in the 1880s, after making his fortune, undertook a major reconstruction program, one feature of which was to destroy the Vieille Juiverie [old Jewish quarter]. The synagogue barely escaped this treatment. The Rue Moricelly is sometimes called by its former name, Rue Dorée. Shrouded in mystery, a discreet vestige of the former Comtat capital in the midst of today's hardworking merchant city, the street does not figure on everyday itineraries.

The Rue de la République leads to the Place du Palais, the historical heart of the city. Along this narrow rectangle the city's two major structures, Saint-Siffrein cathedral and the episcopal palace, stand side by side—an unlikely arrangement that somewhat recalls certain Tuscan cities. The main entrance to Saint-Siffrein is slightly off the square. The seventeenth-century façade of the adjoining palace (which in 1801 became the hall of justice) is harmonious but harsh, its rigor broken only by the entrance gate, topped by a majestic balcony.

Old Jeanjean parks his small van at the entrance to the palace, sits on the tailgate in front of a folding yard table and lays out small bags filled with seeds. Known to all who come here, he is the most striking figure of the square, and his activity seems to sum up that of the entire place. He is, however, nothing more than the last vestige of the old "grain market" in a space otherwise given over today to dealers in clothing and accessories (sunglasses, purses, belts, and so on). You can get both the latest cheap fashions (T-shirts, windbreakers, scarves) and more traditional items (classic men's hats, straw hats, caps, and slippers), as well as nearly everything sold in city boutiques. Some of these stands specialize in a single article: women's aprons, sweaters, socks.

The Place du Palais is also the fabric kingdom. There are actually only two fabric stalls, but one would think there were more because the wares are so amply displayed. One of them, the biggest mobile shop of the market, partially hides and blocks access to the entrance to Saint-Siffrein. A short way onward, next to Gilbert Boniface and his ready-made curtains—mounted so the customer can appreciate them "in situ"—and right in the middle of the square, is the chaotic treasure of Noël Cappo's bazaar: sponges, shoelaces, clothespins, dishcloths, cleaning brushes, floorcloths, bathmats, and tubes of brilliantine piled into plastic baskets and supermarket carts.

The approximately twenty stands along this long, narrow square are positioned as on a street, lined up either against the cathedral and palace or a few meters in from the square's stores and businesses (Prisunic supermarket, Banque Chaix, Bar des Palmiers, and so forth). But there is space enough next to the major stalls (the fabric concern employs five people), whose owners have in many cases been selling here for twenty years and more, for a few "occasionals" with more flamboyant merchandise to set up: scarves, sunglasses arrayed in an open umbrella, the newest sewing machine models, jewelry in small display boxes. These sellers make the goods for sale here seem less homogeneous than they are. A watch peddler carefully goes through his spiel; a young Senegalese squats next to a red canvas cloth selling his poorly tanned bush hats. At the end of summer market mornings, two brass instruments and a guitar playing in a nearby café may be heard above the continuous, subdued bustle of the square.

At the far end of the Place du Palais, the market splits in two, moving into the Rue d'Inguimbert on the right, and straight ahead into the Rue de l'Evêché toward the Porte d'Orange. Lined for all its length with stands pressed close together and close up against the permanent boutiques, the Rue de l'Evêché is a bottleneck where people are continually jostling each other. The sun penetrates only late in the day, which reinforces the sensation of confinement. The products for sale here are fairly diverse. Food predominates, but what is most striking is the extreme specialization of each stand. People come here to buy irregular or superfluous items—"Friday items" par excellence—rather than the usual weekly provisions. At Mistral's big stand you can get olives and brine-prepared products; Fouvot sells herbs and spices; one stand has nothing but socks; another only live fish and birds. Ricci has been selling his *blouses pour dames* (smocks) here for twenty years. Morin's is the place to go for "four o'clock" biscuits.

At the intersection of the Rue Raspail and the Rue des Halles, the way widens to form the Place de l'Horloge. Behind the Fontaine de l'Ange, a work by the Bernus brothers, renowned eighteenth-century Comtat sculptors, the stalls are mixed in with boutiques. One of them, Fructus the fishmonger, is at the foot of the belfry of the counts of Toulouse. Further on, the street becomes less hospitable. A sharp wind blows through here in winter—it's cold at the Porte d'Orange. Though there are only two sizable fish stalls here, everyone thinks of this as fishmonger territory, and it is easy to forget the stands selling *viennois-erie* [baked goods: croissants, brioches], eggs and poultry, and so on. Carefully aligned on cool, fragrant ribbons of algae are bright red mullet and *rascasse* [scorpion fish] next to silvery bream; then heaps of whiting and sardines. Hampers full of smoked herring and sprats are on display at the end of the stall. Wearing a big blue apron, Bachini slices down into the dense dark-red flesh of a tuna.

This seems the outermost edge of the market. That fishmongers should be relegated to it recalls that they have never been well loved. The authorities already had it in for fishmongers at the time of the popes; their cries disturbed religious services. Fish, however, has always been a prized item in Carpentras, from the time of the aforementioned struggles between the rector and the bishop.

On either side of the Rue de la Porte-d'Orange are the poorest neighborhoods of the old city, inhabited almost exclusively by immigrants of North African origin, who make up half of the city's foreign population, this in turn amounting to 13 percent. The majority of them are employed in agriculture. Some are housed on the farms where they work; most live either in public housing projects on the periphery of the city, especially Bois-de-l'Ubac and Les Amandiers, or in this northwest sector, in dilapidated, unsafe buildings lacking basic facilities. A "Ville moyenne" [medium-sized city] agreement signed with state and regional authorities has enabled Carpentras to undertake a vast rehabilitation program, but work had not yet begun in this area, the block known as Saintes-Maries and the Rue Archier, when I began my study. The contrast then was striking between this northern sector of the city, lugubrious, poorly maintained, and the rehabilitated rest, with its newly rough-walled façades, manicured little squares, and recently resuscitated gardens full of lemon trees and aralias.

On the other side of the massive square tower of the Porte d'Orange is a vast, windswept esplanade. After the tumult of the old city and being jostled and cramped against the stalls, one suddenly has the sensation of wide open space. The "Dentelles" and Mont Ventoux are visible in the distance. In the gray light of the olive trees one can make out the towns of Bédoin at the foot of the mountain, Beaumes-de-Venise, Le Barroux huddled around its château. Closer in is the wine-growing region of Caromb, the beginning of the plain.

In the center of this vast square cut through by the circular boulevard is an ever-present "pizza van." This is also the beginning of Avenue Notre-Dame-de-Santé, which runs into the northern outskirts. Down the hill on the other side of the boulevard, a few buses wait to take people back to the neighboring villages. Business here is not brisk. There are not more than a dozen stands to the right of the gate; neighborhood residents buy butter, eggs, cheese, an occasional fresh or dry goat cheese from a small producer. To the left, in the direction of La Pyramide, is a display of gardening tools and machines. This was where the grape market used to be, mostly wine grapes. It was one of the most active wholesale markets, where city residents also came since many in those days made their own wine.

Today wine grapes are sold at the *marché-gare* or directly by cooperatives. This area is quite empty, and the tiny live poultry market is hardly the thing to bring it back to life. This specialty market used to extend the length of the boulevard all the way to the Jeu de Ballon. Though I had been told it was now at the Porte d'Orange, I had some trouble locating it. In fact, it is held right in the middle of the boulevard, among the parked cars on the central strip. There are fewer than a dozen sellers spread out over a hundred or so meters, either professional retailers or farmers, most of them older people who come irregularly from neighboring villages (Flassan, Pernes, Malaucène). Each displays either up front or in the back of the car or van a crate or wooden cage containing four or five chickens or guinea hens. The two retail stalls stand out sharply by their size and the quantity of animals for sale. The bigger retailer, from Orange, has a huge blue marquee. Under the half-lifted tarp of his sizable truck are stacked dozens of cages. A few of the animals are standing on their cages and seem free to move about, to lord it over their imprisoned fellows. Customers are few, mostly North African. Not many housewives are willing to kill and pluck a chicken these days, and there is no longer any wholesale market for this product.

The Porte d'Orange, close to neighborhoods where immigrants live, is in fact renowned for quite a different type of trade. This is where the "slave market" was held when I was living in the city; the term appears in a virulent article in *Le Provençal* denouncing hire of illegal farm laborers. Attracted by Vaucluse wages, hundreds of immigrant workers would arrive in Carpentras at harvest time, most from Tunisia and most through organized channels but without any chance of obtaining regular, legal work. Men wanting to sell their labor gathered at dawn around the gate. Standing, sitting on the stone wall, they waited to be chosen by a "packer-wrapper." Farmers and occasionally other employers drove by in small vans looking for the strongest. In the 1970s there were apparently several hundred such workers. In the early 1980s, the number had dropped to fewer than fifty.

From the market's outer edge, I return to its busy center less than two hundred meters away. A slight distance past the Place du Palais, the Rue d'Inguimbert widens, forming what people persist in calling the Place aux Oies [geese] because of its swan-ornamented fountains but which the mayor's office has renamed Place du Festival. Every July, in the shade of the victory arch, the Carpentras festival competes with those of Vaison-la-Romaine and Orange. The *place* opens to the right into the space that used to be occupied by the city prison. In terms of market products, the Rue d'Inguimbert is continuous with the Place du Palais: there are two bazaars and a few stalls selling fabric and conservative clothing. The only merchant in tune with the tastes of the day is the Parisian Provençal Annick Ceret, in a stall filled with pink and mauve Indian dresses.

Opposite the post office, you turn left off the Rue d'Inguimbert into the glass-roofed Passage Boyer, taken up entirely by "crafts." There are about forty stands in all, open only in summer, selling handmade jewelry, objects made out of raw leather, olive wood sundials, pottery, homemade lamps, cushions covered in Provençal fabric, "organic" pastries. Then a stall selling olives of all sorts, oils, walnuts, and dried cod announces in particularly appetizing fashion the food section of the market. In the Place de la Mairie there are a few *confection*, textile, lingerie, and shoe stalls, but above all there are mountains of eggplants and tomatoes, lettuce heads and cabbages, trucks wreathed in sausages and *andouilles*, stalls selling cheese off the wheel and butter off the mound.

Foot traffic in the Place de la Mairie is extremely dense, in part because there are more mobile shops here than elsewhere. A large proportion of food sellers, particularly *charcutiers* and *fromagers*, choose this system for its refrigeration possibilities. But the layout of the square seems disorderly and confused. The irregular shape is in fact due to the late-nineteenth-century destruction of the Vieille Juiverie. The synagogue was spared, as were a few houses; taller than the others on the square, these buildings recall the time of the overcrowded ghetto. While the *mairie* [town hall] sits in the center of the *place*, it seems to turn its back on it; as in the past, the entrance is on the Rue des Halles. The stalls here, located either around the town hall or in front of the houses, do their best to adapt to the peculiar space.

On Fridays, the fixed shops along the square are transformed. Gardiol lays game animals and poultry on a trestle table. He displays his finest pieces during the hunting season: partridges, a woodcock, a huge boar. Stiff rabbits and golden pheasant hang from the poles of his awninged shop. The Jardins du Comtat puts out a small display case every day, but on Fridays they set up immense stalls on both sides of the store. There are crates filled to the brim with vegetables, seasonal fruit, and greens, while dried and tropical fruits are carefully displayed in wicker baskets, signaling their relative scarcity. In fact, on market day the Jardins' wares are displayed in stallholder fashion and thus melt into the mass. The size of this business, together with the high quality of its produce, helps make the Place de la Mairie one of the best known and valued spots for food.

The arcaded Rue des Halles is a shopping street. Market stalls and fixed-boutique display tables are lined up together between the pillars; the crowd circulates under the arches and in the roadway. The Rue des Halles has sporting goods, shoe, and clothing stores but is also, as the name suggests, one of the city's food and produce centers.[5] On Fridays this specialization is reinforced by the presence of "butter-egg-cheese" stalls and others selling sausages, vegetables, goat cheeses, olives and condiments, spices and teas, not to mention sweets. Carpentras is *the* place for *berlingots*, though this bonbon has already lived its finest hour.

There are also many occasional vendors here. This is one of the places the Africans choose for selling their crafts: handbags, jewelry, belts, all carefully lined up on the ground. Just outside the Passage Boyer some people from Avignon have begun selling minerals and fossils; they want to "test the clientele" before organizing an exhibition at the cultural center. Novelty and imitation jewelry is for sale in front of the small Casino supermarket, and across the way the many-virtued ginseng root is available. On the sidewalk's edge *gitanes* sit selling lemons.[6] In the middle of the roadway other stallholders sell a tangle of disparate objects from mobile stands (trailers or tables on wheels): balloons, hats, sunglasses, dolls, teddy bears, key chains, joke and slogan buttons, and so on.

During the hunting season there is a bird market at the beginning of the Rue David-Guillabert. This year there were only three or four shivering vendors with little to offer—a few thrush laid out on newspaper or in a small crate—whereas thirty years ago this was an extremely active market, renowned especially for its calling birds. Today it survives in inhabitants' memory above all as a toponym, though a few old, nostalgic hunters mention how animated the street was, and the racket the birds made.

Beyond this point, the market stretches along the Rue de la Porte-de-Mazan toward the city's edge. With its relatively low houses and widely spaced businesses, this street already announces the outskirts. Stalls are smaller here, and there are many occasional stallholders selling such things as painted embroidery canvas, beach bags, candy, used cassettes and records, transistors, and wrought-iron work. African crafts are also very much in evidence here. The regular stalls include ones selling paella and pizza, spices and "herbes de Provence," foam and woolen mattresses, and wooden knickknacks.

Just outside the old city is the Place de Verdun, another vast esplanade cut through by the circular boulevard. Everyone here calls it Le Quinconce, and it is the favorite spot for *pétanque*. Though a few cafés and pizza trucks generate a little action, especially in summer, the place always seems a bit empty. No horses have been sold here for a long while; it is now a tool and hardware kingdom. The monotony of these stalls is broken only by a stand selling "American surplus," one with *articles de Paris*, and an occasional mobile shop proposing Ardèche hams and sausage.

The Avenue Jean-Jaurès takes you from the Place de Verdun back to the Place du Théâtre. This wide, shady promenade called Les Platanes is the city's pride, a terrace offering a splendid view of the countryside and the incessant play of the sprinklers, a few big farms in the shade of lime trees, and in the distance the villages of Saint-Didier and Beaucet. Today Les Platanes resembles a vast garden. This space once used for a wholesale *primeur* market has been taken over by florists and a few producers and nurseries. They seem there not so much to sell as to display their talents to potential customers.

In contrast to markets like those of Paris, which tend to be the same every time, the Carpentras market is a fluid, changing reality. Though the warp may be fairly stable, the woof is different every Friday. The actors, products, breadth, and density of the market vary constantly, particularly with the seasons. In summer, the flow of tourist families, the small producers come to sell goat cheese or honey, the rich colors of the fruit, the multicolored stall canopies protecting people and produce from the sun make the physiognomy of the market quite different from what it is in winter: tighter, quieter, simply much less crowded. The market even changes from one hour to the next: the flow of shoppers can be more or less dense, and the clientele varies sociologically: older people come earliest, country people don't usually arrive before 9 a.m., while in summer the Parisians vacationing in the surrounding villages arrive much later, when the market is in full swing. At noon, when the musicians take up in front of the cafés, the streets have already begun to empty.

2. Well-Ordered Chaos

For an observer walking into the Carpentras market for the first time, the domi-nant impression is of inextricable chaos: a labyrinth of densely crowded, narrow streets and squares, the pleasant jumble characterizing some stalls, products spread about in apparent disorder, the profusion of foodstuffs and combination of odors, a general hubbub in which the only distinct sound is the sales pitch of a street hawker, the extreme diversity of both visitor-customers and vendors, the latter including chair-stuffers and knife-sharpeners set up in the spaces left by mobile shops, cheese and honey vendors with small trestle tables next to the opulent displays of professional retailers, Senegalese laying out their pseudo-exotic junk in the shadow of the medieval episcopal palace . . .

This anarchy, while making the market a charming experience for the visitor, worried me at first: my research object seemed disarmingly complex. At the beginning I settled for pacing through the market in all directions every week in hopes of becoming nearly as familiar with it as a longtime city inhabitant. I quickly acquired a precise enough practical familiarity to be able to guide an occasional visitor through it passably well, on a path not much different from the one on which I have just taken the reader. But not getting disoriented in a place is one thing, knowing it quite another.

Thinking on this today, I tell myself that my situation was not any more dif-ficult than that of an anthropologist confronted with a massive, interminable exchange ceremony on the shores of the Pacific, or the stately funeral of an important clan member in an African society. Like me, as I imagine it, the anthropologist does not know where to start, how to get hold of the object. The difference is that he is sure to have before him a "total social fact." The wager inherent in any anthropological proceeding involves the assumption that the apparent tangle of observed behaviors ultimately obeys some kind of all-encompassing logic that it is the anthropologist's task to identify.

The relevance of this assumption for my Carpentras market "field" was not immediately apparent to me. Indeed, one might easily think of the market as nothing more than a spatial-temporal framework for a myriad of independent micro-events (purchases, encounters, conversations, and so on). From this perspective, acquiring knowledge of it would necessarily be an analytic operation: the complexity of the immediate phenomenon would have to be reduced to a series of simple elements. The market may be treated as a set of individual actions, for example, and shopper motivation or buying behavior systematically surveyed. Or we could assume that the market may be reduced to the sum of interactions between sellers and buyers, in which case one would want to take an inventory of the different types of possible scenes, studying the relation repeated in each transaction, the linguistic exchanges this relation gives rise to, and so on.

It is clear that "going to market" has little to do with getting married at Saint-Honoré d'Eylau or attending the funeral of a deputy mayor in a village church. Nonetheless, the fact that actors at the market do not behave according to conscious, custom-bound, and therefore readily formulated rules, that they feel at liberty instead to act as they wish, does not imply that the market is merely the result of a series of individual, independent decisions. Apart from formal, ceremonial moments (the sort that offer themselves directly as ethnographic objects), we continually conduct our daily life in social spaces where everyone seems to behave freely but which are nonetheless governed by a latent symbolic order so familiar that it is difficult to explain. Anthropology here is elucidation of the commonplace, a reconstruction of what everyone knows without knowing they know it.

Listening to Gérard Althabe had taught me that even in places as innocuous and "functional" as housing complexes, where co-residents run into each other every day, a specific "communication mode" can be shown to be at work, a type of implicit logic common to the actors, by means of which they "produce" a relatively autonomous social space.[1]

In fact, if one pays minimal attention to one's own practices, one quickly realizes that though one is not aware of following imposed rules or conventional models when at the market, one does in fact behave there in a socially defined way. The market is the result of multiple, spontaneous, or at least readily explicable (though rarely explained) practices, the effect and indeed the end of which is to constitute the market as such, give it its own specific form. Despite the absence of an orchestra conductor or unconscious structure, the market has a certain coherence and consistency. Each of the micro-events I observe or that is recounted to me is intelligible in terms of a kind of logic-of-the-whole of which it is a single manifestation. The work of the anthropologist here is to restore the unity of the market's meaning, to describe it in a way that will overcome the initial impression of confusion and fragmentation and restore it as a totality. But the very idea of panoptic vision is a delusion; one can describe only from a particular point of view.

To move from apparent chaos to latent order, I would clearly have to show that despite the impression of freedom it gives, a market is a municipal institution and therefore the product of local policy, explicit and deliberate actions which, though determined behind the scenes, are fairly easy to study. In our fascination with the market stage or setting, we tend to forget the machinery essential to its functioning. What appears at first glance a reign of joyous disorder is nonetheless a regulated public space. The impression of an uncontrolled invasion of city streets and squares is thus illusory. What we observe in fact results from continual arbitration of multiple questions and issues, a series of compromises among partners with divergent interests.

Market management is a major matter in Carpentras. Though wholesale and retail markets are now distinct, the mayor's office has insisted on their being managed together. The service in charge of this is headed by the director of the *marché-gare* and has its offices in what is called the Château, a turreted building in the style of Viollet-le-Duc, strange vestige of an old estate now surrounded by eighteen hectares of asphalt. In the early 1980s (at the time of this study), the ruler of this asphalt universe was a jovial, roundish person in a blue suit. I watched him feverishly oversee the installation of the trucks every morning. *Marché-gare* regulars all called him by his last name: Nicolas.[2] On Fridays two women fee collectors worked under his orders, going from stall to stall to collect rent for the spots. The service also keeps records on "subscriber" stallholders and a waiting list for would-be subscribers. The other major actor, Pascal the *placier*, is in charge of distributing vacant spots to occasional stallholders, work he does for free.

How the market is organized is decided by the "fairs and markets" commission, headed by Estève, a fruit and *primeurs* grower, a decisive, plainspoken, commonsensical man. Estève played a significant role in setting up the *marché-gare*, which since its creation in 1963 has been the major focus of commission work. Responsibility for the street market actually falls to an elected official, a deputy mayor who is then appointed "fairs and markets" director. At the time of my study this position was occupied by Jean-Claude Andrieu, the owner of Arts de la Table et Cadeaux in the Rue d'Inguimbert, one of the most elegant boutiques in Carpentras and one of the few able to compete with Avignon shops. Andrieu's shop is made up of two distinct spaces linked by a corridor. On one side, his mother reigns over a world of lamps, coffee tables, ashtrays, and bibelots of the "wedding list" variety. Andrieu runs the other side himself. Here Limoges china sets and Baccarat and Saint-Louis crystal are displayed in a hushed, almost contemplative atmosphere. Young, reserved, and serious, the owner somewhat resembles the objects surrounding him.

Andrieu was devoted to Maurice Charretier, Carpentras's most important political figure. Originally from the Gard, a member of the Carpentras bar, and son-in-law of one of the city's most renowned *patissiers*, Maurice Charretier held the mayor's office from 1965. He was also *député* [member of parliament] for the Vaucluse and minister of commerce and crafts from July 1979 to June 1981. During this time, Jean-Claude Andrieu was in charge of local policy affairs, among them fairs and markets. With Minister Charretier's assistance, he set up the annual Saint-Siffrein fair. Upon Charretier's sudden death in 1987 (he was then a senator), Andrieu became mayor.

The observable configuration of the market is due, then, to these bodies—the municipal service and the ad hoc commission—and the measures by which they limit the market's extension and organize its internal composition. Though all this administrative management is in no way secret, it does escape the eye of most people who come to the market.

The Well-Tempered Market

Where and how far the market should extend is a perpetual, delicate issue for the mayor's office. The space seems too small to accommodate the strong stallholder demand. That which is currently available is occupied by three hundred stallholders, and there are five hundred on the waiting list kept by Nicolas's office. Stallholders quitting the business free up approximately forty places each year for reallocation. In addition to "subscriber" stallholders, there are "occasionals" who request a place when the market opens in the morning. Their number rises in summer and fine weather.

The city has always had to deal with the market's tendency to overwhelm it. This has alternately been perceived as a positive or a threatening development. Though relations between city and market have sometimes been conflictual, the city has generally favored and facilitated the market's rise. In the Middle Ages, the market regularly overflowed the cemetery and the small square next to Saint-Siffrein called the Place de la Fusterie. In those centuries it continually moved into new areas, increasingly encroaching on the public right of way. In the fourteenth century it became necessary to build new walls to integrate the market area, then renamed the Forum novum—the city was actually remodeled to accommodate its market.[3] Then in 1831, to the indignation of all lovers of old stone, the mayor received permission to demolish the medieval walls to enlarge the fairgrounds.[4] The city thus accepted the market's impulse to expand but never surrendered its intention to control it. When new products appeared, the city allotted them a particular spot or legalized spontaneous enlargement after the fact so as to better circumscribe it. In any case, the city had no intention of being submerged by the Friday flow and was concerned to limit the famous "*embarras*" [traffic jams] described by Jean-François Field in the late eighteenth century.[5]

Between the two world wars, the city's vigilant goodwill gave way to tenser relations. Under pressure from sedentary shopkeepers, who were growing in number and getting organized, the mayor's office adopted a policy of suspicion, and stallholders were regularly subjected to police inspections. For shopkeepers, the Friday market, which at the time was shifting to retail sale of food and manufactured products, was looking like a powerful source of competition.

This defensive, pettifogging attitude toward itinerant trade no longer applies or is felt to be necessary. Local boutiques and stallholders are no longer in competition with each other. Sedentary trade in Carpentras is dynamic and adaptable enough to benefit from the crowds and bustle of the Friday market. The city counts around four hundred shops. Businesses on the outskirts—auto repair shops and gas stations, furniture and farm machine stores—require vast sales surfaces. This is where the city's five supermarkets are, the biggest being

Leclerc (2,900 sq. m.) and Intermarché (1,700 sq. m.). Most retail stores are concentrated in the old city center; most are small, and their density is highest in the main market streets. Specialization is spatialized: the Rue des Halles is food; the Rue de la République, clothes; the Passage Boyer has service activities only. Because city center shops are specialized and relatively prestigious (with the exception of a few food stores), they attract a clientele from well beyond the city walls. People come all the way from Sault, Althen-les-Paluds, Sarrians, approximately thirty kilometers away, to buy pastry or crystallized fruit. According to the chambers of commerce and industry for Avignon and the Vaucluse, Carpentras business draws as many as seventy thousand persons for certain products.

It might seem that the presence of stallholders would hurt local trade. They block boutique entrances, and mobile shops partially hide display windows. In fact, in a survey conducted in the late 1970s, only a tiny minority of sedentary tradespersons were in favor of moving the market. The vast majority believe that the market improves their turnover. "Some shopkeepers are not happy to have stallholders in front of their doors, but shopkeepers benefit from the fact that the stallholders are there, they bring them customers. The market brings everyone business. People who can't find what they're looking for at the stallholders' find it in the fixed stores," explains Mme. Martinez, who runs the Hôtel du Mont-Ventoux in the Place de la Mairie, a modest establishment with a café on the ground floor and a restaurant patronized by office clerks and construction workers. Some merchants even say they wish the market reached their doorstep. Pascal the *placier* relates a merchant's complaint: " 'What do we have to do to get some stallholders into our section? We'd rather have stallholders in front of our stores on Fridays than cars.' " Says Boyac, who owns the Jardins du Comtat, two of the nicest fruit and vegetable shops in the city, one in the Place de la Mairie, the other in the Rue de la République: "Purchasing power is double on Friday mornings in Carpentras . . . It's the most profitable day of the week." Many share this opinion. Others, such as Avon, manufacturer of articles he calls "leisure textiles" (embroidery and tapestry-making canvas and materials) and owner of a notions shop in the old city, are more circumspect. They do not see any immediate or direct effect on sales but acknowledge that the Friday market "does get the clientele into the habit of shopping in the city center."

Sales increase on Fridays not only because there are more customers but also because boutiques increase sales surface by setting up stalls in front of their windows that mix in with market stalls and diversify product supply. This is especially the case in the Rue des Halles and the Place de la Mairie. The wares put out on Friday may be of a different nature and price than what is inside; the idea is to align them with those of the open-air market. "On Friday mornings," Boyac explains, "I have to double my efforts, enlarge the display to draw in the customers. Everything gets rotated compared to ordinary days . . . For some product categories, where there's broad demand, I sometimes sell not low-quality but nonrated produce. Oranges, for example. On regular days we sell large-caliber ones, whereas on Fridays we sell more ordinary-caliber ones . . . I sell lower-quality produce on Fridays because I don't want to sell it the other days of the week. For example, today I have only Belgian endive. But on market day I'll have a shipment of French endive, which is good, but still not as good [as Belgian], and I'll sell it at one or two francs less."

With this two-sided arrangement, which enables them to take advantage of the greater socioeconomic heterogeneity of the Friday crowd without losing their everyday clientele, city merchants "play" the market "game." Boyac has fruits and vegetables for families who have come in from the north of the city, others for "his" customers: "connoisseurs," people in the know, shippers and growers to whom he sells "with a certain pride."

Some merchants have actually modeled their shop on the stall setup. They don't just put out an outdoor Friday display but have reorganized the shop itself in "market" fashion. "When I redid the shop," Avon explains, "my idea was to widen the sidewalk into the shop so that people would be partly indoors while remaining outdoors. It's a place for exchange, encounters, and therefore business—that's something stallholders understand."

Market and fixed shops thus seem more complementary than rival, and the stallholders themselves are conscious of this. "There's no competition between stallholders and merchants," says Perdiguier, the big shoe-stall operator of the Place du Théâtre. "It's complementary. The stallholders liven things up, and the animation brings people in. Some small merchants will say that stallholders siphon off their business, but I don't think everyone thinks that way. In fact, whenever there's a shop for sale in the city, it goes for a higher price if it's in the marketplace than if it's further out . . . The market is good business for everyone."

Not only do prices and quality differ on Fridays, but there seems to be a strong, effective de facto division of labor. There are no butcher stands in the market, but many in the city. For *charcuterie* [pork and cold cuts], the opposite obtains. At the Carpentras market, as at others, there are no bakeries or *patisseries*—two specialties that contribute greatly to the renown of city shops. Indeed, it may well be the presence of the market that accounts in large part for the vitality of local commerce. Since the market sells ordinary or down-market consumption products, the boutiques have had to specialize in high-market or unusual items (*produits anomaux* as geographers eruditely put it). This explains why they manage so well despite the supermarkets, a remarkable situation in this *département* where supermarkets are a major distribution mode and customers are particularly mobile (the number of cars per inhabitant here is higher than anywhere else in France).[6] From time immemorial Carpentras merchants' only real rivals have been Avignon merchants.

Still, the presence of the market in the city center may seem aberrant from the point of view of wise public space management. There are serious parking problems; customers have to leave their vehicles farther and farther away; and by subprefecture order, the city's widest fire truck regularly tries to make it through the streets to demonstrate how unsafe the arrangement is. "Not even ambulances can get through a street that's only two meters wide," says Pascal. "Once there was a fire in the Place de la Mairie and the fire truck took more than twenty minutes to get there."

The question was once raised whether it would not be preferable to move the market onto the external boulevards. But 1970s rational urban planning of that sort had to yield to another vision of urban space. The municipality became aware that the market's long history and links to the rural world help create a local identity; that when it comes to "making a name for oneself " and staking a claim to Provençal authenticity, the market is a major asset, that it is therefore essential to preserve its time-honored appearance. "There's something folkloric about the market in the city center—it's great!" says Pascal.[7] The stallholders are of the same opinion. The market is "part of the folklore," they often told me. "It's one tradition that has not been lost."

The city is no longer economically dependent on its market but now uses it to resuscitate the center. Estève, head of the market commission, remarks: "On Saturdays, the city is deserted, as if everybody were at Auchan [supermarket and mall]." And Mme. Martinez laments: "Carpentras is something of a dead city. In winter that's understandable, but in the summer it's a catastrophe. When you pass through the Place de la Mairie on Sundays there's not a soul in the streets, except if you've come to bet on the horses . . . People go to

Auchan a lot. It's closed on Sundays, but the restaurant is open, and people go eat there. I don't even cook on Sundays anymore—imagine that!"

So the city tends to favor market expansion. But this should not suggest that the market is left to develop freely on its own. "The market is in all the streets," says Estève, but in fact the city exercises vigilant control. Opening a new street up to stallholders is a matter for long reflection and a municipal decree. The market can be "swelled up" to respond to stallholder demand, but this is no solution, as Pascal explains: "Enlarging it is a trap because people will say, 'They're taking off the leash in Carpentras'—that's the term they use—'In Carpentras the city council has unleashed another street, so they must have space.' That's even worse, because it means I've got not just fifty more stallholders every Friday [to distribute spots to], but a hundred or a hundred and fifty. It gets almost entirely filled up, and we're back with the problem we started with."

Moreover, the mayor's office does not want to risk "unleashing" if it isn't going to work. Opening Les Platanes (the Allées Jean-Jaurès) to market traffic in 1976, and the Rue de la Porte-de-Mazan, Passage Boyer, and Le Quinconce (Place de Verdun), has been successful, but other experiments have been disappointing. "Extending the market into the Rue de la Porte-de-Mazan, where there are approximately forty stallholders, was a good business operation," Pascal explains. "At first it was very hard because when you establish a new spot, you have to get a clientele. But about three years ago, around the time M. Bernard, the former president of the market, passed away, we opened up the Rue du Vieil-Hôpital and tried to put stallholders in it, but it didn't work. We also tried, with M. Nicolas, to open up the Rue Porte-de-Monteux to antique and secondhand dealers, but that was in winter, when the weather was bad. When you open a square or a street, you have to do it in the right season, make both stallholders and customers aware of it. A crowd attracts a crowd—that's for certain. If you put two or three stallholders at the Porte de Mazan, no one goes there, but if you fill it up with stallholders, everyone goes there."

City managers are continually searching for the subtle balance representing optimal market size and arrangement. If the crowd is too dense, immediate profit is lower, but below a certain threshold "dead" areas get created and that hurts the market as a whole. A good market has to be homogeneous; the animation and entertainment have to be evenly distributed. That balance is particularly hard to reach given that the number of stallholders and, more important, customers increases considerably in summer. The authorities tend not to like seasonal solutions because they give the market the image of a tourist attraction.

With cautious policy of this sort, the number of permanent spots is kept low and spots are distributed parsimoniously, almost exclusively when stallholders leave or quit. But stallholder demand is pressing, and the mayor's office has to respond to it one way or another. In principle, a permanent spot is obtained through seniority on the waiting list, but the mayor's office is ready to make a few arrangements in the name of "social" concerns (a widow with a family to support gets moved up the list) or as a more opaque privilege. The Carpentras market is reputed to be a "good" one among stallholders, one where special favors are the exception rather than the rule (in contrast to the market in Orange, for example). Says Noël Cappo, who runs the hardware and cleaning products bazaar in the Place du Palais: "Usually you've got to sweeten everyone up, but that doesn't go on in Carpentras." A *charcutier* with a permanent spot in a not very desirable area confides: "It's a problem in Carpentras. If you're in good with the *placier*, okay, but in my case, we don't really hit it off. With a small gift—a ham will do the job—friends of friends manage to get in even though there are no spots. I could list at least six colleagues who didn't submit a market spot application like it should be done and who got a spot Place de la Mairie . . . They didn't go through any procedures, they just showed up, and they got places right away. So there's got to be something. Either it's string-pulling or you've got to have your RPR membership card or I don't know what— whatever they like up there.[8] Or else you've got to spread some around. I say I don't know, but if I did know, that wouldn't change the problem one bit."

To manage the market space as well as possible, prevent it from expanding indefinitely or haphazardly, the city not only has to limit the number of permanent spots but organize distribution of vacant spots among "occasionals." Not everyone gets a spot, especially in summer.

Pascal's tasks are to keep tabs on occupied spots and distribute available places to occasionals. His official responsibilities are thus limited. Though he can always say how he thinks things should be done, he is not supposed to handle distribution of permanent spots or manage the waiting list. But Pascal has no such restrictive conception of his role. Continually in contact with stallholders, concerned about problems affecting young people—he is director of the Carpentras youth center—Pascal seems to be the main intercessor between the city and its market.

While duly implementing city policy aimed at controlling market expansion,

Pascal has been contemplating several changes that would enable all stallholders to have a spot. He likes the solution used at Sorgue, has had occasion to see it work, and wants to apply it in Carpentras. An area was set aside there for "all the leftover people. It is of course at the very edge of the market, and they can take it or leave it." Pascal thinks such a space could be set aside on one of Carpentras's boulevards and offered to the twenty to twenty-five stallholders to whom he now has to say, after his 10 a.m. turn through the city on Fridays, "Look, there's just nothing left." With an eye to facilitating integration for those in straitened economic circumstances, he is also trying to convince city hall to reopen the "bird market" in the Rue David-Guillabert to "craftspersons" and "the young people who come in the summer," as was done a few years ago with the Passage Boyer, quite saturated today.

To Each His or Her Place

If on first glance the market seems a disorderly jumble of stalls, its habitual customers know full well that fruits and vegetables are to be found around city hall, fish at the Porte d'Orange, and fabric near the palace. To them it is obvious that the market has been organized. But they think the way merchants and products are distributed occurred spontaneously, or in obedience to no rule other than custom. They generally do not know that in addition to the overall configuration of the market—size, exact limits, number of stalls—its internal arrangement is also largely an effect of the municipality's many interventions.

City hall applies a number of principles aimed at ensuring that the market functions optimally.[9] You don't locate a stallholder in front of a boutique that sells the same type of products he does: "A fellow who sells shoes should not be put in front of a shoe store—there are distances that must be respected," explains Pascal. Likewise, two stallholders selling exactly the same items will not be put side by side. Efforts are also made to separate activities considered incompatible—lavender next to *merguez* [spicy beef sausages grilled on the spot], croissants and breakfast pastries next to fish, and so on—and to isolate the noisiest traders: CD and cassette vendors are relegated to the Rue de la Porte-de-Mazan or the edges of Le Quinconce. Street vendors demonstrating their wares and other specialists selling by the "batch" or "handful" create centers of distraction and entertainment, so there is a tendency to scatter them throughout the market, though each one is judiciously placed so as not to deprive the stallholders near them of customer attention. "You cannot put a *posticheur* just anywhere," explains Pascal, "because he can really bother the neighboring stallholders, not to mention our local tradespeople. They obstruct foot traffic. But if you put a *posticheur* on a street corner or square that is practically deserted, he'll attract people." To take advantage of the hawker's gift for drawing an audience but avoid creating a bottleneck, it is necessary to "keep [him] in the background." Pascal puts two or three in the Place du Théâtre, where the market begins: that way they can set the market tone, while the *place* is big enough for their spieling not to hurt anyone else's business. He also often puts another at the end of the Rue d'Inguimbert, in the very center of the city, next to the "fruits and vegetables." He would never put a hawker in the Rue de la République; there Jacky Thevet reigns supreme.

Somewhat exceptional stalls also get a fine spot—in the Rue des Halles, for example. "In winter I had a fellow dressed a little *à la façon* [traditionally] . . . This man was a genuine street peddler. He sold roots, roots of various bushes, a sensational display of goods. He had roots for all diseases, rheumatism and all the rest. Incredible, this fellow, how hard he worked, and how many people he drew. To me that was something out of the ordinary. And once I had people from Agen with prunes, dressed in regional costumes—growers, maybe. I thought they were great." [10]

But city hall also tries to group together products of the same sort. "Necklace sellers," as Estève calls them, are in the Passage Boyer, and flowers have been moved from the Place de la Mairie to Les Platanes to leave the *place* free for fruits and vegetables. Plans to "unleash" another street invariably involve setting up a particular product category: crafts in the Rue David-Guillabert, antique dealers in the Rue de la Porte-de-Monteux.

This policy aims to restore the morphology of the market of bygone days— or what it is believed to have been. "We try to group merchants together like in ancient times," explains Estève. Up until the early twentieth century the market was largely made up of specialized merchants in fixed areas. Distinct "markets" for wheat and dry vegetables (beans, for example), garlic and charcoal, acorns, potatoes and chestnuts, saffron, birds, and so on, constituted the permanent structure of the weekly market (though each was seasonal). These were wholesale markets, however, where prices were determined. Today's groupings therefore do not reproduce the old order; they merely imitate it. But this type of fiction fits perfectly with the way the city perceives and means to use its market. What it wants above all is a showcase that will attest simultaneously to the dynamism of its business and the wealth of its cultural heritage.

In grouping sellers of the same product together, the municipality is also seeking to create conditions for ideally efficient competition. The stallholders have not always seen it this way. "We had to overcome energetic resistance," Nicolas recounts, "but now they [the stallholders] wouldn't want to leave." In fact, the stallholders' rejection of this arrangement did not involve fear of immediate competition. In a major market like Carpentras, "we aren't afraid of the others," says Perdiguier, owner of the shoe stall in the Place du Théâtre. "Big markets can handle competition." "We don't all sell in the same way," explains a *fripier*. "It's in everyone's interest for the other to exist, everyone attracts a particular clientele."

This is not true of small markets, as I soon observed. In Monteux or Saint-Didier, for example, a stallholder selling the same type of product is considered a rival to be ousted if possible. To attract customers, it is of course necessary for each sector of activity to be represented, but by a single stallholder—otherwise business declines. "In Monteux," relates Delvaux, a *charcutier* of Parisian origin who lives there, "there's a fruit and vegetable seller and some clothes sellers— one does women's, the other men's, another does hosiery more than anything else—and there's a shoe seller, a linens man, a cheese stall. We're one of each sort." This is what is called "a good team."

Stallholders are more concerned about their "spot" than about immediate competition. They are likely to think that the success of their business depends in large degree on where they are located in the market. "You've got markets like Orange, Cavaillon, and Carpentras, which are reputed to be good, but you can have a location in them that's worth zero. For a stallholder, spot is every-thing," explains Avon. Clearly some spots are more profitable than others, but how their value is estimated is fairly mysterious for the noninitiated. There is no clearly formulated general or objective criterion; everything ultimately de-pends on the type of product. Pragmatic intuition of the sort Pierre Bourdieu calls "a sense of the game" is what enables one to distinguish "a royal" from a "spot off the beaten" that will cause you to "miss out" on the market that day.

Overall, stallholders do not like market edges or areas where stalls are sparse. "When you're at the end or in a hole, it's a disaster," says Delvaux. "On the edge of a small market you're still visible, but at the edge of the Carpentras market you're out in the wilderness—no one sees you! Only the guy going to park his car can see you, maybe. One stallholder every forty meters is just no good."

The most desirable and sought-after spots are in the heart of the old city and along the main streets. But the Place de la Mairie is a "royal" for fruits and vegetables, while the Place du Théâtre is preferable for shoes and clothes. Intensity of pedestrian flow is of course crucial, and where it is highest, competitors are an asset rather than a threat. It is never good, however, to be situated in a place where the market narrows down or the jostling of the crowd dissuades customers from dallying. On closer inspection, it is clear that the quality of the urban and business environment is also crucial: it is better to be close to Andrieu's in the Place du Festival than in front of the Arab grocer's at the Porte d'Orange. An extremely subtle spatial hierarchy is thus established. In a small market the game is much simpler: "People in Monteux are churchy," a stallholder explains. "If you're not on the street that leads to the church, it's over, no use trying. If you ain't between the parking lot and the church, you won't make a centime. If you are, you really work! You've got the church and all the bakeries and pastry shops."

Clearly there is competition for the good spots, and it is the municipality's role to arbitrate. Up against pressure from stallholders unhappy with their lot, the others have to fight incessantly to keep their place, and the way to do this is to be there every week. After three unexplained absences, the city has a right to reallocate the spot. Seniority is supposed to determine who gets a better place, but there again, certain sellers question the *placier*'s impartiality: "By all rights I should be in the center, Place de la Mairie, given how long I've been selling at this market," complains one.

Stallholders' wariness of city hall's grouping plans is thus primarily related to their fear of getting peripheral spots off regular customer paths and their attachment to a place that in many cases they have occupied for years and taken great pains to defend. In their quest for stability they are aware of the behavior of loyal customers who from one Friday to the next follow nearly the same market itinerary. Clearly any change in location would be perilous for stallholders. Keeping one's place is also a way of staking a claim to as strong a place in the city as its sedentary merchants have, and of distinguishing oneself from occasional vendors. Paradoxically, an itinerant stallholder will let you know at the slightest opportunity how long he or she has been trading at the Carpentras market—like Perdiguier, who told me his family has been selling there for more than sixty years.

In at least one case, the policy of grouping together sellers of the same type of product seems a great success: florists and plant sellers at Les Platanes are unanimously pleased with their location. This area stands very much apart and has a twofold vocation: trading and strolling. Les Platanes has been city dwellers' favorite promenade since the late nineteenth century—"There were benches and fountains. In the evenings we would get together for some cool air, and in winter the old people would get together for some sun"—but it is also here that the wholesale fruit and vegetable market was held. At that time it was not cut off from city life. Before the flowers and plants arrived, people observed how the space had been invaded by parked buses and cars. Though it took customers a little time to change their habits, today this peripheral section of the market draws many people. The floral pleasures reawaken memory of Les Platanes in olden times.

Clearly, the market with its disordered topology and unkempt appearance is in reality produced not so much by systematic planning and policy as by a series of compromises between different and even antagonistic viewpoints and interests: those of the municipal authorities, sedentary shopkeepers, and stallholders.

But this should not lead us to believe that these institutional actors delimit at will and unilaterally a public trading space that the clientele then merely fills up, as if the reality of the market could be reduced to an imposed material framework. From the institutional actors' points of view, the people who come to the market are a flow to be optimally channeled and captivated. But we should not think in terms of a contrast between active market creators and passive market users. An anthropological description will show that the market is made as much by shoppers and curious onlookers as by institutional actors and stallholders; the event is created and repeated every Friday as much by the former set of actors and their multiple itineraries and operations, both similar and unique, as by the latter set. The actions of the two constitute two "moments" in the single process that "produces" the market. In a city clearly made very different this day from other days, a set of social relations falls into place that is just as unusual.

PART TWO

An Economy of Enticement

Why do people in Carpentras go to the market? It might be expected that respondents would cite their "good reasons"—the produce is fresher, the prices
lower, the selection greater, and so on—as if the market were nothing more
than another mall, this one at your doorstep though open only once a week, and
as if all that happened there were an exchange of goods and value. But the price
of carrots or the quality of socks is strangely absent from people's accounts
of the market. They speak more readily of the ambiance, or remember unexpected encounters ("The mayor was just starting his reelection campaign");
they remark the absence of Jacky Thevet ("He must've gone to the beach!") or
the presence of "le petit Seguin" at one of the stands ("It seems he passed the
bac").[1] In sum, instead of enlightened rational-consumer discourse justifying
one's choice to shop at the market, I collected attestations of pleasure.

And wondered about the nature of that pleasure. It seemed to be of the sort
one takes in playing a game.

Every market is a social space constructed on the model of the game. A separate time and space are conventionally determined (market hours, like stallholder spots, are fixed by city hall), and these limits constitute a pause or break
from everyday social life, one given over entirely to a specific activity, the buying and selling of products, in which the actors agree to follow well-established
rules, the first of which is that they encounter each other as partners in the same
game and are therefore formally equal. Not only do the rules determine transaction modalities; they also suspend ordinary rules.[2] At the *marché-gare* people

come together as men, "colleagues." Far from domestic obligations, they practice an intense social interaction that stands in contrast to the relative solitude of working in the fields. At the street market, one need only listen to people's conversations to understand that the ways of proceeding here are quite different from any others and the rules of civility and *politesse* more relaxed.

But not all games are alike. The phenomena we group together under the notion of game are linked by little more than what Wittgenstein called a "family resemblance," and even the game of trade is characterized by highly varied forms and modes.

A game is a "free activity"—this is the first characteristic Roger Caillois distinguishes. Still, since the game of market exchange generally brings together noninterchangeable partners (some sellers, others buyers), the degree of freedom varies by position occupied. The fruit or vegetable producer is free not to accept the exchange mode practiced at the *marché-gare*; he can bring his goods to market directly if he likes. He is nonetheless obliged to sell, and quickly, or risk losing his merchandise. This constraint is not as significant for the *rabassiers*, who will in any case manage to sell off what they gather—truffles can always be put away for a better day. Conversely, the shipper or broker does not absolutely have to buy that day or on the market (unless he has urgent orders to fill). Most actors at the street market, on the other hand, are there by unconstrained choice. Everyone is free to go to market or not—by definition. And though stallholders (in contrast to sedentary merchants) need to "keep their spot," they can always miss a market on their circuit.

Once the game has been accepted, the stakes in it can be high or not so high. The *marché-gare* is a place of serious business. Every "deal" represents a gain or loss, and repeated "bad luck" can imperil a farm's prosperity and perhaps its very existence. The atmosphere of the street market is much more one of free entertainment, though some actors have to spend, of course, if others are to earn. It is never indispensable to shop at the market; there are no products there that cannot be found elsewhere. This is why exchange relations remain secondary or are underestimated in many customers' accounts of their visit. The market is an end in itself, whether one shops there or not. Even supposing I don't spend a centime this Friday, I will nonetheless have "done the market" (or "taken a turn" through it). This is true for more than just customers: treating the market as a moment of pleasure rather than a "mode of distribution" is also a rule of behavior among stallholders. To entice the market customer, to induce him to buy, it is crucial not to seem as if one is there to do business. Accordingly, stallholders tend to think of their risk as spread out over their market circuit as a whole and across the seasons. A stallholder's eye is not riveted on how much he will take in that day.

3. The Art of Taking One's Time

"All week long, I yearn to go to the market," says Mme. Coste. "For us, Friday takes the place of Sunday." Once the owner of a small grocery next to the Porte de Monteux, where she still lives, Mme. Coste is retired today and lives alone. She has known the merchants in this neighborhood forever, can shop comfortably here, and readily acknowledges that the medium-sized Ifaprix supermarket on the Boulevard Albin-Durand is "very convenient." But every Friday at around nine she sets out from her house for the market. First she negotiates her way through the crowd in the Rue des Halles, where she sometimes buys a little garlic sausage at the big *charcuterie*. Her destination is Gardiol's, Place de la Mairie, where she will buy a chicken or rabbit. She chats for a good quarter of an hour with old Gardiol and other habitués who come there for fresh poultry. And never fails to run into her neighbor and friend, Mme. Germaine, who left her house at about the same time but has followed a slightly different route. Then she takes a turn through the Place du Palais, "just to see, really," though she may purchase some woolen stockings or an apron there, after which she turns down the Rue de la Porte-d'Orange and, not far from home, makes a long stop at Verdier's, the butcher in the Rue Raspail, where she is perfectly at home, knows everyone, and jokes with the butcher's apprentice. She's home again by about eleven.

The meaning of the market for Mme. Coste, as for many, is first and foremost a place where one "takes one's time." Time is not measured on Fridays. She took an hour and a half to do her bit of shopping, to buy products that are in fact available at Gardiol's and Verdier's any day of the week. Going to market also means entering and enjoying an urban space that is not on her daily rounds, a space transformed that day into a vast fairground with festival trappings. Whether she buys any sausage or not, Mme. Coste never misses the show in the Rue des Halles. Last, it means using the center of her city as a public space where the reserved relations of everyday life yield to generalized "commerce": "You see people at the market, that's almost why you go." The exchange game unfolds along these three dimensions.

The market is an art of "wasting" or "taking" one's time, spending time generously, lavishly, in a way that goes against the usual accounting perspective we have on it. This presupposes first that one organize things in such a way as to be free that morning. Peasants here traditionally did not work on market day, and growers try to maintain this custom, though it isn't easy to take Fridays off during the major producing period. Friday is often a harvest day, since the *marché-gare* is open Saturdays (closed Sundays). In winter this is not an issue, and men in from the countryside often stop awhile at the wood and grapevine market (set up on the site of the *marché-gare*), the habit being to leave the wife off in town and meet up with her again there around noon. In city offices, Friday is of course a workday, but people "manage," and an absence that at other times would be judged illegitimate is tolerated then. At the Bibliothèque Inguimbertine, Mme. Ayme and her colleague arrive on Friday with their shopping bags. Around ten, when the market is in full swing, they slip out together for an hour or so and no one says a thing to them about it.

But being free to go to market is above all a state of mind; a question not merely of how to organize one's time but of general attitude. One needs to be *open* to take in the market, open, like a visitor entering a foreign city, to whatever may be discovered there. Mme. Patio remarks: "At the market it's almost as if one were going to a show—a salon or exhibition." Like an art lover "doing the galleries" just "to see," you stop here and there, go back a ways, at times borne by the crowd, at others making your way against the current. You are more attentive to stalls you pass than to any given itinerary, and you stop at the least occasion. You finger a towel, assessing thickness and absorbency; crumple a fabric unrolled off a bolt to see how readily it wrinkles; hand-weigh a melon, taste an olive, extract a shirt from a pile of clothes, ask the price, how well it washes, comment on the quality—as much for the benefit of the other customers as for the stallholder. For many customers, the rule of the game is to act as if one intended to buy. For the stallholders, meanwhile, as we shall see in

58

detail, everything—stall arrangement, manner of speaking to customers, and so on—is done to make the market spectacle catch the passerby's attention and induce her to play an active role.

Still, the selling arrangement does not monopolize attention. People are just as receptive to the spectacle offered by others' transactions, the proceedings of others' exchanges (the savvy housewife, the intimidated fellow who doesn't dare say no, the foreigner laying on the affability, overheard conversations, the strange getup that one over there is wearing, the fact that M. and Mme. Raybaut are out shopping *together* today, and so on. Last, they remain open to both habitual and unexpected encounters and are always ready to move off to the side for a bit of conversation.

This state of openness is observable not merely from the outside; it seems an essential, conscious component of "going to market" for the actors themselves. Everyone says they spend more time strolling and chatting than buying. Most analysts, geographers but also sociolinguists and anthropologists, attribute to actors a primarily utilitarian and economistic vision of their own behavior and try to show they are generally not aware that it is governed by the logic of social relations and symbolic meaning. But in this case people rarely say they are motivated by exclusively rational or economic choices. It is always "the others" who are subject to the gray imperatives of well-grasped self-interest. As for oneself, one goes to market to "have a walk" or "take in the sights" more than to buy. Of course one should shop there because prices are lower, products fresher, selection greater, and so forth, but that is not why people say they go. Instead, everyone finds a reason in his or her particular situation. Mme. Coste says she goes to the market above all to meet up with people. Regarding her purchases: "I've been going mostly to the shops since I started living alone." "I don't buy much at the market either," adds her friend Germaine, "but I go anyway, to have a stroll. It's my Sunday." Both explain that living alone means they have few purchases to make, intimating that those who live *en famille* surely don't use the market the same way.

"We don't buy very much," says Mme. Patio. "We mostly go for the flowers. Except for vegetables, we don't buy. As you know, there's only me and my husband." "The rural customers come in to buy work overalls, whatever they need, a cap, a big thick sweater," specifies M. Patio, once director of the local branch of a major bank. This is also Rousseau's opinion, a city notable and former industrial canner, who adds: "Tourists buy food there. They get a change of scenery buying local products, all sorts of oils, cheeses, spicy things,

Provençal things. For us, given the relations we have with the supermarket [Intermarché took over what was once the space of his food-processing plant], we don't buy much at the market. It's rather exceptional for us."

It seems to me that most of my interlocutors minimize the purchases they make at the market. If everyone bought as little as they say, the market would have long since declined and disappeared. In fact, the people of Carpentras do a significant proportion of their provisioning at the street market, approximately 10 percent according to estimates by the Avignon chamber of commerce—higher than the national average of 7 percent.[1] But the way people answer suggests they are implicitly laying claim to a symbolic, playful relation to the market. This may be a way of appropriating the widespread cultural model of the "Provençal market," a figure par excellence of the Mediterranean area's reputedly warm sociability and emphasis on social relations. People readily establish an opposition between the market, where what they appreciate above all is the "ambiance," and the supermarket, where they go to "do the shopping," though this does not preclude speaking in other contexts of the Auchan mall as a place for "outings." "People are attracted by the parking lots, the big stores. They fill up the car there, then they come stroll in the market," says Nicole Grossage, wife of a former stallholder. Conversely, and to better demonstrate how important this local event is to their lifestyle, foreigners to the city tend to exaggerate how much shopping they do there.

The market is presented as a festive moment. It breaks up the daily monotony, if only by rendering the familiar city space unfamiliar. Even residents feel the change in city center streets on Fridays, with the array of bright colors, the heavy mix of smells. They easily forget those times when the market hardly resembles their enchanted descriptions of it: rainy Februarys, chill mornings in the Mistral wind, or all the "small" market days, when a handful of bundled up customers wander uncertainly among sparse stalls and only longtime habitués—who call themselves "real stallers"—are there, to "keep their spot."

It is significant that in speaking to me of the market, people spontaneously refer to the festival model of Saint Siffrein's Day: "Market days are big these days—it's Saint Siffrein's practically every time." In fact, this annual fair, held on November 27, is of quite different proportions. There are all the standard fair attractions, from a shooting gallery to cotton candy; a major exhibition of farming equipment, new and used vehicles, household appliances, and so on, and dozens of hawkers and product demonstrators of all sorts. On Saint Siffrein's Day you can get a haircut at the stand in Les Platanes, buy a fireplace,

60

taste wine from the Caromb cooperative wine cellar, learn about the dangers of drugs at the local police stand, or order "miracle" asparagus for the following spring (all the same size and they all "arrive" at the same time). But it is true that the overflowing disorderliness of "big summer markets"[2] (or market days just before Christmas) does call to mind the impression of joyous chaos associated with memories of the fair.[3] The presence of a great number of spielers on Fridays may well be what evokes for people the fundamentally different atmosphere of Saint Siffrein's Day (different because focused on rural activities). "Fair merchants holler, bark, call out—it's a show, the new and unexpected, noise, lots of action. This one's cutting glass, that one's sharpening knives. In the old days there were even what were called tool salesmen who sold sets of big keys and other things. They used to sell kilos and kilos of them," recounts Nicolas. Similarly, the recent increase in knickknack and "this and that" stands seems more in keeping with the traditional fair model, where the superfluous and novel reign.[4] "There didn't used to be trinket sellers at the market," says Mme. Coste. "It was only on fair day that they had everything."

To better depict today's market as a place of entertainment where buying is secondary, people like to remind you that in olden days things at the market were more serious (though in other contexts they evoke in great detail what remains in their memories first and foremost as a festive day). "The market used to be only useful things," says Mme. Coste. "It was for food. We'd come home loaded down like donkeys. You ran into people then too, but you didn't go there for that." "We don't buy there," explains Mme. Patio, "but come to think of it, my mother-in-law used to buy everything at the market, because in those days that was how you did things. She went to the market to shop, and when she saw people, it wasn't that she was wanting to see them. There was a time when everybody waited for Friday to come around just so they could go shop." Says Mme. Barrau: "Today we go there for a stroll, but back then, people never went to the market for nothing, they went to shop. They waited until Friday to get their provisions, and then they got them for the whole week because they usually only went out on Fridays. When the peasants finished selling their produce, they came to buy manufactured products they didn't have. The market was only for business."

People insist, moreover, that the market of olden times was not just a place for city residents. "People used to travel twenty-five kilometers to come here. They came to buy. They came from Sault [40 km.], they came from far away. They were a country clientele that was used to buying in the open. When they had to buy coats—at the time I made fur-lined jackets and suits—they came to Carpentras to buy them," says Grossage, who once had a clothing stall. His daughter-in-law adds: "Stalls used to be big. Now the wind has turned and there are little stands, food and crafts, things like that. Trinkets and little things sell well."

Even if people don't buy much, or claim they don't, the market is not merely a show. Whatever the pleasure one gets from the ambiance, one is not merely a stroller there. You have to participate in the event; otherwise it wouldn't be the market. People always go to buy, or at least with the vague intention of buying something. "We go to the market a lot to stroll, but that becomes an aim, because we wouldn't just go there to stroll aimlessly. I hate walking around aimlessly, taking an aimless walk, doing anything aimlessly. So we go to the market—and there you go!" explains Mme. Patio, and continues: "If you really have nothing to buy, theoretically you shouldn't go, if you've really got nothing, but you've always got a little idea of something. Seeing the selection gives you ideas, there are choices to be made, you take it into your head that this is better, that's not so good, and there you go! There are people who stop at the café on their way through the market, but not many, because when you want to go for a stroll you do that differently—on Saturday afternoon or Sunday, for example. That's when you go to the café."

One of the most characteristic types of behavior in this connection is the purchase-as-pretext. Every Friday, after taking his daughters to middle school, Pierre de Villette, a winegrower who also "does" apricots on the hills above Beaumes-de-Venise, walks through nearly the entire market to the Place de la Mairie to buy three small goat cheeses from a producer he knows. This habit has made him an excellent observer of the slightest variations or innovations from one market day to another—knowledge I greatly benefited from. And many of my interlocutors say they set themselves the purpose of buying a specific but relatively secondary item that they justify in terms of either its specificity—the ham that Grossage buys in the Rue des Halles has "a little extra taste of thyme"—or loyalty to an old routine: "We go to the market out of habit," says Mme. Barrau, "since time immemorial. I don't go to the market anymore to shop, except for cheese, and I always go to the same seller, opposite the *mairie*, where my mother used to go."

Certain other purchases, though relatively marginal in the household economy, are not a matter of pure alibi. People go to the market to buy dried fruit, spices, dried cod, slippers, an apron or cap—so many articles they could surely find elsewhere but that are easier to buy there. When, like Mme. Delavigne, you have long had a family home in the Comtat or on the other side of Mont Ventoux, it is considered good form to buy a few kilos of "Bergeron" apricots (indispensable for good jam), which can only—so the idea goes—be found there.

For some social groups, the market remains a nonnegligible supply source. People from the country stop in the specialized shops (hardware, household products, and so on) and buy shoes and clothes, not to mention hunting and fishing gear. North African immigrant workers can find live poultry only at the market, and also buy sheets, blankets, and household linens to send back to their families. But such "serious" purchases do not prevent their being receptive to the show: they are among Jacky Thevet's most regular admirers.

Whoever penetrates the market, even with the firm intention of not buying anything—one has only come to "stroll through," though one does happen to have a few bills in one's pocket—is in fact always ready to discover an unexpected or unsought object (a miracle can opener), to afford herself a small treat in passing (a rattle for the baby, a bouquet of tulips) or be tempted by an unexpected bargain (three T-shirts for the price of one): the unplanned, the adventure, as it were. Even those who've planned their purchases in advance or have a carefully laid out itinerary may indulge a capricious desire they did not know they had.

The stallholder's art consists in taking advantage of this indeterminate or unfixed desire. He knows that the attention of every shopper, whether his path is erratic or predetermined, is of the floating variety, that she advances with her nose in the wind, that they are therefore potential customers. All he has to do is catch him up in his own freedom, reflect back to her an image of herself as an idle onlooker susceptible of buying any old thing, and so draw her in by imitation. Hawkers have an accomplice, called "the baron," to bring in the crowds and get them to buy. While stallholders do not use this lure, they are well aware that if one person is curious, others will be too. "There's a very peculiar phenomenon," remarks Grossage. "Sometimes early in the morning there aren't many people on the market square, the customers haven't arrived yet. But if you're lucky enough to have two customers around your display, you'll see at least four others come—there and not elsewhere. The other stallholders have no one, they're standing there with their arms crossed. The fact that you've already got people around your stall—is it a magnet phenomenon?—makes people say, 'Hey, there must be good stuff there,' 'What's going on?' It's an event, and suddenly there you are with four or five customers trying on and buying things from you when no one else has a soul . . . We call these customers 'calling birds,' but it's independent of our will. A baron is a fake calling bird."

People implicitly let themselves get taken in, so the market is a world of false appearances where multiple decoys are continuously "calling" them. Stage-managing or the magic of the word can make anything desirable at any moment, and Octave Mannoni's description of the hawker's "labor" is valid for many types of behavior particular to the market: "The *bonimenteur* [spieler] is a slightly clearer case than the preacher, because what he has to sell is real, and because his way of 'improving' it ['*bonir*', *bonifier*] is not really to talk about it. The object for sale will be 'good' [*bon*] if it is sufficiently veiled and if there is desire, the sort that has no name. The *bonimenteur*'s use of metaphor is highly poetic: he speaks of faraway lands, caravans, stars, or the moon. It doesn't hurt that he recites his pitch by heart; on the contrary, the authority seems to come from further away. He speaks of all that is not present, that which '*n'a pas lieu*' [doesn't have a place, doesn't take place], to use Mallarmé's expression, touching upon what each person is missing, what each is wanting, and setting in motion unconscious desire. Quickly then, because this state will not last, he offers the latest lure, the tin or plastic treasure, the ridiculous acquisition, to be grabbed up by not yet disenchanted hands."[5]

Everything is done to capture and focus indeterminate desire. First, the stall is an open space: "You can come and go as you like at the market, you're not stuck like in a boutique" (Mme. Coste); "You're freer there because it's outside, out of doors" (Mme. Germaine). The stallholder also lays out his wares so that they are entirely within viewing and reaching distance. The products on display are directly accessible: foodstuffs are unwrapped or put out in bulk directly under the customer's nose, giving him the sense that he can touch and handle whatever and whenever he pleases, and though not just anything goes— "Leave the melons be, I'll choose one for you!"—the visitor-customer can assess the quality of a fabric with his fingertips, taste an olive, ferret around in the socks, and, at the extreme, more or less clandestinely, squeeze a sausage to see if it's good and firm. This is what Mme. Patio appreciates about the market: "There's greater selection, and you can see, you can touch the merchandise. At the market I always touch, touch if it's soft, if it's rough, if it's close woven." Every stall invites the shopper to take her time, and let eyes and hands rove over the objects on display.

Stallholders are perfectly aware that the meaning and effectiveness of this selling technique are due to the contrast with sedentary shops. In a boutique, much of the merchandise or stock is hidden from view (though today, particularly in clothes, there are new display strategies of putting everything out on hangers and shelves). The stall is an open space where all that is available is on display. Though the stallholder may have to go back to the truck for an extra crate, nothing happens out of sight. "When the merchandise is presented outside like this, people readily move in to look," explains Perdiguier. "They look, the prices are there, they're free to choose themselves, touch the wares. It's an extra attraction for the customer. He doesn't have to go through a door, or go in without knowing what he might like inside. At the market, all merchandise is automatically on display, he can see it. Nobody asks him anything, he chooses himself. The prospect of going through a door keeps lots of folks out. Here it's out-of-doors, and they can look even if they don't need to buy, whereas if you go into a store, you have to go out again, and it's always a delicate business to leave if you haven't bought anything. You can't put everything into a store window, and going in is more of a delicate business than with the market, where you can see everything. That's kind of our advantage—the stallholders' advantage."

The boutique is the realm of closed drawers and stacked boxes, and having stock and a selection presupposes going back and forth incessantly between shop and stockroom. Display windows do show a selection of products but maintain a distance between object and potential buyer. Embedded in a window display or buried somewhere in the stockroom, the object is more readily imagined to be unique and unobtainable, desirable because inaccessible. Displayed en masse and accessible to the touch, its power of attraction becomes more physical, playful. The customer is invited to rediscover the pleasures and privileges of childhood: wanting everything, being able to touch everything, not having to commit oneself. The stallholder operates through enticement and inducement, calling the potential customer to look, touch, and handle, rummage around not only to find what she is looking for but also to look for what, afterward, she will be happy to have found, to lay hands on an object she didn't really have in mind. The stallholder is not concerned with need, but speaks the language of desire. "People come to the market to do their shopping for the week . . . but not really," says Laville, a stallholder I met in Monteux. "Actually, I don't know why they come. In a store, people come to buy what they need. At a market, you hook people in, you even sell them things they don't need." "People will buy just about anything at the market," acknowledges Mme. Patio, "a thing for cutting *frites* [french fries]—it doesn't matter, it's tempting." In this respect, the only type of boutique that really resembles the market stall is the secondhand shop, which both imitates the spatial arrangement of the "no obligation to buy" shop and plays on sudden desire—an inexplicable passion for an old enameled salt box, for instance. In both cases objects are displayed to a virtual customer like a reflection of the unbounded multiplicity of her potential desires ("Now what nice little thing can I find in all that?"). The ideal receiver of the stallholder's message is thus not the rational or penny-pinching consumer but the *enfant-roi* delighting in the spectacle of all that has been put within his reach; the customer consentingly enticed, seduced, with whom an implicit shared understanding develops: I am here to get taken in, I know I'm going to get "taken," and I accept the game, delighting already in the account, the story, I will tell of it.

The greatest number of items must therefore be displayed, and the stall has to be maintained in as great a seeming disorder as it is in reality deliberately organized. This is a highly perfected trap for catching the customer up in his own freedom. "If you have to leave soup pots and saucepans in a cardboard box," explains Espenon, who "does a bazaar" in the Place aux Oies, "if you can't display them, you won't sell as much as if you just pile them up. You just can't work the same way as in a store—it's that simple. For us, the nicely wrapped item in a nice box won't sell. We get a toy in a pretty box, nicely packaged, the first thing we do is take it out and show it like that. How many times have we bought nicely packaged items, for Mother's Day let's say, or some such, to have stuff like they have in the stores—it gets you zero! That's not the thing, they don't want that, they just lie around, and if you tell them, 'I've got the box,' they say, 'Just put it in a bag.' "

This principle is so decisive that a small market where stallholders can spread out as much as they like can actually be more profitable than a big one where allotted space is meager. "There are items I can't put out in Carpentras," Espenon continues, "I don't have room, whereas at a market like Caromb you have as much space as you like. There you set yourself up, you display your merchandise better, and it works. There are a lot of women who come to market because they can finger things. Women like to rummage around. I've often noticed that when a stall is too neat, they don't dare touch. This doesn't help sales much. A tumble-jumble, a mess they're not afraid to rummage in—that's what they like. People don't dare go into a store and start digging around. Everything's neatly arranged on the shelves, so you don't dare. They may do a little damage to our stuff—don't think the merchandise can take it; things get broken sometimes and we have to throw stuff out. The thing is, letting them run their hands through it, pick it up, put it down, choose it, 'This one? No, that one'—in the end, they buy."

Noël Cappo uses the same technique. Working alone at his hardware and household products stall and handling a steady stream of customers (he sells a multitude of inexpensive products: floorcloths, soap, shoelaces, and so forth), Cappo makes a virtue of necessity: "I put things out disorderly because I'm alone and my time is limited . . . I think disorder attracts some customers, especially for the little doodads I sell. Markets aren't supposed to be organized! You've got to be able to dig around a little. People like digging around."

This arrangement seems to share features with the one used in supermarkets and department stores, as some stallholders themselves remark, among them Perdiguier and Nicole Grossage: "At the market, you arrive, you touch, you come, you go. It's a bit like that in department stores. At the market they sell Gruyère and then just a hundred meters away clothes or shoes. That's what supermarkets are, the same advantages. We offer a whole diversified thing to the public."[6] It also often happens that supermarket or mall managers try to imitate the street market model, within the constraints of their spatial arrangements. The people of Carpentras, however, perhaps adopting some of the widespread criticisms of mass consumption, often told me that in the Auchan supermarket they feel "channeled," as if the felt freedom of the marketplace had been replaced by the surreptitious, invisible, diabolical pressure of a type of organization that in a thousand ways forces one to consume. "They've got this catch-the-sucker way of selling," explains Espenon. "They put two or three big-selling items on sale, they give you three for two, they draw in their crowds, and they know that once people are there they'll leave with eight hundred or a thousand francs' worth of merchandise." Or as another stallholder put it: "In supermarkets they set two or three low prices and the rest are sky-high." To listen to the people of Carpentras, these types of buying incentives actually create an attitude of wary reservation. People try to take advantage of the deals, the appealing "special sale" items, while remaining calculating, savvy consumers. We may hypothesize that behavioral logic in the two cases is different.[7] The fact that supermarket merchandise is displayed en masse and is directly accessible is due to a kind of rational arranging of products in space that precludes all surprise. Also, because this type of display facilitates price comparison, it responds not to the need for a low-cost adventure but to the pleasure of imagined savings at the expense of the big capitalists. The appeal of stallholders, who play on customer openness and whim, is the opposite of the invisible manipulation that customers undergo in the labyrinthine prison of supermarket or department store aisles. In fact, stallholders too "catch" the customer, as they readily acknowledge, but in another way. "People come to take a stroll, a look," acknowledges Espenon. "They buy some little thing, sometimes next to nothing, sometimes they buy something and think to themselves, 'I wasn't expecting to buy today!' Opportunity makes the thief."

Might it be that people experience Auchan as a pressure machine because they compare their experience there with a given cultural context, of which the market experience is a part? The subject's relation to supermarket-type setups is necessarily a function of his or her personal story and mode of social integration. It is hardly surprising, for example, that the writer Philippe Sollers, upon visiting the Suma supermarket built on the lot where his childhood home once stood, feels something like disgust: "The ultimate anonymous parade, of satisfied, unconscious, self-regulated, consummate misery. We all digest! We're all the same! . . . Standing in their patient, resigned lines . . . pious almost."[8] "Supermarkets overwhelm me with boredom, eradicate all desire, render me incapable of choosing," writes Colette Pétonnet, but notes that "a Tunisian intellectual living in Paris for the last ten years says that pushing a cart through the aisles gives him a feeling of omnipotence, absolute freedom of choice."[9]

The attitude of ready, consenting openness specific to the market may well explain why people often have the impression of buying little, of going instead "for the market itself," whereas they have no trouble acknowledging they buy a lot at Auchan. The fact that people go to the market without planning to buy anything means not so much that one will not buy anything as that one goes with a mind free of all need and is thus ready to buy just about anything. One always thinks one is there for one's pleasure and one always buys nearly inadvertently. Even the person who goes to shop can get drawn into the game: the market makes an enchanted moment out of a tiresome household chore. It is impossible to treat it like a buying and selling location where you come to satisfy predetermined needs. It is an arrangement for enticing people, inducing and seducing them, and the knowing consumer's cold rationality or the housewife's parsimonious management cannot resist the charm. Once taken in by the market, one no longer perceives oneself as consumer or cautious housewife; one becomes instead an economic actor in spite of oneself, unconsciously, since so many noneconomic reasons may be given for one's behavior. It is precisely because it seems to each person that he or she is not there to buy that the market does such good business.

4. Familiar Strangers

Why does a buyer at a street market feel free and easy, free to come and go? In part of course because of how the space is organized. The stall is an open structure, without marked limits. But the buyer's sense of freedom is also produced by the type of social relation established with the seller. As their comments suggest, people at the market feel they have been freed from the sort of minimal commitment you make simply by entering a boutique. "You don't feel the same type of obligation as you do with regard to the merchant or salesperson," says Mme. Blanc. At the market, just as no door closes behind you, so no firm tie need be tied. Going through a boutique door, even one marked *entrée libre* [no obligation to buy], means putting oneself into the buyer position because of a sort of implicit contract. In this connection the equivalent of the boutique is not so much the stall as the market altogether: consenting to enter the market involves exposing oneself to making a purchase, however unexpected. And one stall is just like another. Spending time looking over the wares does not commit you to anything. It would be very peculiar behavior to enter a city *charcuterie*, ask if they had sausage meat, then walk out saying, "Okay, I'll think about it." But since the market is an invitation to walk along and take things in, hesitation and even caprice are perfectly acceptable.

People feel especially free from obligation at the market because the exchange relation is engaged in with a stranger rather than an "acquaintance." "It's not closed—this is psychological," comments Rousseau. "You can talk together, then leave, more easily than in a self-enclosed shop where there's a saleswoman asking you what you're looking for. At the market one is not known." Going into a store means initiating a relation with a fellow citizen who is assumed more or less to know you. One is always somewhat "on a visit." At the market, Reynaud notes, "you don't have the feeling of being *chez quelqu'un* [at someone's]." The stallholder is not "someone from here," and thus at the extreme he or she is no one, or at least is not relevant to the network of relations in reference to which people define themselves. The stallholder's stall, temporarily taking up room on the public way, is in no way a private space and creates no contractual obligations, whereas the opposite obtains for shops— one goes *chez Gardiol* or *chez Jouviaud*—and even for the Auchan supermarket. One always feels slightly guilty leaving such businesses without buying anything.

In reality, customers have their habits, at the market as elsewhere, and wandering among the stalls does not preclude a few necessary purchase stops or a certain type of loyalty. The stallholders are well aware of this. "My mother gets her potatoes at one place, her cod at another, her olives at a third, and vegetables somewhere else again," explains Espenon. " 'I only shop there,' she says. I hear people talking together and saying 'This is my bazaar, I always come here, you can't imagine how nice they are.' It's not true, we're no nicer than the others, but there you have it, it's like that. Of course people at the market will check if anyone's got a sale on dresses or shoes. They check if sometimes someone puts something out. But they've still got their suppliers."

This kind of loyalty is not perceived as a constraint, however. People simply do not feel obligated to buy as sometimes happens at fixed merchants', particularly in small cities or individual neighborhoods. As Mme. Patio explains, "You don't dare buy only twice and not three times, because you want to avoid questions like 'Why haven't you been in? You weren't sick, at least?' To stop stores from asking, we sometimes don't go there at all. It's not really because we don't want to." She appreciates the freedom of the market for this reason, while acknowledging that she almost always patronizes the same stalls.

It is therefore essential for customers that stallholders seem, rightly or wrongly, like people from elsewhere. It is true that as itinerant tradespeople traveling from one market to the next on their circuit, they incarnate the figure of the nomad, the person from nowhere. People cannot imagine meeting up with them on the streets of the city in a different setting or on occasions other than the market.

But if we look a bit more closely at stallholder circuits or rounds, it is easy to show that the way they are arranged and the logic behind them have little to do with nomadism or wandering. The vast majority of stallholders have a weekly round covering five or six markets, generally not far from each other and always the same. The fishmonger Payard's round is typical: Cavaillon on Mondays, Vaison-la-Romaine on Tuesdays, Wednesdays off, Orange on Thursdays, Carpentras on Fridays, Apt on Saturdays, Sorgues on Sundays. Regular stallholders differ from "market men," the *sans domicile fixe* (homeless), as they're called, who move throughout France on unfixed itineraries and at unset paces, in that they are regularly present at the same markets within a limited regional space.[1] "We are not stallholders," explains Perdiguier. "We are itinerant merchants. Sellers like us are called *landiers* because we're always at the same markets. The others are called *voyageurs*."

What stallholders continue to call their circuit is in fact a series of round trips between home, where they return in the afternoons, and the different markets they sell at. Limiting total distance traveled is a primary concern: "The point is not to have to jump around too much, do too many kilometers, because obviously that requires getting up early and home late," explains Nicole Grossage. Says Espenon: "After knocking about for a number of years, I developed a core of markets for myself around Carpentras, to make the travel profitable and limit the bother." He lives in Beaucet, fifteen minutes from Carpentras. In fact, most of the sellers one meets on Fridays are not strangers at all. A quarter of them actually live in Carpentras, and most reside in the Vaucluse, primarily in the region delimited by Orange, Avignon, L'Isle-sur-la-Sorgue, and Carpentras. Having a round presupposes that the markets in the region constitute an organized network, and this is the case in the Vaucluse and surrounding area. It is clear from the market map that the area's markets are organized in such a way that no two big ones are held on the same day. The same rule applies to small town markets to the extent possible.

It has often been noted that markets are not purely local, isolatable phenomena, but become "aggregated into veritable systems endowed with particular topological and chronological properties."[2] The historian Dominique Margairaz, for example, has shown how these systems were put in place in the eighteenth century in France through the combined effects of economic liberalism and a *dirigiste* approach to space.[3] Stallholders are fully aware that a certain system coherence is a necessary condition for exercising their profession: "We'd be in a fine mess if all the markets were scheduled on Saturday." The fact remains that for them a circuit is always a matter of personal options.

External, objective analysis of how market networks are organized in space and time, such as that offered by spatial economists, should not obscure the fact that the success or decline of a market within the system also depends on stallholders' choices from among several possible markets, some of which are held on the same day (in this case Cavaillon or Saint-Didier on Mondays, Arles or Apt on Saturdays, and so on), and that these in turn follow their own particular logic. Circuit organization represents a compromise between two principles: the desire to "travel in an area close to home" and the tendency to specialize in a particular category of market.

Stallholders generally choose markets of the same type. They distinguish between small village markets, "neighborhood" markets in big cities (including those at the Avignon walls and "housing development markets" in working-class Avignon suburbs such as La Jolie), and "markets in somewhat major cities" (such as Carpentras or Apt). This last variety, says Perdiguier, "pulls in extraordinary numbers [of sellers]. For all of them to have some business, you need more [buyers] than a neighborhood or small market gets."

The profession is not the same from one type of market to another. Laval, a fishmonger who specializes in "village markets" and "does" Saint-Didier, explains thus: "Over here we don't make what the Carpentras stallholders do. You can work alone in villages, but at bigger markets you need personnel, so you've got to double what you take in to earn the same amount. I'm not ambitious, what I do is enough for me, I don't try to pile it on." His friend Bonnet the *fromager* jumps in here: "I *am* ambitious. And I'll make it, but it'll take time. I'm breaking myself in on the small markets. It's happening slowly, little by little. I've got a truck with three meters of fridge space now, next year I'm going to get one that will go six meters. I'll keep the markets I have with this truck, and little by little I'll get on to the big markets. I'll do one a week, then two . . ." Doing small markets is clearly either a choice or a way of learning the ropes. This explains why such markets often feature mobile shops owned by Carpentras or Avignon shopkeepers and managed by or franchised to stallholders.

The opposite trajectory is also possible. Espenon, for example, gave up most of the big markets he used to do, particularly Montélimar, where he went twice a week as manager of a mobile shop: "You've got to be young to do that. A thing like that has to be driven at 70 an hour [approximately 45 m.p.h.], and you've got to take it to the end of the universe. I had to leave here at five in the morning—and when you look at gas prices these days!" He chose himself a village-to-village circuit instead: Saint-Didier every other Monday, Caromb

74

on Tuesdays, Velleron every other Wednesday, the little market on L'Isle-sur-la-Sorgue on Thursdays, Perne on Saturdays, Monteux on Sundays. Delvaux, the *charcutier* at the Porte d'Orange who lives in Monteux, relates: "At first I ran all the way out to Bagnols-sur-Cèze, Vaison, Istres. I tried the housing projects too. La Jolie wasn't bad, but once you're known in the projects, everything runs on credit, and that gets you zero! So I fell back on Vedène on Tuesdays and the round I have now [Entraigues, Le Pontet, Pernes, Monteux]." The fact that stallholders specialize in a single market type goes a long way to explaining why a stallholder at Carpentras on Fridays is likely to be at Sorgues or L'Isle-sur-la-Sorgue on Sundays, Cavaillon on Mondays, Vaison on Tuesdays, Valréas on Wednesdays, Orange on Thursdays, and Apt or Arles on Saturdays. Meanwhile, the combination of professional necessity and concern to stay close to home explains apparently atypical rounds. Deredjan, for example, who sells clothes in the Place de la Mairie, goes to Valréas and Orange, but since he lives in Bollène, he does that market Mondays, and Pont-Saint-Esprit, on the other side of the river, on Saturdays. Macaire, an olive, nut, and dried fruit merchant, stays home in Pernes on Saturdays (after doing Cavaillon, Vaison, and Valréas on other days) though it is only a small market, and prefers to do nearby Pontet on Thursdays.

The nature of the product sold must also be taken into account. If you're in exceptional-purchase goods (luxury secondhand clothing, for example), you need to "drain" a greater surface area. Avry, who sells foam mattresses and lives in the Gard, has big distances to cover. On Mondays he's at Forcalquier, Tuesdays in Nyons, Thursdays at Miramas, Saturdays at Apt, Sundays at Château-renard. But if you're in food you can cover less territory, keeping in mind that with perishables you can't move too far from supply points and will need to do nearly a market a day. For Rodriguez, who sells *viennoiseries* at the Porte d'Orange, four markets a week suffice (Carpentras, Orange, Sault, Mazan).

Last, from one market to the next the clientele is socially different, and this too determines stallholders' choices. For bottom-of-the-market products, Sorgues with its large immigrant population is preferable to Apt; luxury secondhand clothing sells better in Aix-en-Provence than in Bollène. Still, stallholders can adapt their products to local clienteles. Some do so without realizing it after a bit of hands-on experience: "In Pontet, for example," remarks Delvaux, "I work a lot with Spanish products. In Monteux it's ready-made dishes and *patisserie charcutière*; in Vedène I sell a lot of cheap cuts, pig's feet and tails, *croustillons* [spareribs], things like that. Yeah, it's true, in fact, I hadn't really thought about it, but depending on the market, one thing sells rather than another." His charcuterie ethnography proves highly relevant: the suburbs of Avignon have long been populated by Spanish immigrants; Vedène is a town that has long been working class; and the people of Monteux, while not particularly well off, will treat themselves to *bouchées à la reine* for the family meal after church on Sundays.[4]

Other stallholders have explicit tactics in this matter and make direct use of their sociological intuitions. "In fact," explains Laval the fishmonger, "I don't improvise at the Saint-Didier market. Sales vary above all for Mediterranean fish, which is much more expensive. People are finer connoisseurs in some villages than in others. In Bédoin, for example [a prestigious resort town on the slopes of Mont Ventoux], there are a lot of people who sail, who know a lot of different types of fish and still buy them. I can sell fish like pollock, pandora, things like that, in Bédoin, but not here. People in Carpentras are also connoisseurs. There are a lot of *pieds-noirs* there, they know Mediterranean fish, and they'll buy at any price."[5]

But sometimes variation in demand remains unexplained. "There's no reason for the clientele to have the same needs or tastes from one market to another," observes Espenon. "Take Tergal (artificial silk) flowers, for example. If you put a Tergal rose into a bouquet of roses, you can't see the difference. You can leave it in the sun, you can wash it, it's rain-resistant, it's wind-resistant. So you go for example to the Pernes market and let me tell you, I hardly sell any Tergal flowers, but at the Carpentras and Monteux markets I sell lots!"

Whatever the parameters determining choice of selling venues, and even if stallholders modify their strategies over a long-term career, circuits are generally stable and regular, at least for subscriber stallholders. Moreover, a circuit clientele can be transferred from father to son. "I took over my father's and grandparents' circuit for all except the Bagnols market," says Perdiguier. "They would leave with a cart and spend the night in the market town. On market days, we're almost like the stores—it's our heritage. The customer has to be sure we'll be there the following week." Many Carpentras stallholders have been occupying the same place for generations, and, paradoxically, they never fail to cite this to customers as a strong point in their favor. Though stallholders have no formal right to their spot, a circuit can be transmitted from parents to children. "We unload in the public right of way. Spots can't be sold, and being in the business without a spot is no good. The only way to transmit it is through the family; the children have to take over the business," says Perdiguier. If there are no descendants to inherit the circuit, one can make arrangements to sell it almost like a business—if the *placier* and city hall agree to look the other way. "A guy who retires here sells his markets, he sells his circuit, his equipment, everything," clarifies Laval, "whereas in Paris that's strictly prohibited. It's even prohibited here—market spots belong to the city—but it happens anyway. For example, I take a guy on my round one week, I introduce him. 'He's my *commis* [assistant],' I say, 'he's my cousin, I'm quitting, I'm going to take care of production, he'll do the selling.' " This way, even though the faces change, the same business continues to occupy the same spot.

It therefore requires a whole set of imaginative representations, often fueled by narratives from the stallholders themselves, for customers to be able to project the image of a nomad onto the familiar figure of these itinerant tradespeople, ultimately so sedentary, most of whom can readily say they *are* "from these parts." A whole imaginary to be able to see their lives as having something in common with tales of the wandering, adventurous stallholders of yesteryear, trundling up hill and down dale, traveling in groups for fear of bandits, back and forth over the highways on their carts from market to market several days in a row.

But the image of the stallholder as passing stranger is understandably strengthened in customer eyes by the presence on the market of the "voyager" variety. Every market morning, people notice stalls they have not seen before, new faces that may well not be there the following week. There are generally two or three "homeless" stallholders, often hawkers or discounters selling factory outlet linens or dishes at cut prices at markets throughout France. Many of them go round Provence in the summer "for the sun." There are a lot of them at the big Saint-Siffrein fair. Their way of life is similar to that of "industrial stallholders," that is, amusement fair vendors. They live in RVs and their circuit, they say, is "the whole of France." They constitute a separate world in the eyes of regular stallholders. They are said to marry only among themselves and hardly send their children to school; they are suspected of swindling customers, "and this reflects on the market as a whole," but they are respected for their energy: "They do make money—but not easily," says Perdiguier. "I admire them, they do fine work."

In addition to these nomadic professional traders, the irregular and above all seasonal presence of small retailers, craftspeople, producers, and other more or less amateur sellers gives the impression of a disparate gathering of "people from elsewhere." Many occasional stallholders are very irregularly present;

others come to market several weeks in a row but without anyone's really being aware of them; they are never in the same spot, either because of the spot drawing (see chap. 12) or because their wares are on wheels so they can "park" wherever they like. Moreover, they never fail to let the customer know they may not be there the following Friday.

"We go where there's room, we work by word-of-mouth, tips we get on where to go," a craftsman who sells objects in flame-engraved wood explains to me. He lives in Lambesc and does not have a real round, but peregrinates anarchically over a vast territory without concern for distance or travel costs. "On Mondays I stay put, there's no market worth going to. On Tuesdays I go to Vaison or Aix or Istres. On Wednesdays I'm at Le Buis, Valréas, or Salon, Thursdays sometimes at Orange, sometimes at Aix. Fridays generally at Carpentras. Saturdays, Arles, Sundays Sorgues or Martigues."

Most occasional stallholders do small business in wares such as children's clothes, toys, small leather goods, gadgets, slogan buttons and brand-name pins, and so on. But during the summer you find occasionals of greater scope who sell only on small markets, not Carpentras, because they are there to "have a rest." A hat-selling couple from Saint-Etienne manage to take a semivacation this way. "We have friends on L'Isle-sur-la-Sorgue. We come down to see them with the truck so we can arrange to sell on the quiet little markets."

The craftspeople in the Passage Boyer are something of a special case. They are seasonal (Easter to September) but have fixed spots nonetheless. People call them "students," sometimes "hippies," and are particularly likely to consider them strangers because of their appearance: overalls, mended jeans, sandals or bare feet, loose, open shirts. The objects they sell—pottery, "organic" pastries, lamps in turned wood, "Provençal" cushions and place mats—have clearly been patiently, more or less skillfully handmade and evoke a lifestyle that does not correspond to the usual norms, recalling instead the potters, painters, and other artists who settled in the region in the 1960s to "live elsewhere and differently." In fact, most of these sellers (23 out of 39 by the count I took on a Friday in July) are children of the area who want to escape the monotony of a small family business or the dead end of life as an office clerk and are constructing themselves imaginary membership in an artistic milieu.

Pierre, for example, sells beaded necklaces and bracelets made by his girlfriend Cathy to a clientele of "tourists and young people from the region." His family lives in Monteux, where his father works for the Ducros industrial herb and spice company. Apprenticeship to a television repairman did not lead anywhere, and working as a packer for a Carpentras shipper, as his father suggested, did not tempt him in the least. Cathy was familiar with markets; while preparing a first-level accounting degree, she often accompanied her father, a former mason who had switched to selling poultry, cheese, and eggs at the Pernes, Monteux, Saint-Didier, and Apt markets. With her "girlfriend," who was learning stenography, Cathy began making the jewelry they now sell at the Carpentras and Monteux markets and also "at school" when it's in session. The three of them like to think of themselves more as creators than traders. "It brings in a bit," says Cathy, "but what's nice is to show what we do. And then at the markets you meet other jewelry makers and see what they do. I never make two pieces alike. I make what I want, not what sells."

The considerable number of *gitans* and Senegalese spread throughout the city reinforces the standard idea that the market is by nature a welcoming place where everyone can find a place for themselves however distant they may be from the local culture. In fact, the gitans live in the region, most of them in Avignon, and do the rounds of the big markets (L'Isle-sur-la-Sorgue, Cavaillon, Vaison, Salon, Nyons, and Marignane, for example) all year round, selling wicker baskets and lemons or garlic bought at the Avignon MIN.[6] The same ones are there every Friday, a dozen members of a single family who divvy up among themselves the slightest vacant spaces between stalls. Mother, daughter, or cousin occupies the bit of curb next to the fishmonger in the Rue des Halles. But no one feels they know them. You buy "from the gitan," not from a particular one among them. And their selling tactic is to play the gitan just as people imagine them, squatting on the ground and extending a hand with two or three lemons in it. This pose, close to begging, conceals a certain prosperity: "Our small family business brings in good money because everyone needs lemons," explains Thérèse Cérès of Pernes.

The Senegalese, who go to both the big markets (Cavaillon, Vaison, Arles, Orange, and so on) and the smaller, more touristy ones (Bédoin, Malaucène), are there every week from April till September, but no one pays any attention to whether they're the same from week to week. "I can never recognize them," admits Pascal the *placier*. With their so-called primitive crafts—imported directly from their native bushland, they say—they are of course particularly "other-worldish" since their business is to sell the exotic.

Friday merchants are thus strangers to varying degrees and in varying ways. But it is essential that the market tradesperson one is dealing with, however familiar, appear a stranger. Mme. Patio needs Espenon and his general bazaar to evoke to some minimal degree the wanderings of the Gypsies, even though he resides in Beaucet amid the oak and olive tree hills where she herself likes to stroll on Sundays. In reality, these "strangers" are often much more familiar than city merchants. Mme. Ripert goes much more often to look at the vast display of goods Jojo Spinelli sets up every Friday than to the perfumery in the Rue Vigne or the jewelry shop in the Rue de la République, and Mme. Sorel has much more regular relations with Bachini, a fishmonger at the Porte d'Orange where she goes every week to buy her red mullet, than with the butcher of the Rue Raspail, from whom she may order a leg of lamb on those occasional Sundays when her children come for lunch.

The stallholders themselves, while playing on what makes them people from elsewhere in contrast to sedentary merchants, are fully aware that the tight network of relations they are part and parcel of every week gives them a kind of de facto citizenship. A fishmonger related to me how, after a mistaken first name was published in an obituary notice in the local newspaper, everyone expressed their sadness at his demise. Stallholders who have been transmitting the same spot from one generation to the next understandably have a feeling of rootedness. "You'll often hear customers say that their grandfather was supplied by us," remarks Perdiguier. "It's a little like a tradition. We've known these families for a long time, and we often speak together of relatives, of everyone, and there are very old people who ask for news of my parents." More recently established stallholders may also feel "at home" there, and recognized as such, when they see generations of customers succeed each other at their stall. "We're *chez nous* at the markets we go to, especially ones we've been going to for a long time," says Espenon. "It almost seems like you've got a fixed store, because these are customers you see every week. Every week you've got the same guy, the same lady, the same kids who come for toys, you end up knowing them, they're almost like family. We've seen little girls we sold toys to who are married women now, twenty-four, twenty-five years old, and they come buy toys for their children. I hope to have the third generation, and when there's the fair—we don't do fairs, people don't want to walk around in the crowd with a toilet seat or a watering can when they know we'll be in their town two days later!—people come say hello. We shake two thousand hands in the course of the day—and don't make a cent."

5. Delights of Free Trade

The market situation requires a face-to-face between two types of actors: customer-strollers, who may have a particular purchase in mind but nonetheless remain unconsciously open to all the market has to offer, open to the adventure of it, to sudden sharp desire for a just-discovered object; and traders, "strangers" to the city perceived to move like nomads from market to market. To the whims of the first must correspond the freedom of the second, for it is essential that the person who buys for the pleasure of buying be sold to as if in a game. The stallholder's secret is to make clear through a multitude of signs that he or she is not just any tradesperson.

To the customer's openness and unconstrained vagabonding corresponds the stallholder's representation of his or her own work. Stallholders see their profession as one of those rare activities where one can remain master of one's time and movements, and it is precisely this autonomy that they bring to the fore when stage-managing the market relation. The encounter is between a tradesperson not subject to the customer's will (in contrast to the situation in a store) and a buyer who doesn't feel trapped into any obligation to buy. Each may rightfully feel himself master of the game: the trader can, at least theoretically, change markets, and the buyer can very easily change merchants. The freedom that informs street market exchange, and the different ways it is manifested, are essential to the market game.

In the course of their conversations with me, all the stallholders I spoke with spontaneously evoked what they consider their particular privilege: "It's a trade where you've got freedom." To begin with, their working hours leave them a great deal of free time. "We do what we want," says Blanc the cheese vendor in my three-way conversation with him and Laval the fishmonger at Saint-Didier. "Especially me. He [Laval] gets up at four in the morning, I get up at eight, and I don't work in the afternoon. We get a perfectly decent wage for four hours' work a day, it's really good, we can do other things. If I had a house to build I'd build it, you can have another job—which I do in fact, I've started doing packing with the guy who bought the business I had. I take a vacation whenever I want, I do whatever I want." "Not quite like you say you do," objects Laval. "The clientele comes to buy cheese. If you were only there every other week, they'd get around to thinking you're a lightweight." And there are certain business management requirements, as Delvaux points out: "Some people tell you, 'Ah, you're sitting pretty. You're your own boss. When you want to go out, you go out; when you don't want to because it's too cold, you don't.' But they forget that when we don't go out, nothing comes in. And the expenses keep running up."

Because stallholders "navigate" every day from one market to the next (the word is Delvaux's, who gave up his dream of sailing faraway seas for the lot of itinerant *charcutier*), they have the feeling the initiative is always theirs and that they can change circuits whenever they like. Sometimes they do just follow their mood, rather than concentrate on how to maximize profits. Nicole Grossage recounts: "On the road to Cavaillon one day we got a flat tire and arrived at the market a hair after eight. The head *placier* grouched and my husband had his tantrum: 'I chose this work so no one could give me a hard time. You can keep your spot. I'm leaving and I'll never set foot in your market again!' And we haven't been back there since."

Most stallholders are careful to attend the markets on their circuit with strict regularity, and "hold down the spot" even when takings are small. In winter "you don't do good business"; there are even days when "you'd do better not going out," but "you hold onto the spot." Though Perdiguier enjoys "getting a change of scenery" every day, he readily acknowledges "it's hard work. You have to get up early in the morning, and you have to work on Sundays. I haven't had a Sunday for myself since the age of thirteen. I remember when I was twenty, I had to leave after the others to go to rugby practice, by bike, and I always got there late. You can never miss a market, come rain or wind; people's confidence is based on that. The customer has to be sure that you'll be there to trade next week. They're used to seeing me. They often buy shoes without trying them on, or for their kids. If they don't fit they bring them back, like in a shop."

For others, however, this constraint is only really an effect of their free will; they can always choose "not to go out." The Grossage family has had a spot in the Place du Théâtre for two generations. In some respects, they say, "it was like a store. Since we had fixed spots, people kept coming back. We supplied the mother, then the daughter, and it kept on like that because there was a kind of loyalty. But then one day, say the weather's bad, you don't absolutely have to go out. If you've got a store you have to open every day. At the market, if you don't feel well and you want to take a week off, you leave a note with the *placier*, you stay away for a week, and that's that. You can even miss two weeks, it's no tragedy. The customers come back!"

The young generation of stallholders is particularly concerned to take advantage of this feature of the job: "The freedom exists—that's obvious. But the first people to mention it are the ones who destroy it by the work pace they impose on themselves," says Martin, who sells secondhand clothes. "They have to be at the market regularly every week and they do six or seven markets a week, so freedom is really a relative term!" In fact, Martin, like Françoise in the stall next to his, settles for being present at Carpentras regularly enough not to lose his spot, adding a few extra markets (Nyons, L'Isle-sur-la-Sorgue, Aix) as soon as the weather gets nice.

For professional stallholders, such amateur behavior or poor attendance ("They don't hold down the place!") is where "young people" or "newcomers" go wrong and explains why they often "come a cropper." "How many times have I seen guys who don't unload," relates Perdiguier. "The other day it was raining and one of them says to me, 'You must be dead broke to unpack when it's pouring like this!' And at nine he went home—after doing a hundred kilometers to get here. At nine-thirty it stopped raining and we did a small amount of business. He didn't make a centime. Have you seen who stays around at Easter time when the weather's bad? Only the old stallholders. It makes sense, in fact. Let's even say I know I'm not going to sell anything— but the customer who comes because he needs something, if I'm not there . . . People just getting set up don't understand that."

Though stallholders may have a more or less demanding vision of their work—and it is true that the felt obligation to "hold the spot" varies by business size—they share the idea that their line of work is a better guarantee of inalienable autonomy than any other activity, an idea sometimes formulated as "At least there's no one to get on your ass!" "The independence we have is unique," explains an occasional seller of wooden toys. "We aren't accountable to anyone. Freedom like this is priceless." First, one is "one's own boss," a situation particularly appreciated by stallholders given that for many this work is a means of escaping the blue-collar or office work to which lack of skills and/or educational degree would condemn them. Second, it is relatively easy to set up as a stallholder: reduced administrative formalities, limited up-front investment.[1] "You do need three million ["old" francs; approximately €4,500], though. You have to get fridges, a scale. I had two thousand in pocket when I started," recounts a cheese merchant. "I got started on small loans."

Stallholders' attachment to their work, perceived as different from all other kinds, is often indissociable from the independence it has enabled them to acquire, in some cases with difficulty and through self-abnegation. Delvaux the Porte d'Orange *charcutier* is pleased to have become his own master, but he managed it only after some hard times.

> I used to sell at the market for a boss in Paris. We did markets at Breteuil, Porte de Choisy. We did the Porte d'Auteuil and the Point-du-Jour market in the Avenue de Versailles, and Ornano, Billancourt, Clichy, and Choisy-le-Roi. Then I decided to set up on my own. My father's a native of Avignon, my mother's from Carpentras, and my father was sick and tired of Paris. He retired early. He owned the apartment we lived in, so he said, "If you want to stay in Paris you'll need at least 60 or 80 million. You'll never be able to get yourself set up. If you want to come with us, we're going to Monteux, and with the money from the apartment you can always buy yourself a mobile shop." Otherwise I'd still be in Paris. It's really not the same kind of work. In Paris, nine out of ten times you make the stuff in the cellar, whereas here when I leave my *atélier* [kitchen] I've got the grass, trees, a willow . . . We left Paris in July as if we were leaving for a vacation. I really screwed up on the formalities, though, and I couldn't get started until November. The bills started coming in, people started getting unpleasant . . . In the beginning things really didn't work. The first time I went to Carpentras I made forty-five francs [€6]. The worst was in Orange—seventy centimes! A single slice of rolled *petit salé* [salt pork]—I remember it like it was yesterday! For six months I was bringing in about sixty francs per market. I did the maximum to hold on, but it just wasn't happening. So I fell back on the circuit I have now. Today I'm okay, it's not bad work. Like I told you, I'm someone who can't stay in one place. I earn my living okay, but you've got to live a little—that's why I'm here. But if I'm still here when I'm pushing fifty, still in this work, then I may just think about getting a store. It's less of a hassle.

84

Not only is the stallholder his own master, which is also the case for sedentary storekeepers, but like an artist with a violin under his arm or a poker player in westerns, he has the feeling he can use his talent anywhere. Stallholders often believe they earn their living by exercising a certain gift, what in other milieus is called a feeling for public relations. They are therefore more than ready to adopt the most widespread image of the market—a place of warm social relations—and make it a principle of their identity. The big word in the profession is contact, rapport. "To be a stallholder," says Perdiguier *père*, "is to have good rapport with people. The supermarket and all those things, they don't have enough contact. From my side of the stall, I've got a pretty good idea what the customer wants. People come by and they start talking—they need contact." Says Martin the secondhand clothes seller, who has read Guattari and Baudrillard[2] and never fails to explain to me that he could be in my place if he hadn't chosen freedom and wagered on "*l'imaginaire*": "The market is relations with people. A sale is ultimately an instantaneous relationship between two persons—that's really what it is. The market hasn't given me any knowledge of this or that, it's something deeper, it's relations with people. The market is a concentrate of human relations."

This (rather than any wish to sell a particular product) is why people choose to be stallholders. Mme. Varet, for example, "loves the market"; it doesn't matter what she sells (she's switched from cutlery to baby clothes). The same is true of Valérie, long unemployed, who has a job selling "organic" bread and croissants. She wouldn't leave the market "for anything in the world," and like one of her seller friends who gets his stock every Monday at the degressive auction market in Hyères, near Toulon, she would like to "move into flowers" if she can get up the funds to buy a cold room. A recently set-up cheese seller also chose to be a stallholder "because it's another life." After not making it in *charcuterie* he immediately switched: "I started in charcuterie. I bought all the Catalan and Toulousain specialties and leaned hard on that. I didn't have a fridge, I didn't have anything. I did that for three months—torture! I had to throw everything out, lost five thousand francs. So I said to myself, you've got to do something, you can't stay in charcuterie. You've got the truck, you've got everything. I said to myself, I'm going to find something in foodstuffs where you can manage after the first month. I looked at all the cheese people, saw they had a fair amount of business, so I said, let's do cheese!"

Stallholding, a trade befitting a free man, would thus seem almost a calling. Relates Perdiguier *fils*: "Even as a child there was only one thing I liked—going with my parents to the market. It was already the only thing when I was in middle school. For me, coming to the market was a reward." Not an occupation, then, but an *art de vivre*. Many obviously chose it at first not to have a boss, not to have to get a high school vocational degree or do an apprenticeship program. But ultimately they are there for love of it. "I can't wait to go to work," says Noël Cappo. "I'm telling you, everyone who does this work loves it. I go at it with all my heart. I think I must have it in the blood, because when I'm sick, when I can't go out . . . As soon as I can go out again, I go to the market. This year is my last year, I think, because the doctor says I shouldn't have been working these last ten years. So I drag myself around as best I can. I'll probably still be thinking about my markets when I retire. I got started in this when I was forty-six. Like I told you, I don't do it for the money, though of course everyone works to make money. But really, if I were retired and in good health and a stallholder said to me, 'Come with me for nothing—what do you say?' I'd go. That may seem strange, but when I see a stallholders' market, it's a real pull."

It is true that this "vocation" has often been a matter of last resort, and boasting of the freedom one enjoys and the relations of friendship and trust one establishes may be a way of looking on the bright side of a bad situation. A *charcutier* related to me how he found himself selling at the market after "failing" at the head of "a hundred-twenty-square-meter superette with three cash registers . . . They built a highway that didn't go by the store. Everything used to run in front of my store on the road to Sauveterre, and people came to do their shopping from the city or on their way to work in the city because we carried everything—bread, meat, everything. But now, with the route they have to take, it's done for, over! All the customers were friends—I'd worked there ten years, then managed it ten years—I bought the business from my boss. When my kids got married, the church was full. The customers came to congratulate us. And now! It's hard. I was really disappointed. I'd worked so hard. That's how I started doing markets. But I have a wonderful time now. I love the contact, and being outside in all weathers."

However great their love for this work, stallholders do not deny that they often see it as a phase on the way to the ultimate success of having their own shop. That trajectory is in no way exceptional in Carpentras. A good number of tradespersons in the city, such as Boyac of the Jardins du Comtat, began selling at markets. The Grossages too are a typical case: "You start as a stallholder, then you get a store. We've all tried to buy a business. Only fools stop at stall holding."

The Grossage parents started selling on the market in 1948. Grossage *père*, descendant of an old Jewish Carpentras family, was a tailor by trade. He did "custom-made," then began selling the clothes he made on the market.

> We made skirts, jackets. My brother still makes all his own coats. He's at the market, near the Crédit Lyonnais. It's women's ready-to-wear, but he makes them himself . . . When we sold you something, you could trust us entirely—no need to try it on, it fit. We took measurements, made pleated skirts because they were in fashion. They were already pleated, all that was left to do was sew in the waist. In the early fifties there were plenty of people on the market who made the clothes themselves, guys who came from Marseille, who made coats and came to sell them. Then things changed. I stopped making, but we continued to sell big pieces—coats, major items. We bought a business, but continued to sell on the market. At the time, the only people here were people with big stalls, I mean solid when it came to stock. They had high turnovers. I had a twelve-meter stall, we unloaded a hundred fifty, two hundred coats. There were trucks fifteen or twenty meters long, there were two or three thirty-meter-long merchandise trucks—that amounts to ten city shops' worth of stock.

Son Alain took up his parents' market circuit in the 1970s. Alain is an artist who is very well known in the Paris galleries and fully up on the latest *Art Press* articles. At the time, he sold on the market and painted. "We came here once for vacation," explains his wife, Nicole. "His parents were already in the business, so for Alain this was the ideal solution because it left him free time. We did the market, we took the spots his parents had." They hardly changed a thing in the family business: "About ten years ago, in spring, when you start selling dresses, we had from six to seven hundred dresses out at the stall in the beginning of the season. Our clientele were forty- to forty-five-year-old women, not really from the city, the country rather. They'd come down with either their mothers or their daughters and they all got clothes at the same time. So we dressed the younger ones too, especially in summer, and then the grandmas. But in recent years we've sort of given up the grandmas' department."

Nicole Grossage herself has just opened a boutique in the Rue d'Inguimbert next to Jean-Claude Andrieu's "table arts" shop. She sells brand-name leather goods. "It just happened like that," she tells me.

> We had Paris family in manufacturing, then we discovered there weren't enough leather goods shops. We said, there's something for us to do here. I have to admit that the last five years I couldn't stand the market anymore because people have gotten really aggressive. In the old days, country women came down on Friday mornings with

their husbands in their little vans and did their shopping: cheese, vegetables, and at the same time clothes for the kids, the husband, city clothes as well as work clothes—it was nice. We had easy relations with those people. They trusted us. We had a country clientele that was used to buying at the market. After we sold them something, they would always come back, because there was a kind of loyalty. Now they all have cars, and they either go to the shops a few kilometers from where they live or to Auchan. We could laugh together when we made a sale, joke, talk about a load of things. It was different. We could talk. Sometimes the customer would say, "Yes, I like that, but I don't want to buy anything today," and then "Good-bye." But these last five years, with the supermarkets and department stores, people think they're at home wherever they go, they think all is due them. The market clientele has changed. Now they check the labels before looking at the article. They used to want a coat that would last several years, they looked at the quality. Today's market is not at all like that, it works for little stuff, and for food. For big items, it's over! Stallholders were people who had been here a long time. We didn't see young people arriving like this every other day. And things have also gotten much harder between stallholders.

88   "In our time," adds her father-in-law, "there was a kind of respect, everyone in his spot. Now it's the jungle."

As Nicole Grossage tells it, the change in the quality of human relations on the market is what explains the fact that today she runs one of the most luxurious boutiques in the city. Obviously, however, the move from stall to boutique followed the logic of social ascension. Not only do the Grossages now have their fine boutique, but the husband has become a full-time artist (at the time of this study he was preparing an exhibition in a gallery near the Centre Pompidou in Paris). And it is of course much more chic to sell handbags and belts to a clientele in the know than light flower-print dresses to large peasant women.

What is unusual in the Grossages' case is that they have broken all ties with the market. The stories that stallholders enjoy passing around often suggest that, on the contrary, being a stallholder is such an irresistible passion that you never really give it up. They list examples of stallholders who cannot really resign themselves to retiring or who, after opening a shop in Avignon—a sure sign of success in Carpentras—or elsewhere, ended up either hiring people to run it so they could take up their circuit again or simply gave up to get back to the market. "Even some who don't need the money go back on the road after 60," says Perdiguier *père*. "They can't stop. You don't give it up, even at 70, 75. I know a guy who's a *posticheur* in Bandol. He's got a fine house with everything you need, and he's gone back on the road! 'Industrial stallholders' just never

stop." And old Grossage recounts: "Irma—you know, the fabric merchant—
she was getting up in years. She took over a fabric shop in Avignon and stayed
there a month, then ran right back to the market. Some stallholders really get
bitten, they just can't stop . . ." "It's the same with the Daspases," adds his
daughter-in-law. "They've got their shop, but you still see them on the market.
They like to be outside, to move around, not to stay in the same place all the
time."

There are two stallholders at Carpentras who seem to me to represent a gen-
eralizable contrast between two different though not antagonistic ways stallholders see their job, two ways of acting the stallholder part, two styles in the art of
handling the customer, both of which define the social space particular to the market. At one end of the Place du Théâtre is Perdiguier with his vast mobile shoe
shop; at the other, Martin with his stand of sophisticated secondhand clothes.

Perdiguier and his family incarnate the model of the traditional stallholder,
a veritable dynastic heir. The people of Carpentras know the Perdiguiers well.
They have been selling what they call a "traditional" shoe for several generations and are also specialized in slippers and work shoes. "Luxury boutiques
don't have these articles, naturally"; as for "city stores," they don't have the
space to carry them anymore, whereas department stores, which carry a limited
number of models and items, are not serious competition. Through loyal, rational "exploitation" of this "niche," the Perdiguiers have developed a thriving
family business.

"We've always done this," explains Perdiguier *père*. "I learned to walk in
the midst of shoes, and I think I'll retire in the midst of shoes. I began in '34,
but my father started in '19." The grandfather worked first as a coachman, then
began to make the rounds of the markets with a horse-drawn *jardinière*.[3] Preciously preserved memories of this heroic period serve as a founding legend.
"He left here, went up to Orange, from Orange he went to Vaison—he went all
the way round. He didn't come home in the evenings, so the animals wouldn't
have so far to go, and he slept in the *jardinière* to save money. Grandmother
took the cart and went out too. They waited for each other, because there were
thieves." Dynastic continuity has been ensured since then; this is the third generation. Perdiguier *fils*, around forty, works at his father's side on the market
and feels he has the same calling: "I've always loved being outside. As a child
it was all I thought about, but my cousin, who's an industrial designer, never
really took to it, he didn't follow." Perdiguier *fils* married the daughter of a
butcher-charcuterer in Avignon. "We stallholders," remarks the son, "unlike

hawkers, we don't really marry within our trade. But it does happen. My father didn't marry a stallholder, but my uncle did." Perhaps because she was not born into it, his own wife gave up the market and became a youth social worker. They have two young children, who will be allowed to choose their occupations freely, he says, but it is clear that he expects them to take up the torch of the "traditional shoe."

Seven family members still work in the business. "There were as many as ten once": five on the market (father, mother, son, an uncle and aunt), two managing the voluminous stock stored on one side of the courtyard of their vast home in Saint-Saturnin-lès-Avignon: "We turn over more than fifty thousand pairs once or twice a year." Theirs is a sizable registered business that allows them to live with a certain ease and comfort: "Plenty of work for us on the market!" They have no intention of opening a boutique, because they are stallholders "in the soul": "Staying in the same place all the time waiting for people to come . . . I prefer going out to get them. I don't know if I could ever get used to being indoors all the time—that's the problem when you've lived forty years outside," says Perdiguier *père*. As members of the Syndicat des Commerçants Non-Sédentaires [nonsedentary merchants union], father and son are among the rare stallholders who help run the profession in Carpentras, harmonizing stall spot fees, creating new markets, and so on. And when vacation time comes (they rotate, each couple taking a different three weeks off), they visit stallholder markets. "We have an RV, and we go to Portugal, Italy . . . When there's a market, we stop to see how it operates. It attracts us. I go in to see how it works, question the stallholders—it's how we make our living, after all. And lord if it isn't pretty much the same thing everywhere you go. We've seen markets in Yugoslavia, Switzerland, that run just like ours in France."

For other stallholders, on the contrary, doing markets is a freely chosen way of life (or at least experienced as such) and one they always think of as temporary. This is the case for Martin, but also for many "occasionals," vendors that the Grossages and the Perdiguiers call "newcomers" or "young people." Selling wooden toys on a small cart or old records off a garden table is a way of earning one's living without overly committing oneself. The impression of precariousness that these vendors associate with such activities is in fact a decisive element in their choice. "Doing the stallholder" allows you to work at your own pace, have free time, establish relations with customers that are not perceived as work relations ("We provide service"; "It's supercool"). But it is also a way of being able to quit from one day to the next, avoid or defer irreversible commitment, remain open and available to every adventure at all times.

In his own way, Martin is a strong figure on the Carpentras market. All regular visitors to it have noticed this still-young-looking man with his big, gentle, light-colored eyes and rather long blond hair who sets up his decor on the steps of the Place du Théâtre. Since Martin is near the entrance to the market, people always take a glance in passing at the lace-hem skirts and loose, *broderie anglaise* blouses that he displays as if they were precious objects.[4] But he is quick to repeat that the market is for him a way of living "without becoming integrated," "earning a bit of money without dragging a ball and chain"; that he is, in a way, just passing through.

Martin lives with Laure in a big, somewhat austere stone farmhouse with two big cedar trees on either side in the middle of the countryside. Laure writes novels under a pseudonym that was surely chosen in reference to the woman who inspired the poet who once lived in the immediate vicinity. She also sells at markets now and then, sharing a spot with Martin or Françoise, who sells secondhand clothes too but also new ones in craftsy, folksy style (sweaters of local wool, light Indian cottons).

About once a week, often on Fridays after the market, Martin goes to Avignon to pick up his wares. He buys from a wholesaler who gets the stock from Holland. He then brings the clothes home to sort, repair, starch, and iron. In winter he does only the Carpentras market; in spring he also goes to L'Isle-sur-la-Sorgue, and in summer to Aix-en-Provence. Between mending his merchandise and selling it on the market, he takes classes in modern dance. In summer he regularly attends "off" plays at the Avignon theater festival. He and Laure have a whole group of friends, some in secondhand clothes and other goods, who often go to each other's houses, and in this too they differ from traditional stallholders, who today at least are not likely to socialize together outside the market. But Martin's pride and joy is his house, the one he's building himself out of stone near Beaucet, on a hillside terrace today overgrown with green oak and wild fig trees. He has designed it down to the slightest detail: "The fanlight on the staircase is for watching the sun set behind the mountain." By regularly checking all the salvage shops in the region, he has collected all he needs in the way of used earthenware tiles; he handpicks each door and window lintel. Martin makes use of his friends' various talents; one has even come specially from the Ardèche: "No one makes a timber frame like he does." He works at the task impassionedly every day: "You have to have built your own house in this life."

"The market leaves me the time to do what I want," he explains to me at the counter of the café in Saint-Didier. First, there are fewer constraints than with a shop: "A boutique means stability, a whole relation to settled legality that the market doesn't require at all. Some of my friends have secondhand clothing shops—that puts obligations on them, whereas with the market, you don't have to do more than one a week." Second, selling secondhand clothes at the market is a good way to make a living while remaining oneself; one doesn't have to compromise. "I only sell things I like. It's that or nothing. I often cart things around that'll never get sold because they aren't salable, in the sense that very few people would want to buy them." Furthermore, he believes that what he sells "brings people something other than just the object": "They buy something that brings them a kind of dream." For him, selling secondhand clothes is a challenging way of making money and has nothing to do with ordinary trade: "Selling an astrakhan coat at a very low price is a provocation. The clientele that can buy it are people that can let go at a given moment, hop the tiny barrier that everyone's got in his head. These are objects that have already been worn, it's old stuff, but 'It's not in bad shape,' they say to themselves, 'I'm going to buy it.'"

Above all as far as Martin is concerned, the market allows him to make a living without really committing to the world of work. Being a stallholder is in his eyes neither a calling nor a profession. And if the activity deprived him of his freedom, he would change:

> I feel marginal with respect to the world of work. Ultimately I feel comfortable on the markets, but I might feel just as good if I were a customer. Right now, the way my existence is unfolding means that I work the markets to earn money, but really, I don't feel like a stallholder, I don't feel implicated in how stallholder work will develop in the future, what markets are going to become. Doing the same work as they do is just a semblance of resemblance—it's not real. People put themselves into what they do—I don't. I don't represent someone who can be integrated, and I don't know whether I'll be doing the same thing in six months' time. "Stallholder" means delimiting oneself in relation to a job, and that's something I've always refused to do, at the deepest level. If people think I can be defined by the work I do, that's their problem, not mine. The spot you have isn't permanent; you can lose it if you don't come for a month, it's something you have to fight for. It seems to me it would be hard anywhere else to have the marginal position I can have in Carpentras. Knowing people,

individuals, in Carpentras is important, and enables you to dig out a little hole for yourself, but as soon as the problem of a spot begins to make things more difficult, the relative possibility for people like me to exist may well disappear. The day I don't really have the energy to hold onto my spot anymore, I'll find something else to do to meet my needs, whereas someone who's been doing shoes for twenty years . . . ! I can do without markets because my human relations go beyond the market.

Clearly this discourse is to some extent addressed directly to me. It is hard to imagine Martin saying the same to his neighbor Perdiguier or his friend Bonis, a truffle broker and erstwhile fedora maker. His refusal to be defined by the activity of stallholder is also a way of reminding me that he could have done and still can do something else; that if he didn't have to worry about avoiding any compromise with "society" he might today be interviewing stallholders about their way of life for the Ministry of Commerce and Industry, for example. Martin doesn't think I'm asking him questions as a stallholder, he's no market actor. He wants to be a friend who, just as he occasionally offers me a taffeta dress, is helping me with my work by giving me information I might need about the others. At no point does he tell me about his life. Instead he adopts the position of a sociologist of the market, making ever more numerous allusions to cultural references he assumes we have in common, speaking of La Borde and his own "*psy*" [psychoanalyst] friends, of a meeting with David Cooper, of a woman friend of his in Pina Bausch's dance troupe.[5]

Martin's declarations are nonetheless characteristic of the distanced relation to work that so many stallholders say they have, especially occasional or marginal ones, for whom the market is a means of making a living as a dilettante without relinquishing or alienating one's freedom. But there are two modes of being free on the market. For some it is a choice of radical nonengagement. This may conceal a number of failures or disappointed hopes, but nonetheless represents a certain existential value. For others, Perdiguier and his ilk, it is a fully accepted and appropriated calling, regardless of the fact that they "became" stallholders by taking up a nonnegotiable family inheritance.

These are not solely discourses of self-justification; they are modes of self-presentation that help produce the specific social space of the market. In order for the customer to feel freer here than elsewhere, she must find herself face to face with a tradesperson who in various ways stages his own fundamental freedom. The stallholder has to demonstrate that he is not an ordinary shopkeeper subject to the customer's will and a slave to his work. Certain sales techniques are used at the market that are unknown in other commercial spaces, and their

93

effect is to signify to the customer that the stallholder is just that—a market stallholder—and that the customer is entering a specific exchange situation. The liveliness of the talk and joking that accompany market transactions, the generous if not sumptuous display of wares, stallholder cries and calls are all ways of saying that these tradespeople are there for the pleasure of it, because they love their work, and proclaiming that stall holding is more a "communication" or public relations art, a "science of contact," than a business activity.

At a stall where good humor reigns and the banter is quick and rife, how could one imagine that the stallholder, who always says something to make you laugh, is there because the demands of his work force him to be?

"And what shall I add for the demoiselle?" asks Favre in a teasing tone from behind his groaning counter of fruits and vegetables.

"That'll do for today," comes the lady's reply—she is clearly in her sixties. "Besides, I don't have another *sou* [penny, money]."

"No more *sous*? No problem—I'll take you hostage!"

We know that all he is trying to do is sell his olives. But with this type of talk, the stallholder creates a situation that leads people to think he's there only to have a good time; that selling olives and dried cod is a game he wouldn't live without. Likewise, when you hear Brunet say to old Mme. Daval, "Let's make up our mind, my pretty!" or Noël Cappo rebuff an honest *dame* who has demanded a better-quality floorcloth with "It's the same price, whether you like them or not!" it's hard to imagine them as grasping tradesmen cowering before capricious customers. At the market you can give a potential customer the heave-ho, and the general feeling is that it's better to do without all those bothersome people who don't buy anything and only waste your time ("dead rats" in professional jargon).

The effect of these comic little scenes is to shatter the usual type of market relation, effacing the reserve and distance that it normally implies and concealing the service relation inherent in it. The customer is hardly king here. You can make fun of him, send him quite openly to the devil, and you never refuse the pleasure of a good line that will make everyone laugh, even if it means losing a sale. Showing the customer you don't need him is an act of defiance that "passes" on the market. For a shopkeeper it would be suicidal.

The stallholder has to seem like an "entertainment" specialist making fine use of his smooth-talker talent, rather than a professional tradesman worried about his markup and turnover. Selling has to seem almost like something extra, as if his real purpose were to give the public a good time. Not all stallholders

94

practice the same type of joking to the same degree, but the fact that some do gives the market its overall tone. The same is true for stallholder barking—"Let's try some strawberries, finest strawberries! Two baskets for ten francs—I'm giving them away! It all has to go, so come and get it! Come along, ladies, we're doing strawberries today"—and more focused appeals: "Come along, little lady, take a look. Don't they like strawberries at your house?" In fact these selling techniques are not much practiced in Carpentras; only fruit and vegetable sellers use them. And yet they are inseparable from people's idea of the market. Linguists have eruditely shown that stallholder calls are utterance sequences that obey precise rules (limited vocabulary, simplified syntax, abundance of linguistic markers, and so forth).[6] For their part, the customers take away the impression of an exuberant spontaneity suggesting that here, at least, doing business is a game, and first and foremost a word game, a somewhat gratuitous verbal riot. Above and beyond the advertising message, the stallholder is signaling to the company at large that the market is an exceptional place where speech can be wild and provocative and no one will take offense. Here, in deliberate contrast to modern types of goods distribution, there is no hesitation about jostling the customer, forcing him out of his reserve, as in the souks of the Arab world where stallholders come very close to grabbing onto you as you pass. The hawker likewise takes over the street with his boisterous clamor, like a leader haranguing the crowd. Shedding the respect normally paid to citizens' desire to be left alone, he plays at transforming a public space usually given over to passive, silent coexistence into a sort of jolly free-for-all.

The way goods are displayed is also a means of staging the playful relation the stallholder is understood to have to his work, transforming the street into a spectacle of which he or she is the artisan. At Annick Ceret's stand, cotton prints flutter in the breeze like the great wings of some pink or purple butterfly; we are plunged into a world where a harmony of color reigns as if by nature. It is clear that Annick loves what she sells, that she is here because she likes to display things that please her. She herself wears one of the fresh wide skirts we see hanging from a clothes rack. She seems to be moving about in her daily habitat, amidst objects intensely familiar to her, and it is hard to imagine she is working. In this setting, which seems to have sprung up by magic, there is no trace of effort or labor. And yet she has spent at least an hour and a great deal of energy setting up the metallic frames and canopies, unloading and hanging dozens of dresses. For her as for other stallholders, the stall must not show any signs of the work that went into setting it up. It should be an expression of the pleasure to be had at the market, not the laborious erecting of a structure from which to sell.

Annick Ceret may be considered somewhat untypical because of the esthetic aspect of her wares and the suggested identification between seller and what is sold. Still, each stallholder in his or her own way works to give the impression that they are there for love of their art. Standing behind his carefully aligned tubs of olives of all sorts and provenances, Mistral is somewhat the figure of an expert, always ready to launch into an interminable account of the olives' respective merits. And Espenon amidst his movable hardware shop is readily taken for a veteran handyman. As for Huguet, who sells a few small jars of honey and royal jelly from a garden table, he is seen first and foremost as a practiced beekeeper for whom the market is an occasion to share his passion and the wondrous product of his hives.

One mustn't show the pains one takes or complain of one's lot, and there is to be no feverish agitation unless one is parodying the busy tradesman. Nothing must mar the spectacle the stallholder makes of the joy it is for him to be selling on the market. He is not overwhelmed by his work but absorbed in a leisure activity—or gives as many signs as possible that this is what's going on. For convivial relations to develop, people have to feel free and relaxed—this is one of the conditions of a properly functioning market. It is crucial not to have a happy world of customers on one side, the toil of those who serve them on the other. The stallholder must work without seeming to.[7]

The relation the stallholder entertains with his work also becomes manifest in his face-to-face encounter with the customer. His tactics for inducing a customer to buy range from ostentatiously relaxed behavior, not to say patent disinterest, to friendly attention. The essential point is to appear detached from all concern about profit, moved more by a taste for meeting people and the pleasure of "joking it up" than an obsession with one's cash box. This kind of behavior, which the stallholder knows stands in contrast to how sedentary shopkeepers behave, is used to establish a certain sense of *connivance* or tacit shared understanding and agreement with the customer, a sales situation specific to the market.

The stallholder's art is to offer his victim a soft flank so as to skewer him when the time is right. "I wait for the customer to ask me," explains Perdiguier. "In any case, the deal's not done until the customer asks. There's no purpose hanging around behind him saying, 'Try them on, try them on!' The customer's an adult, after all." Perdiguier knows full well that the stallholder's strongest suit is to stand back and let the customer move around as he or she likes. "In a shop," he says, "when you've gone in, it's hard to leave. Going through the door keeps people inside. At the market customers feel free because there's no door to go through. That's why some stores are set up so you're in them without realizing how you got there. At the market, people are free. They can see everything, choose, you don't force the sale. They pick up the merchandise, try it on . . . I don't say anything, just, 'They fit? . . . They don't fit?' Nothing more." With this approach he takes full advantage of the openness of the particular selling arrangement. It is because the customer feels he is there just to "look around" that he may well leave with a pair of new shoes, without realizing he has "acted out," without realizing he has been supplied what he is not in any "urgent need" of. "After all, they'll serve me well next winter," said an old peasant I observed outside Perdiguier's stall.

But Perdiguier also knows how to intervene when the customer doesn't want to be an "adult." "There are people you have to tell that the shoe doesn't fit. They're incapable of knowing if it fits or not. I'm sure there are customers who, if I gave them a 44 and their size is 41, they'd say, 'Okay, they fit.' Then there are customers who aren't satisfied unless you come press down on the shoe toe." He adapts his principle of nonintervention to the occasion and the customer. "In fact, it depends where you are, it's linked to the mentality of a given city. In Apt we shoe a lot of the people who work at Saint-Christol [missile-launching base on the Albion plateau]. They're army captains. They didn't know at first how to buy at a market. We had to take care of them like in a shop. When they enter a shop, the salesman takes charge of them from start to finish, whereas on the market we personally prefer the customer to be in charge of himself."

Because the market is an exchange space in which the customer need not be either coddled or kowtowed to, a stallholder can hook onto a customer and not let go—unthinkable in a city boutique. As Perdiguier puts it, "Some let people do as they like; others grab onto the customer."

Now set up in their leather goods store, the Grossages insist retrospectively on the fact that they had more freedom to maneuver behind their stall counter. They could use the customer's sense of freedom to "corner" him. A customer is all the more easily cornered when unsuspecting. They see this tactic as specific to the market. In a boutique the customer feels from the outset exposed, even threatened, simply because he has gone in. He has to be handled considerately. "In the shop," says Nicole Grossage, "if a customer says, 'I'm going to think about it for a bit,' you don't insist. But at the market you can't let her leave like that! If she leaves without buying, the competition will get the sale, so it's a little battle every time. You say to yourself, if I don't get it the neighbor will, and that will mean I'm incapable. In a shop you can't make a big deal of it. It's just not possible to force a sale, otherwise the customer won't come back." "There's something else at stake on the market," adds her father-in-law. "The fact that we're all outside means there's no barrier, so you hook onto the customer and you spiel. In the shop you can't allow yourself to force the sale. Forcing a sale means folding up the item and putting it in the bag when the customer hasn't even decided yet. It's already in the bag and you hand her the bill."

Even the rather rough tactic of "cornering" presupposes a degree of skill and tact. One has to know how to adapt one's weapons to the customer's personality and social status. "There's an angle for every customer, a different way of talking. You know very quickly whether you've got a sale. When you've got some experience you can feel it—you sense the moment when you can push the sale," Nicole Grossage explains. "And then the customer leaves, she's bought her thing. Maybe she didn't really want to buy it, or didn't really know what she wanted—but she's delighted. Each time, every customer is a circus, something else again. You don't talk the same way to a peasant woman from the Ardèche and a tourist. Every time you make a sale it's like a little comedy, whereas here in the shop, the customer's already made the choice before coming in."

Martin the *fripier*'s way of working is not dissimilar to Perdiguier's. He too leaves customers alone, affecting indifference. But paradoxically, Perdiguier can play this card precisely because he inspires confidence in much the same way a long-established city *boutiquier* does. He has regular customers who periodically buy the same article. (There are some who come up to the front of his stall and say simply, "Give me a size 42." They can't imagine he could have forgotten their shoe style.) But Martin's apparently similar behavior obeys quite different logic. He wants to appear a stallholder "unlike the others." He's dealing not with "customers" but with people like himself who share his tastes. Martin sells to friends for their mutual pleasure.

Strictly speaking, Martin does not have a display. He hangs his clothes on big racks at the perimeter of his spot, so customers penetrate his space unawares. He never plants himself behind his counter like ordinary stallholders separated from buyers by the mound of merchandise they lord over. Rather he stands off to one side, near his truck, and seems more busy with his personal affairs than with the customer. He rearranges a pile, folds a shirt, talks calmly with friends who have come to see him at the market. You have to really want to get

98

his attention. At most he will nonchalantly announce the price to a customer looking insistently at a dress or jacket.

After deliberately catching his eye, two young women call out, "We're just looking." "Go ahead, rummage around," says he, his hands in his pocket, and returns to his conversation with Laure. This is a way of granting the two women precisely the freedom they seek. Clearly they want to be treated more like curious visitors than customers and to rummage about in his merchandise without any assistance from him. Though his stand is in perfect order, his invitation to "rummage around" means that buying here can be a personal adventure. It suggests that with a little talent you'll find real finds and that he has no business interfering with "the other's desire." Without a move on his part, one of the women takes off her jacket and slips on a fur; the other decks herself out in a hat with lace veil. They stand admiring themselves in a long freestanding mirror.

"What's it made of?" calls the one in the fur.

"*Sconce*," replies Martin. "It's gorgeous!"

Embarrassed silence. The women seem all the more awed for not knowing what animal *sconce* [skunk] could refer to.

"And how do you think it looks on me?"

"It falls perfectly. Look at the sleeves."

A few seconds later, laughing and delighted, the two leave for Boyac's to buy vegetables for the pot-au-feu.

At Martin's stand, one is invited to look at lovely things at leisure, to partake in the joy of discovery and the pleasure of dressing up. You slip a damask jacket on top of old jeans; you imagine yourself dressed in that low-necked gown at a great ball in *The Leopard*, for an instant you possess the fur coat of your dreams. Martin doesn't disturb the game. He is not there just to sell, and everyone at his stall must be able to savor a moment of happiness. When a customer moves off after a fine sale—a well-cut, perfectly preserved astrakhan—he confides in me with some distress: "What a pity that girl doesn't take the pleasure she should in buying it! Hers is the dissatisfaction of someone who's been spoiled." Leaving his customers free to "rummage around" as they like and not to buy is for him a way of shattering (or "deconstructing") the market relation and disengaging himself from the shopkeeper image. Martin instates a relation of *connivance*: at his stand: we are "*entre nous*" because we are assumed to share a common cultural universe, and he is there as a slightly more knowing companion proffering disinterested advice to people of his own world. The clothing he sells is a highly effective mediator: it attracts people for whom being fashionable means never slavishly following what's in fashion but making winking allusions to it, a whole ethics marked by the cult of the singular, the piece of clothing that expresses one's personality, the rejection of stereotypes, a taste for baroque combinations of the quaint and the modern, the exotic and the everyday.

One of the key elements in the particular enticement and inducement game called the market involves the stallholder's staging of his or her own freedom. Her activity must seem more like a labor of love than labor; his concern to turn a profit must disappear behind the show he takes such visible pleasure in creating. Meanwhile, the customer herself is all the more open and willing as she is continually being shown in every possible way—from being mistreated to being ignored—that she is not needed. And just as the art of self-presentation works to dissociate the stallholder from the usual shopkeeper image, the market's specific power of attraction is in how what is sold is presented, the many uses of verbal magic or appearance manipulation by which ordinary objects are transformed into market products.

PART THREE

Commerce of the Imaginary

"I have customers who only buy from me on the market," says David, puz- zled. He owns a shoe store in the city but unloads every Friday in the Place de la Mairie as well. "They know I've got the same style for the same price in my shop, but it makes no difference. 'I'll come get them next Friday,' they tell me." This behavior is characteristic of market regulars. For Mme. Ripert, the sausage she buys at Maurin's stall is entirely different from Auchan sausage, even though there is a sort of kiosk amid the supermarket aisles offering "salt pork from the Ardèche." For Mme. Delavigne, Carpentras market is the only place she can find little cotton blouses—as if she could not at any time procure a similar item very near her Lyon home. This kind of illusion is neither purely subjective nor strictly local. From *Le Monde* to *Marie-Claire* by way of *Trouvailles* [Finds], the national press too would have us believe that lettuce is always crisp at the market, eggs new laid and body-warm, frying pans as heavy and sturdy as in the old days, corduroy pants particularly wear resistant, jeans much less expensive, and so on.

Everyone is more or less convinced that market products are different from all others, different from what you find elsewhere in terms not only of quality and price but also, as David's shoes suggest, of substance, as if the fact of being displayed at a market endowed them with a specific nature. This presumed difference, this je ne sais quoi, is assuredly one of the main sources of the market's enticement and inducement power. The "market difference" is recognized well beyond the little market world; indeed, it serves as a mark of quality for an international clientele. The "market product" is the secret of his cuisine, insinuates the renowned French chef Paul Bocuse, and his *Cuisine du marché* is an international best-seller. Any self-respecting *restaurateur* now accompanies his *magret de canard des Landes* with "its little assortment of market vegetables."

What, then, is a market product? The better question is, are market products specific to markets? The shopper wandering from stall to stall hardly wonders about this, absorbed as she is in the spectacle of profusion and diversity. But from even a slightly distanced vantage point, just this side of having surrendered entirely to the charm, it is clear that there are very few products that cannot be procured elsewhere. The only real specialties of the Carpentras market are the "organic" pastries, the sundials, beaded necklaces, and other baubles sold by "students" in the Passage Boyer, the miracle healing roots, and the live poultry, which has made a comeback thanks to Islamic prohibitions. The city of Carpentras itself does not have any secondhand-clothing, book, or CD and cassette shops, but one need only go to Avignon or Aix for those items; the market "monopoly" is thus highly relative. Yet however few and ultimately secondary market-specific products and businesses may be, they are absolutely essential to the market image. The market cannot be reduced to the series of products available at it. For visitor-customers it has meaning as a whole—this is reflected in the words *ambiance* and *atmosphère* that so many use in describing it—and even its marginal components help define this meaning. For the market to be the market, you need Perdiguier's reassuringly solid "maison" to rub shoulders with Jacky Thevet's madcap antics; you need a Gypsy girl holding out a handful of lemons and Liliane Fresquet with her folding table and little goat cheeses to be not far off from Mistral and his comprehensive olive selection. And for "traditional" tone, the Carpentras market would not be what it is without the proximity of the truffles, though as explained, this little weekly event unfolds among the initiated, off to the side of the main market bustle and flow, almost in secret.

Most of the merchandise for sale is therefore in no way original, but the customer is thoroughly disposed to think it is. Olives that would be taken for Tunisian if found in a jar at Ifaprix supermarket are assumed on the market to come exclusively from Nyons. The cut flowers, shipped from the wholesale market at Hyères just like those at fixed florists', seem, when displayed at Les Platanes, to have been snipped from the surrounding gardens. The stallholders are the first to admit that their merchandise is very similar to what is available in the stores. "We all have the same suppliers, so automatically you've got the same articles," explains Espenon, whose stall offers an accumulation of unrelated items, from corkscrews and wrenches to toothpaste and *savon de Marseille*. "We have a lot of suppliers who also deliver to stores," he adds. "A wholesale perfume salesman in Avignon where I get my stuff also supplies all the shops in the region." One would gladly believe that the embroidery canvas painted with Provençal landscapes can only be found at the notions stall that sets up every Friday in front of the palace, but Avon, who manufactures the product, explains that "stallholders are like any other client" for him and that he doesn't sell any items made specially for the market. What's more, as with David the shoe man, stallholders who also have a shop (clothing, shoes) say they sell the same products at the same prices in both venues.

103

6. "The customer doesn't go by price here"

Products are reputed to be cheaper at the market. The press fuels this idea by presenting markets as places where bargains are still possible and available to all. "Those markets on the outskirts that Parisians keep running to" ran a headline in *Paris-Hebdo*, spring 1980. When taking food price samples one October day in 1982 at the Prisunic supermarket, the Jardins du Comtat, a number of shops in the Rue des Halles, and several spots at the market, I found nearly identical prices for fruits and vegetables, fish and poultry. Dairy products were cheaper at the market than at Prisunic, but the fixed *crémerie* in the Rue des Halles had better prices than either.

Stallholders acknowledge that their prices are "the same as in a shop for the corresponding article." Their attitude toward supermarkets is not devoid of ambiguity or contradiction. At times they are concerned to demonstrate that they are not more expensive—and everyone gives an example: "I've been told that items I sell at three francs fifty go for eight francs fifty at Auchan," relates Espenon. "One day a lady showed me a toilet-paper holder—she went to get it at her house—and she said, 'Look, you sell exactly the same one for six francs!' She'd paid eighteen francs at Auchan. I said, 'You may have saved forty cents on a kilo of lentils or a can of chickpeas, but for the other stuff, you got had!'" Moreover, the technique of selective "dumping" is not unfamiliar to stallholders. "We keep our prices fairly low, to be able to keep up the fight with supermarkets and department stores," explains Noël Cappo. "There are things I bought a long time ago. We keep selling them at the same price, we don't mark up, and the customers realize this. We have doormats that sell for ten, twelve francs, whereas everywhere else they cost forty." At other times, on the contrary—and like sedentary shopkeepers—they acknowledge their impotence against mass marketing: "We can't fight those people—they're financiers. They buy the products at such and such price and sell them at the same price, except they pay for the merchandise ninety days later" (Nicole Grossage). "They sell some things we pay more for. We can't really fight for price equality" (Noël Cappo).

Actually, stallholders agree that prices are a secondary factor in running a successful business. They don't think competition among stallholders involves price particularly or that "slashing prices" is necessarily a good strategy. The following is Delvaux's rather humorous account of his experience, chosen from among a number I collected.

At first you pay attention: "Hey, that guy's selling it for ten francs more!" But I soon stopped worrying. I'm more afraid of the guys who sell higher than me than of someone who'd sell below me—on condition that he sells way below me! Those guys don't last long. No, in my case I know what price I've paid, I know what price I can charge, I fix my price and that's that. Someone could set up next to me who sells sausage. Let's say I'm selling at sixty-five. If he wants to sell at sixty, let him sell at sixty—I don't care. That's not going to make me change mine to fifty-nine—it doesn't have any effect on sales.

Once in Vedène I wanted to have a good time with *croustillons* [spareribs]. I went directly to the slaughterhouses in the morning. They asked me what I wanted—at the time they must've been seven francs a kilo and they were going to give them to me for four, so I took them. I get to the market and I put them on sale: I'd gotten a deal so I wanted my customers to get a deal. The first customer to arrive, she usually buys a whole tray and sometimes two, so I say to her, "Look, today you're going to get a bargain." I hadn't put out the prices yet and she says, "That's good, because I need two trays today." When she sees the price, which was nearly half what I usually sell them for, she stops in her tracks and she says, "How's that possible?" So I explain the deal. "But are they fresh?" she asks. "Yes," I say, and show them to her, put them right under her nose. "Oh give me frankfurters instead!" she says. Then comes the next customer and she says, "Wow, they sure are cheap, your *croustillons*—let me have some. You're sure they're fresh now?" Okay, I said to myself, I get it. I let her go, then I took away half of what I had, changed the price back to what I usually charge, and I sold them all. I added to the heap as I ran out—there must've been twelve, fifteen kilos. I sold them all in the course of the morning, but at the normal price.

Since I had my three kids I've never put anything on sale again, I mean it. And you know, sometimes we get whole batches, deals. Well, I'm the one to profit. Low

106

prices are no good. My colleague Robert had a shipment of apples, crates of apples from Entraigues. He put them out at two francs a kilo, whereas everywhere else the price was five or six. He didn't sell a single crate! Then he left a pile at two francs and put another at the normal price, and he sold them all! He'd sold maybe two kilos at two francs. And they were exactly the same! You can do the experiment yourself: you stand here as if you're the producer with a pile of crates, one expensive, the other less expensive, the exact same merchandise. You can bet on it, the more expensive ones are the ones to go. They complain that they pay too much, that we're all sharks when it comes to prices. But they're the ones who make themselves miserable, not us!

Low prices are not necessarily a good selling point; customers may well imagine that sellers at the market are more likely than shopkeepers to try to sell off "junk"—*daube* in the professional jargon. People think that because the stallholder is a "stranger," he or she doesn't have to take the same precautions as a city shopkeeper, especially since the cheerful, trusting atmosphere at the market pushes people to buy. "I don't understand how it works," says Mme. Patio, "but you buy more readily when you see things at the market, because you just don't think about it. If you thought about it, you wouldn't be so quick to buy." A *charcutier* in the Place de la Mairie confirms: "People are a little afraid of cheap pants and shoes." My observation confirmed that people are particularly wary of clothing. "The prices, obviously. There are times when it really is cheaper," acknowledges Mme. Patio, "but then, are there defects? Is it end-of-line stock? Are they factory reject sorts of things? You never really know."

According to the stallholders, market habitués do not have their eye on the price tag, in contrast to consumers trained at Auchan or vacationing campers who are willing to waste time if it means saving money. "Tourists go by price," remarks Delvaux. "They'll drag themselves through the market three times for a three-franc difference—you can ask my colleagues—for a two-franc differ- ence, on peaches or anything else." Delvaux's own mobile shop is parked on the outer boulevard at quite a remove from the center; he needn't worry about sat- isfying a tourist clientele, which is not the case for many of his colleagues. Still, rather than do "low" or "sale" prices, stallholders prefer to "make a gesture." Rather than lower the price to "bring in" undifferentiated passerby customers, they "weigh the order on the heavy side" for the same price or "round down the bill," to establish personal, lasting relations with particular buyers and give them the pleasure of being recognized as "a good customer."

7. "Pumpkins are rounder at the market"

The vast majority of market products are the same as elsewhere and sold at the
same prices. Whatever "market look" they have is due to form or presentation;
the difference is an effect of staging or wording. Producing this appearance
is part of the stallholder's art, practiced not so much to deceive the customer
as to satisfy her wishes and expectations, and this game works all the better in
that, as suggested, everyone wants to be taken in. The market is an enchanted
world where stallholder talent combines with customer desire to make products
appear different from what they are. As I heard someone say around Venturi's
stall, "Pumpkins are rounder at the market."

The archetypal "market product" is a heavy melon bursting with sweetness
because the Provençal sun has been so generous, or a head of lettuce so visibly
harvested at dawn that day that you can almost see dewdrops on it, or firm, fragrant strawberries that still bear the trace of the pebbly soil they were grown
in just south of Carpentras. In the minds of most customers, shopping at the
market means first and foremost laying in a supply of fruits and vegetables,
natural rather than industrial products. As Nicole Grossage explained to me,
"The market sensitizes people to food level. The market's brand image is the
food; it's where you find fresh, higher-quality produce." In fact, as I was able
to confirm in interviews, most of the fruits and vegetables available on the market, either at stallholders' or in sedentary shops, were purchased from the MIN
in Avignon, a major wholesale market featuring an extremely broad range of
produce from a great variety of sources.[1] In the appropriate season, melons and

strawberries are always available at the *marché-gare*, whose function of course is to ship out local produce. But you can't get Spanish oranges or Israeli avocados there.

"In winter," explains Boyac, "we go mostly to MINs. There are actually very fine suppliers at the local Carpentras market, but I'm more in the habit of buying from Avignon suppliers. You have to admit that the Carpentras market is smaller. Sometimes I go to Marseille; they have a bigger selection than in Avignon. Starting in May we do Carpentras, where we can get at least 20 percent of our potential salad needs, and little things. We're in an area where there are so many supply markets that it's easy to buy. We buy about 20 percent from rural markets and all the rest from the middlemen, the wholesalers, who get the merchandise externally." Contrary to what one may readily imagine, then, he only occasionally buys directly from growers, and when he does it's through wholesale produce markets.

Despite the illusion they produce, the vast majority of market fruits and vegetables have therefore been grown almost industrially, using the most modern methods. Melons are grown "above ground" under plastic sheets in heated air, watered continuously drop by drop, with the sugar level automatically monitored. They have only the most distended kinship tie with the melons grown long ago by Provençal peasants.

In *Empire of Signs*, Roland Barthes comments on the effect of how certain Japanese dishes are presented: "It is the very essence of the market that comes to you, its freshness, its naturalness, its diversity." The "market product" is a "compound object . . . at once nature and merchandise, commercial nature, accessible to popular possession."[2] And indeed, the term "freshness" on everybody's lips, together with the idea of "genuine nature" available and affordable to all, right in the center of the city, sums up quite effectively the market ideology, the set of propositions that function both as arguments for market sellers and self-justifications for market buyers. "When you buy vegetables at the Intermarché [supermarket], they seem nice," says Mme. Ripert, "but when I get them home they're rotten or too green. It's at the market, ultimately, that they're freshest." Mme. Coste would agree: "You can't say supermarket fruit is not as pretty, but it's not as fresh." The superficial, deceptive beauty of supermarket produce thus stands in opposition to the "freshness" and the "real" though not necessarily visible quality of market produce. Clearly produce rotates more quickly at the market; fruits and vegetables do not lie around several days in the enclosed space and stale air of the store and they are not wrapped in plastic. But touting the "freshness" of the butter lettuce or tomatoes is a way of obscuring how they are handled: machine-sorted by size, crated, transported several times, spending long hours under truck tarps and in shippers' dusty warehouses. The word "freshness" is a denial of the whole complex process by which produce moves from grower to shipper to wholesaler to retailer; it is a way of signifying the product's direct relation to nature. In itself it is a myth of origin according to which, thanks to the market, this lettuce head has arrived as if by magic from the soil in which it was grown to the plate from which it is eaten.

Through his selling setup, the stallholder stages two competing representations of nature: its universal, generous fecundity, but also a more intimate image: the well-tended nook, the lovingly cultivated little garden behind the house. Most fruit and vegetable sellers in Carpentras, whether stallholders or not, choose the first representation and play above all on the abundance and diversity of the produce they sell. The impression of lush, prodigious nature is due to both the accumulation of foodstuffs and the way the stall is organized. A stall is made up of a long, multiple-sectioned wooden table that can stretch for eight or ten meters, behind which extremely busy vendors run back and forth from mounds of tomatoes to pyramids of citrus fruit, passing in front of a cash box quite visibly set on an upturned wooden crate. The table is about eighty-five centimeters high, to enable the customer to take in the entire panoply of produce at a glance. The most precious items are set in baskets slightly inclined toward the customer so that their contents may be seen better. But stallholders also manage to make it look as if everything is within reaching distance. Merchandise is displayed unwrapped, in bulk; products that customers can select themselves and hand to the vendor (avocados, usually sold singly; Spanish melons; bunches of bananas) are up front, below table level.

The number of products is striking, and the way they are arranged tends to create an impression of "mass": mounds of cabbages and celery root, heaps of *batavia*, *scarole*, *frisée*, *feuille de chêne*, butter and other lettuces, pyramids of oranges and tomatoes, mountains of cauliflower heads, leeks set upright in big bouquets, and so on. There is no empty space; the structure of the table disappears under the heaps of produce. Stocks are continually replenished so that product volume never seems to sink, at least when the market is in full swing. Colors are alternated for the pleasure of the eye but also to intensify product contrast and increase the impression of profusion. The purple of the eggplants shows nearly black next to the gleaming tomatoes; the lemons seems tarter when positioned next to spring-green spinach.

The implicit pictorial model is of course the horn of plenty, where the whole of nature is summed up in an assembly of fruits from the four corners of the earth. On stalls explicitly of this type, ginger, hot peppers, sweet potatoes, and even Caribbean mango squash are close by the usual local products: strawberries and tomatoes from the surrounding irrigated market gardens, long or round squash with the flower still attached. The most exotic fruits—litchis, mangos, passion fruit—are next to the dried fruits and nuts traditionally consumed at winter evening gatherings and on Christmas Day (the "thirteen desserts"): apricots, dates, hazelnuts, walnuts, Provence almonds and the *longette* variety from Spain, strings of dried Baglama figs, golden sultanas or Malaga raisins, so tasty despite the seeds . . . "I like going to Llorca's," says Mme. Coste, "because there are fruits everywhere, and tropical fruits. They're tastefully arranged. It works well today to show things off. You make good money if you've got a few baskets out in front."

In this garden of Eden, distance between continents and the alternation of the seasons are abolished. Shop interstices are garnished with pineapples and limes—and bunches of grapes, surprising in the month of March. Paradoxically, the "dead" season is the lushest moment on the market. "Contrary to what you might expect," explains Boyac, "the selection is much greater in winter than summer. Summer is local, fifty products maximum, whereas in winter we easily reach a hundred, a hundred twenty items. Green beans from Senegal, strawberries from California—we can get anything we want. In summer you can't find cauliflower or endive, but in winter you can get cherries, melons, strawberries, peaches, apricots. In the three to six months of winter, all products can be found."

At the corner of the Rue des Halles where it meets the Place de l'Horloge, Roux plays on quite another representation. His stall is made of a simple plank of wood less than three meters long laid on trestles and covered with an oilcloth. In front he has carefully lined up a few bunches of leeks; handwritten in chalk on a small slate board above them are the words: "leeks, untreated, 6F." Next to them are a couple of pretty parsley bunches and nicely bound chives; in the center of the stall a big platter of cooked beets; nearby, a wicker basket holding a few eggs. In the back are several crates containing spinach, shriveled-looking *reinette* [pippin] apples, a few fleecy green cabbages. Red and yellow tulips in a small metallic bucket add a note of brilliant color. The price of every product is marked. On the side and at a lower level he's rigged up some cursory scaffolding out of a few plastic crates and put out boxes of turnips, carrots, *belle de Fontenay* potatoes and smaller ones of the *ratte* variety, still covered with soil.

The nature that Roux stages is that of the Sunday gardener: cherries eaten straight off the tree, patiently transplanted lettuce whose progress is observed daily. These are patently healthy vegetables, untampered with, straight from the vegetable garden, still full of flavor, authentic flavor hearkening back to the time when vegetables were grown in manure-fertilized soil, well before the invasion of chemical varieties or pesticides. Several signs are meant to show this: the turnips sport their greens; the leeks are uncut ("Shall I cut off the green for you?"); a few downy feathers are still sticking to the eggs; the lettuce is gritty and there are even one or two small slugs ostentatiously inching their way along the leaves. Obviously the concern here is to display the product in all its rawness; quality, the message goes, is not a matter of appearance. The puckered apples are assumed to be much better than shining, size-sorted granny smiths. 113 Holders of similar stalls seem to want to evoke the patient family labor that went into the product. While some leave their leeks just as they were when pulled out of the ground, others wash and arrange them carefully in even bunches; at some such stalls the carrots are covered with compost; at others they have been cleaned and the roots trimmed.

Here nature is evoked not by means of a display of abundance and diversity but with small amounts of a low number of products. To give the impression that the seller is offering everything he has, no unpacked merchandise is visible. Moreover, the products are displayed separately from each other, and oilcloth shows through pretty much everywhere, as if the three-meter plank were much too long for the little one has to sell. Here what is underlined is the product's scarcity, its rarity. Everything works to suggest the patient effort that went into obtaining the treasures here offered up to the customer's admiration. The fact that produce at this type of stall is often sold by the bunch or unit rather than by weight reinforces the impression of scarcity.

Moreover, the selection of products here does not follow customer logic—"I need carrots and a bouquet garni for the *daube*";[3] "This guy's got tarragon but not lettuce"—but rather the logic of the gardener torn between constraints of soil and climate, her concern to grow good produce, and her own momentary fancy. To whoever wishes to hear it, the stall recounts the cycle of the seasons (I don't have strawberries yet; We don't carry anything wrapped in plastic), the nature of the soil ("The asparagus? It's from Velleron—it's all sand down there"), and the gardener's adventures (I tried pumpkins this year—it worked). Putting a dead rabbit or a bouquet amidst the cabbages, henhouse eggs next to snap peas, a bunch of daffodils close by the raw fava beans; adding a few items gathered wild (a basket of *girolle* mushrooms, a punnet of blackberries, a few branches of sweet fennel) evokes the multiform activity of the traditional domestic economy.

The piecemeal look of this selling arrangement also strengthens the impression that we are not dealing with a professional tradesman here, but rather with a peasant of the sort Chayanov described, who occasionally comes to sell his surplus on the market.[4] Sometimes the crates are set out on canvas on the floor, as was the practice in the nineteenth century. Or the stall is a low, small, rudimentary construction made of found materials (old crates, garden or camp tables); the produce is set on old crates or displayed in household objects (straw or rush baskets, platters, salad bowls, washbasins); the cash box is a small biscuit tin. And the seller, often sitting on a folding chair, a cap pulled down low over his brow, sometimes still wears a blue canvas apron like gardeners of olden times.

This arrangement, designed to evoke the peasant economy (which has long since disappeared from the region), is in fact not frequently encountered on the Carpentras market. The small number of stallholders who play this card serve as a reference for the many more whose allusions are so subtle they are not always perceived—gardener's baskets instead of crates, slates bearing the words "*haricots du pays*" [local beans] in clumsy handwriting, bouquets of flowers that here can pass for decoration—or whose knowing winks at the customer allow doubt to subsist: a question like "So you don't want any of my plums?" is meant to be heard as meaning that the fruit comes from the seller's own garden.

This kind of display is more frequently found on L'Isle-sur-la-Sorgue, for example, where the Sunday secondhand market along the river pulls in a big tourist clientele. Narrow-range stallholder trade has held up best in places with many tourists. It was at this market in any case that I found the most fully evolved instance of such a stall. The very structure of the table across which seller and buyer usually interact has disappeared, and piled up on overturned plastic crates in an indescribable jumble are a few very round pumpkins, huge squashes, onion bunches, the scale, some celery stalks, and, in place of Prévert's *raton laveur*, a guinea pig with its own sign: "I'm a guinea pig, don't touch me."[5]

This type of display may lead the customer to believe, or at least suggests to him, that he is buying lettuce or leeks directly from the person who patiently transplanted and hoed them. In reality, Roux's fruits and vegetables come from the *marché-gare* (the section called *le petit marché*, used above all by producers who have only small quantities to sell), though he does have his "own" little producer, a neighbor of his in Pernes.

Very few growers sell fruit and vegetables directly on the Carpentras market. It should be recalled that the Comtat is a region not of small multi-item growers but of intensive, specialized farming for wholesale nationwide marketing. The surrounding farms have pleasure gardens, not vegetable gardens— lawns and flower beds that suggest second homes. Their owners have a Labrador or Siamese, not a barnyard full of hens or a rabbit hutch. The current state of Comtat agriculture is more accurately evoked on the market by the occasional stall selling one product only—unshippable "split" melons in the summer, for example. Here the seller, patently not a producer, rolls out his bulk item roughly and calls out to the customer to liquidate his stock as fast as possible. Paradoxically, selling a single product not by unit but by "lot," a practice occasionally used by discounters for dishcloths or socks, does somewhat evoke the specialized-sections market of olden times that some Carpentras inhabitants still remember. Stalls with highly diversified products arrived here fairly recently.

Nothing is done to provide fruit and vegetable growers easier access to the stallholder market. I witnessed an interesting incident in this connection early in my research. During the winter, when the *marché-gare* is closed, a few producers had begun to go to Les Platanes on Fridays (where farmers used to sell their produce before the advent of the *marché-gare*) to sell lettuce they hadn't been able to dispose of on the wholesale market. City hall decided to prohibit this because the producers had not requested spots. Clearly the producers weren't looking to sell regularly on the market, just to use it occasionally to unload products that couldn't wait until Monday.

There is only one local grower regularly present on the market; he is one of its most striking figures. Every Friday *le père* Jeanjean parks his little old two-horsepower van in front of the Palais de Justice and sets up his humble stand, a garden table laden with small bags of seeds: *marmande* or *pierrette* tomatoes, long Provence leeks, carrots, and the like. His weights and copper-plated two-tray scale are set behind the table on a crate. "I've been coming here forty years, in all weathers," he repeats whenever you talk with him. "I'm of resistant temperament. When you love your work, you hang on."

115

In reality, though Jeanjean is indeed a producer, he also runs a national-level business that exports all over the world. "We're big producers of tomato seed," he explains to me, "export markets primarily. We produce near on five tons of tomato seed—and just think of it: it takes a thousand kilos of tomatoes to get you four kilos of seed." Under these conditions, selling on the market is "a pastime, a hobby," as he himself acknowledges: "It's my day out. I see all sorts of people I know, from here, from there. It's a distraction for me." Jeanjean is not there to do business. People come to see him to "chew the fat": "I've got customers who are eighty-five years old still coming to get seeds for their gardens. They're not big customers, but I'm telling you, if I'd recorded all the things that've been said around my stand . . . !"

Leaving his business to prosper under his son's control, he continues to play the small producer on the market, one who has never made it and so can't stop working. "The market is a presentation thing," he says. He is also the old, experienced peasant ready to proffer all sorts of advice and counsel: "That's the work of a real seed seller," he explains. "Not only does he sell the stuff, he offers his ideas at the same time, assesses things in ways that people can't usually do—that's Père Jeanjean's occupation." He is fully conscious of playing his own character—"You're always *en représentation* [playing to the audience] here, it's a specialty of the Midi"—and also knows that as such, he's a market attraction: "I've always been a figure on the market. There was a lady of nice appearance, and for several Fridays she stood in that corner over there watching, and then she'd leave. So one day I said to her, 'And this good lady, what might she need?' 'I'm not a buyer,' she answered, 'but I come often just to listen to you speak, because it's a mixture of Provençal, with a little French . . .'"

Paradoxically, then, the only real peasant on the market, the only stallholder selling directly to the consumer, is a fake merchant. He is there exclusively for his pleasure and that of others, not really to sell. In a way, he is the opposite of the occasional May '68ers and other marginal presences selling their goat cheeses here and there—real producers of genuinely local products who have indeed come to sell them, but fake peasants. The two figures are two modes of the general practice of simulation that gives the market its touch of authenticity.

8. "Let me have some pâté, but *your* pâté"

Given the type of agriculture practiced in the region and city inhabitants' multiple connections to the world of the countryside, only "vacationers" fall for
the line that the garden lettuce or bush peaches were picked "just this morning." While this does correspond to a conventional image of the market, it is
not a serious selling point in Carpentras. "Homemade" products, though, are
another story. Since people cannot really believe that the cabbages or artichokes
Venturi sells were grown on his own land, they enjoy telling themselves that
the *charcutier* makes his own sausage. They go to market in search of products
sold directly by the producer as in bygone days, and that expectation has to be
met one way or another.

In fact, one cannot really go to market without at least glancing at the multicolored beaded necklaces and slightly stiff western-style leather belts in the
Passage Boyer, or being tempted by the small, makeshift stalls displaying a
dozen small goat cheeses, a few small jars of honey, a little royal jelly, and
five or six spice breads. Such stands are few, but they are scattered throughout the market, and all offer nearly identical products. Perhaps it is to them
more than the other types of stalls that the market owes its overall character.
Their handcraftedness is ostentatiously conveyed. On an extremely clean linen
cloth laid over a rickety camp table, small quantities of two or three products
are carefully positioned. Goat cheeses, which may be hard and dry, fresh and
moist, *demi-sec*, or laid out in olive oil with a bay leaf or two; a few bottles
of olive oil bearing a label of the sort once found on the cover of schoolchil-

dren's notebooks and here marked "cold-pressed extra-virgin olive oil"; last, perhaps, a few sprigs of vervain, stalks of lavender, as if to show that all the treasures of the home producer are for sale here. A sign specifies a tiny locale of origin: "Ferme de Fonblanque, route de Mérindol, Faucon," "Les granges, Montfroc," "Campagne Redontiers, Murs."[1] This is both a guarantee of the product's authenticity and an invitation to those who appreciate it to come and buy on site.

Occasionally, and with a redundancy at first surprising, a small handmade sign marked "raspberries for sale" is set next to three or four punnets of just that. This is a way of saying that the sellers are first and foremost country people, for whom trade is a secondary activity; that only after some hesitation have they decided to sell their produce rather than consume it themselves. Writing out "Honey" or "Apricot jam" in a pretty, round, almost childlike hand when there can be no doubt about the product's identity lets the prospective customer know that what is on offer here has nothing to do with what she can get on supermarket shelves. The neatly glued-on label marked "Cornichons" guarantees that this is a homemade product prepared with loving care, a work signed by the author, one that calls up childhood images of a grandmother's pantry cupboards or cellar shelves. Some labels go so far as to note that this is "genuine" beeswax or spice bread, in contradistinction to mass-produced substitutes. The spice bread's genuineness inheres in its being made according to an old forgotten recipe—which the maker is only too happy to divulge should the customer show the slightest interest: half honey, half rye flour, natural spices. . . .

To convey still more convincingly that the product is homemade, it is insinuated that the honey is from the vendor's own beehives, that she herself has spun the wool for the sweaters or cut out the sandal leather. The presence of practicing craftspersons at the market—chair-bottomers, for instance—reinforces this illusion. In fact, though the product itself is handcrafted, the customer is not necessarily dealing with its maker; any direct relation between producer and buyer is exceptional today. At the solar watch seller's stand in the Passage Boyer, the sign is there for all to see: "Atelier des Ormes, Le Barroux." The vender confides that he didn't make them himself; then, concerned to preserve his image, explains he buys them from "a friend." And though we are quite willing to believe that Liliane Fresquet, whose stand in the Rue des Halles resembles those of the other goat cheese vendors like two peas in a pod, came down from the mountain to sell off her week's production, in reality she lives in

Avignon and also "does" L'Isle-sur-la-Sorgue, Cavaillon, Vaison-la-Romaine, Salon, Nyons, and Marignane—for her boss, a producer in Bagnols who pays her by the month.

When there is no claim to offer exclusively homemade products, the vendor makes sure to position advantageously those that are. "In the food business, *charcuterie* and the like, there are still many who make their own products," affirms Nicole Grossage, who may be assumed to know her market. "People want it because it's homemade, whereas in the supermarkets everything comes wrapped in plastic—straight from the factory and that's that! Here you've still got homemade hams and *pâtés*. In the city there're almost none." In fact, from what the *charcutiers* at the market told me, very few of them make their own products anymore, but they do strive to meet customers' expectations, even if that means letting them believe that what has actually been bought from wholesalers comes out of their own *ateliers*. As Delvaux explains with a touch of humor:

> It's important to people that we make our own products, so we have to lie. When I have them taste a pâté, they say, "Oh, it's good, it's really good!" If I don't say I made it myself, they don't think it's as good. In the beginning I made almost everything myself, while trying to fill customer orders at the same time. That hurt me, obviously. Here I don't make anything myself. It'd help if I had a shop, I could work in the back. But I don't, so I started buying. In the beginning that raised a few eyebrows, but later people came and said, "All right, let me have some pâté, but *your* pâté, okay—homemade!" It wasn't mine, I'd bought it at various places, so I'd say, "Here, this one is new, it's a new recipe." You cut off a bit, give them a taste. "You made it yourself?" "Yes, yes." The product helps, but a bit of hype really makes it easier to put things over.

The enchanting thought of the *charcutier* behind his stove or the cheese vendor herding her goats up the slopes of Mont Ventoux does somewhat contradict the image of the stallholder as continually on the move—from one market to another. Doesn't the customer's illogic justify in advance all the little manipulations to hoodwink her? Moreover, it is a matter not so much of misleading the customer on quality as of staging the "market product"—precisely those products the customer has come in search of—through a number of presentational artifices. The stand is set up so that whatever is manifestly "homemade" is directly under the customer's nose—e.g., stuffed tomatoes or peppers presented in a Provençal earthenware baking dish as if they'd just come out of the oven—in a way that suggests the same is true of all the other products, the big sausages hanging in bunches, for example, or the little ones strung like a rosary, which the vendor grabs with his whole hand when cutting them down, as if to evoke the movement practiced by the sausage maker. Other stallholders use similarly metonymic arrangement—ultimately more suggestive than deceptive. In the Rue des Halles, Vieini puts the fresh *fromage blanc* in its ceramic bowl and the farmhouse yogurts in little wax-paper-covered glass jars at the forefront of his display case. And in the Place de la Mairie, next to the truck stand where Jaquet sells *salaisons*, [2] he sets up a little table laden with irregular-shaped breads. "Baked in a wood-burning oven" reads the sign.

To preclude the thought that the product might be industrially manufactured, close attention is paid to its appearance. It is good for blood sausages to be oddly shaped and *andouillettes* not to be all the same size. "Country pâté" should be coarse, with small chunks of unground meat showing. When handmade products look imperfect, the contrast with the regularity of mass-produced ones is sharper. The hope is that the *saucisses de Francfort*, objectively indistinguishable from the vacuum-packed version piled into supermarket cases, will look better if positioned not too far from slightly clumsy, flour-dusted ravioli. Next to Dannon yogurts and bottles of Yoplait sits the *fougeru* cheese with its fern frond, the *brie de Meaux* on its straw mat, the rush-encircled *livarot*—all reassuring signs of rural authenticity that work to ward off any agro-industry images: they would be so out of place here!

How the product is handled in transfer from seller to buyer also counts. The very fact of selling butter "loose" off a big mound, cutting the *beaufort* or *tomme* cheese off a wedge from the wheel, evokes vacations in rustic rented cottages or the cowshed discovered off a turn in a path through mountain pastureland. The "market product" includes the set of gestures and discourse that accompany the transaction. With small successive touches, the vendor intimates his intimate knowledge of the merchandise, which thereby becomes a rare, unique object to which such things as pasteurized cheese and cellophane-wrapped cold cuts are utterly alien. Vieini the cheese man offers a taste of his *saint-nectaire*, recommends the *comté* today rather than the *emmenthal*, indicates a perfectly ripe *coulommiers*, guarantees that the *bleu de Causses* is just right, reassures an ignorant customer: "No, no, the *maroilles* is not too strong!" Such familiarity with the merchandise is more than a mere selling point; it's an indirect way of affirming that these are indeed his cheeses, that though he assuredly did not handle the milk they're made of, he has perhaps meticulously overseen the ripening process in his cellars. When you ask him for a "good" *reblochon* and he peels back wrapping paper on which one may read "Reblochon des Aravis" against a background of snowy mountain peaks, when he pinches it gently with a satisfied air and has you appreciate its soft springiness, how can you not imagine that he has his regular small purveyors, and that they in turn regularly visit a few old, isolated, dark-wood Savoyard chalets in the far-flung reaches of the Vallée du Grand-Bornand, like those pictured on post office calendars? Like the others, Jaquet probably buys his *salaisons* from wholesalers. But to watch him lovingly slice a few thin rounds of *saucisse sèche* or *rosette de Lyon* and pass them around—"which costs me!" he notes—commenting all the while on their respective virtues, how can you not believe that he has somehow had a hand in their making? Questioned on this point, he is determined to play the game through to the end: "A friend in the Ardèche makes them for me."

Delvaux actually does make some of what he sells: "Pork sausage, *merguez*, country pâté, head cheese, various types of *boudin, boudin à la viande*[3]—there you have it, not so bad!" He must nonetheless play the part of *charcutier*. In checkered smock and capacious white apron, he recommends his "specialty"— snail brioche—to a hesitant customer, explains his recipe for spinach pie, and keeps to himself the little "thing" that makes his rabbit pâté so very tasty.

9. "I sell Provence"

The real market product is unique, or should appear so, not only in that it is pre- sumably "homemade" but also because it is assumed to be local. In fact, people tend to confuse these two features. They don't shop at the market for standard, soulless, or no-brand products (sold under a supermarket name) such as those lined up repetitively on Auchan or Leclerc shelves. They don't go there for *paupiettes* [rolled veal cutlets], but for Laville's painstakingly prepared "head-less birds," or on a quest for lavender honey of incomparable flavor. And in the end, isn't it the quest itself that makes the market product unique? If it is true that in customers' minds the market is the place to find "local products," it is also true that products become local because the market is where people go to look for them.

M. Patio's weekly experience is a fine example. "The olives at the market come directly from Nyons," says he. "I'm sure they're local olives, from just around here, and they're very good. In the stores they come in a plastic bag, they're from Algeria or Greece, they're not very good, they're sold packaged, not in bulk. But the genuine Nyons olive—*that* you find at the market, loose, bathed in oil, olive oil, with a little garlic, rosemary—they're glorious! They've got all the freshness of products from right around here, truly. I'm sure they're Nyons olives, they're to my taste, that's how I like them, and I always go to the market for my olives."

This discourse may be reduced to a set of mutually reinforcing utterances, the logic (or tautology) of which is indicative of the implicit representations shared by regular market customers: market olives can only be local, therefore fresh and good; they are local because they are said to be from Nyons, but they are believed to be from Nyons because they are sold in traditional market fashion (loose); they are local because they are displayed and seasoned in conformity with local culture (olive oil, garlic, rosemary); last, they are local for M. Patio because he affords himself the leisure of a long, circuitous trip to the Place de la Mairie to get them every Friday. All of these are signs of the "localness" he "likes" in these olives.

The notion of local product is in fact highly ambiguous, designating both what is made or grown in the region and everything that in one way or another evokes the traditions of the Comtat or, more vaguely, Provence, the Midi. The "market product" is in large measure an effect of this confusion. People represent the market as a place where the products of regional farmers and craftspeople are sold and ancestral customs perpetuated. It is recognized as serving a twofold function: a center for selling and buying, and a "conservatory" of peasant memory. In fact, the Carpentras market's particular vocation for selling Comtat produce came to an end in the early twentieth century. Since then it has traded in industrial products identical to those found elsewhere in France and Europe, and though local farm produce is sold there (melons, strawberries, tomatoes), nothing distinguishes this from produce grown elsewhere using the same ultramodern techniques. Extensive use of forced ripening techniques and importation of products from still further south (Spanish strawberries, for example) have even meant the end of the Comtat's privilege of being the first to offer these fruits thanks to the Provençal climate.

Customers think that market products can only be local. To satisfy their expectations, stallholders have to create meaning, piece together appearances, invent reputations. It is up to them to recreate the zest for Provençal culture that everyone comes to buy on Fridays. The most elementary means of doing so is to identify available products as much as possible with regional toponyms. Cavaillon melons and Carpentras strawberries are nationally valid labels of quality, like Soissons beans [white], *belle de Boskoop* apples, and Sisteron lamb. But for the initiated (local natives or fervent readers of the Michelin *Guide vert*) and "local color" fiends, the stallholder will further refine this "product geography": the sausage is from Sault just as the cured ham is from Malaucène; Condorcet, Dieulefit, and Bouvières *picodons* (sharp-flavored goat cheeses) are to be distinguished from those from Banon; the peppers are from Cavaillon; the eggplant is Cheval-Blanc eggplant; the *chasselas* table grapes are from Thor;

the peaches are Cabannes peaches, and so forth. Naming the products this way works to differentiate them from others that look exactly like them.

Product provenance is often indicated even when it refers to no specific quality. Lemaresquier in the Rue de l'Evêché buys his eggs at an industrial chicken farm in Le Pontet but never fails to specify that they are "local." Announcing that the tomatoes are from Monteux is a way of giving an imaginary identity to this stereotypical product grown there as elsewhere under a plastic tunnel or in a hothouse. Customers are particularly responsive to this argument on the market, whereas in other contexts they are much more attentive to the famous quality-price relation. To my great surprise, it is important to Henri Levêque (as he told me several times) that the croissants sold at the market are from Thor, a village on the banks of the Sorgue river where an industrial bakery is located. For this nonnative vineyard owner, the market is of interest only in so far as it offers authentic manifestations of local culture. It is therefore unthinkable to him that the same croissants might be sold in the Forum des Halles in Paris.

Another stallholder technique is to stage the "typical product," the one that everyone represents as characteristic of local practices and habits. At a *charcuterie* and readymade dishes stand, zucchini flower beignets, *caillettes*, *panisses*, a small bowl of *tapenade*, and a few *fougasses* are carefully positioned center stage.[1] The vegetable seller makes sure that his little round squash, which so impress Parisians, are displayed up front; likewise for bunches of *blettes* (Swiss chard), and at Christmastime he hands you your parsnips and cardoons wrapped in sheets of *Le Provençal*. If need be, the stallholder invents the "local" by playing on a few firmly anchored culinary clichés. "If you don't put spinach in the *boudin* here, you won't sell it—that's something you've just got to know! If you don't put garlic in just about everything, you won't sell anything," says Delvaux, who, like me, has a certain experience of Paris. "There's even got to be garlic in the country pâté—*I'd* never put any. You've got to make garlic sausage, and there's got to be garlic in the *saucisse sèche*!" To accommodate this *idée fixe* (and since as we know he doesn't make all these products himself), he is not loath to add an imaginary hint of garlic.

For the product to be "typical," the seller should be too. In accordance with the logic of appearances characteristic of advertising rhetoric, clothes not only make the man but also guarantee the quality of the cheese. It's not enough to make and sell little rosemary-flavored goat cheeses; the seller must also have the appropriate look. The "character" she plays must be in harmony with the product she sells. Above all, nothing must get in the way of imagining he comes from a place where rosemary grows wild and goats graze. Delvaux has learned that one does well to throw in a slight Provençal accent with the garlic—it isn't easy to win people's confidence in Carpentras if you talk *pointu*.[2] When Delvaux "came down" from the Paris area a few years ago, he didn't have the accent, of course. He had to make up for a missing sign ("He's not from these parts") by taking another sign to the extreme ("It's all homemade")—he had to make everything himself. Today he spikes his sausage with garlic and his patter with idiomatic expressions, regales his customers with *farcis* [vegetables with ground pork stuffing] and can *galéjer* [joke] on the fly, not to mention selling public [i.e., secular] school raffle tickets. He has learned to "do" local color and can therefore resell wholesale-bought *charcuterie*.

Product selection and the way products are grouped together at a given stall are also means of inventing the local. The "olive merchants," as people in the city call them, are particularly remarkable in this respect, and actually identify themselves as local-product specialists. There are fewer than a dozen of them, strategically situated (Rue des Halles near the bird market, the intersection of the Rue de la Sous-Préfecture and the Place de la Mairie, Rue de l'Evêché near the Place de l'Horloge, and so on), and their displays are big, attractive, strikingly decorated. They have olives of all varieties in big wooden buckets, each with a serving ladle; the customer is invited to compare the merits of the *picholine*, the best-known green olive, the *lucques* (longer and a bright blue-green), the *salonenque* (pear-shaped and slightly bitter), and to sample a range of black olives: *tanche* of Nyons, which Carpentrassians like best; *grossane* from the Vallée des Baux; the small, purplish black, very flavorful *cailletier*, also known as *olive niçoise*. Each variety is prepared in a variety of ways: *nature*, in brine, in salt. There are pitted and stuffed olives, *olives piquées* (flavored with olive oil, bay leaf, and whole garlic cloves—*"fachouiro"* as they are still sometimes called), *olives cassées* (cracked or *"escachado"*), and so on. The blatant diversity and abundance are a kind of proof that here we are all enlightened amateurs, far from the overcrowded beaches where you stand in line for yet another *pan bagnat*, far from all the fake Provences gotten up for tourists hankering after a change of scenery.[3]

Varying combinations of other "local products" are also displayed at such stalls: dried fruit, dry beans, herbs, *tisanes* [loose herbal teas such as lime blossom, vervain], oils, and dried fish. Mme. Bressy, who has had an olive stand in the Place de la Mairie for forty years, also carries walnuts, salt cod, and bottles of an olive oil from the Baronnies that she describes as "a bit gruff," touting its amber-green color. What all these products have in common is the crucial role they played in the ordinary Comtadine diet of the nineteenth century. The elderly persons I met seemed to take considerable pleasure in remembering cod and spinach *tian*;[4] walnut, almond, and fig desserts; salads, chickpea soups . . .

Farmers in the Comtat gave up growing this type of produce quite some time ago. Apricot, cherry, and peach orchards, along with vineyards, have taken the place of almond and olive trees, and land which once produced only pulse vegetables is now devoted to sprinkler-watered *primeur* green vegetables and fruits. Olives, walnuts, and the like are therefore "local" not so much because they come from the region but because they are brought together at specialized stalls, because they evoke *la Provence éternelle*, for residents and foreigners alike. The display of seemingly disparate foodstuffs in such stalls obeys a clearly defined imperative: bring together everything that recalls vanished cooking and eating practices in stalls that individually and collectively resemble a museum of popular culture. The products themselves are quite marginal in current consumption habits. They are traditional, but for the most part fake-local. The olives were bought at the MIN, and many were imported from Tunisia. Local olives are extremely expensive; they and other products have become luxury items. "Cod *tian* was our Friday meal," says Mme. Coste. "It was the poor man's meat. Now cod is too expensive." "We ate a lot of chestnuts, figs, and walnuts," recounts Mme. Favier. "That was dessert in our families. It's all become very expensive, we don't buy those things anymore."

To respond to the vogue for "country products" or regional crafts, stallholders are ready if need be to invent the local out of whole cloth. Because olive wood evokes the Provençal landscape, a number of objects, from napkin rings to cheese boards and salad servers, are now made out of it. Few of these can claim to represent a local tradition, but in the national context they take on regionalist meaning. Avon the "leisure textiles" specialist, who produces locally in the city outskirts, has a product that can be called local for another reason: the images on his embroidery canvases (embroidery itself ineluctably evoking a grandmother sitting by the fireside with a cat on her knees and an eye on the street scene) are inspired by local nature and life. "Our biggest clientele are stallholders," he explains. "We sell first and foremost on markets. Stallholders help us sell notions better, in part because they are dynamic young people who like these things, know their products well, and are not bogged down in the negative aspect of tradition. They partake in a tradition, but a tradition that is evolving, whereas your traditional 'center-city' notions shop is often constricted by lack of shop space. All creative or semicreative sewing items, kits that comes in separate pieces that you sew together, for example—we sell those things best on the outskirts of town and on the markets." He continues:

> My father is preparing a series of embroidery cloths with regional themes for next summer—there's a strong demand for them. We're going to bring out a dozen regional subjects: monuments, scenes of local life. That's never been done before. We also have a manufacturer who supplies us with images of fields of lavender. That sells well on the Sault plateau—in summer we sell between a hundred and a hundred fifty. If we manage to give some style to a home-and-regional collection, really get it going, I think we'll have a good niche, as long as it isn't bottom-of-the-line tourist exploitation stuff. We try to maintain a level of quality and esthetics that will ennoble the region. I'm also trying to recreate a kind of regional dress that won't look like a costume, with authentic fabric printed here. I've designed the patterns, and I'm having them sewn by seamstresses in the region. My studio is in Carpentras—entirely local. I aim first to please people from here, but tourists buy it too, of course. You've got to admit, Provence sells well. It's a bit sacrilegious to say so, but it's true: the Provence phenomenon sells. In stallholders' displays there are durable products too—underwear, Rhovyl shirts—and there are impulse buys, articles that tourists may, in fact, find tempting: wicker baskets, goat cheese . . .

In his concern to promote his products systematically, the farsighted Avon is conscious of being part of a movement of civilization that extends far beyond Comtadines' love of their region.

> In my business, there's a phenomenon that's not strictly regional—I'm referring to the environmentalist trend. *La mercerie* is a very old skill area ranging from weaving to spinning to dyeing. This was a major silkworm center. I think there's a desire at this time to rediscover those values. I think we can achieve a balance between consumption of manufactured products and the need for creation. We're going to organize a conference in the spring that will bring together manufacturers, tradespeople, and craftspeople in the sewing-notions and leisure textiles branches. The plan is to set up a center for the creation and promotion of leisure textiles that won't be commercial but rather for training instructors and monitors for old-age homes, town activity centers, and other groups, in such disciplines as silk painting, lacemaking, macramé, sewing, and embroidery. Among other things, the center would inform people about sales outlets in the region where they can get supplies . . . I sell dreams, a potential dream—I think that's what lasts.

CHAPTER NINE

If the market product cannot be or appear Comtadine or Provençal, it should at least be able to claim a local origin of some sort. Market products are always typical or local, no matter how distant or imprecise the provenance. Noblet, who buys from a wholesaler, will tell anyone who wants to listen that his *salaisons* are from the Ardèche or the Tarn. And Delvaux will unabashedly explain how he proceeds: "This smoked ham is Italian, but if I ever said so I wouldn't sell any. I'll show you with the next person who comes up—you'll see. I'm going to tell him, and you just watch, he won't buy any! Whereas if I tell him it's from Corsica he'll buy some and think it's very good. Like this other Italian sausage. This morning I didn't remember to take off the label ring. Just watch: on Sunday [at Monteux] I'll take the ring off and the sausage will sell itself. If it's Italian, nothing doing. But Corsican, Auvergnat, Breton—that'll do fine!"

Brittany, Auvergne, Corsica, the Ardèche—so many essential locales of *la France profonde* whose very names are enough to evoke untrammeled nature and small-scale traditional production. The ham and sausage may not be from these parts, but they *are* from a particular expanse of French countryside—and that's what makes them desirable. As localizable if not local, they link up with the set of products that give the impression of being "exotic" because of their assumed origin and the way they are displayed. "You can find everything on the market," people say. There are Indian dresses and incense, bulgur wheat for making tabbouleh, papayas, mangoes, and sweet potatoes from the tropics alongside *beurre-hardy* pears and bunches of green onions. A stand in the Rue de l'Evêché sells red chili powder, "*ras el hanut*" [Moroccan spice blend], "*qirfa*" [Arabic for cinnamon], saffron, and other Oriental delights, loose or in small transparent bags (rather than boxes like at Auchan) next to different varieties of rice in metallic bins. Though the habitué comes to the market above all to satisfy his desire for products "from these parts," he also enjoys the cosmopolitan dimension—on condition, of course, that each foodstuff come from an identified elsewhere.

If you want to sell the famous Agen prunes, it's advisable to wear a "regional" costume, regional in the way a chair may be "a period piece," that is, one that is likely to suggest some particular area, though people won't necessarily know which. Miracle-cure hawkers of the sort Pascal likes so well are also to be seen on the market occasionally. The *placier* places them expertly so they will be able to "create an event"—as this man is doing, for example, as he appealingly touts the multiple virtues of the roots set out before him on an

129

oilcloth: "You just take the plant and scrape it . . . You take this wonderwork-ing pomade—you can't get it from Rhone-Poulenc [pharmaceutical company], it's made only by nature, the sun, the rain, the cold—and you massage the pain with it and this wonder-working pomade will make the pain go away. Lum-bago, sciatica—you can treat the ill directly with Tanus root, the only plant in the world capable of treating sciatica or lumbago. Let any doctor here say it isn't so! Nature gives her all to feed us, and she does the same to heal us. The ancients were forever telling us: plants are all that's good for the human body. When you've got a headache, don't poison yourself with aspirin. Use this pomade instead and give your head a massage." To sell this natural prod-uct, these roots out of the depths of the ages whose secrets are known only to a few initiates in the remotest reaches of the countryside, you need a vendor with a canvas smock over corduroy trousers, a red cotton scarf knotted around his neck, a broad-brimmed black hat. The costume is from nowhere and ev-erywhere, but such mysteries require such folklore. The semantic surcharge can come perilously close to the absurd—and therefore become counterpro-ductive: Why sell peanuts from a pony-drawn cart? The phenomenon might surprise the Senegalese sellers, who for their part have chosen to wear Noah-style dreadlocks.[5] And what are we to make of that young man in a striped sweater with his slightly romantic air, there from time to time selling skeins of raw wool from a wooden handcart?

Aerial view of Carpentras looking south down the Rue de la République. In the center foreground, the Place du Palais with the façade of the episcopal palace.

Carpentras, Place du Palais. The episcopal palace (present-day hall of justice) is on the left.

Old Jeanjean selling seeds in the Place du Palais

Mobile shop *charcuterie*

At the *marché-gare* wholesale fruit and vegetable market

Inside the truffle circle (see chap. 11)

Weighing a truffle *lot* (see chap. 11)

Truffle broker noting price (see chap. 11)

The author in the field

10. Ordinary Authenticity

Stallholders make an ordinary product into a "market product" by giving it
its own identity, making it appear to come straight from nature, the countryside and country traditions [*terroir*], the *atelier,* the farm or vegetable garden.
But other "market products" appear specific to the market because they either
evoke vanishing trade sectors, such as sewing notions, or seem to target a local, specifically rural clientele assumed to have preserved the lifestyle of olden
times.

According to the people of Carpentras, there is a whole range of products on
the market that are of interest above all to "others," i.e., the villagers who "de-
scend" upon the city on Fridays. Rousseau says they are "country people" who
"come to buy their clothes, hardware, china, small jewelry." Nicole Grossage
remarks that in contrast to food, both country and city clothing have clienteles that are "traditional." In fact, people do their marketing differently by
social category. Just about everyone shops for fruit, vegetables, and *charcuterie*
on the market, but immigrants are more likely to buy linens and blankets, and
it is unlikely for well-off city residents to buy a pair of shoes or a jacket. They
might purchase a fifties blouse from Martin, but not a checkered apron-dress
from Ricci's garment stand. A whole segment of the market seems to speak, or
answer, to popular or peasant tastes.

Mme. Patio, a true city dweller, declares: "I don't really trust clothes that
come from the market. Maybe they're exactly the same as in a store, but they
aren't presented the same way. The way they're put out gives you the idea that

there are a lot of them and that everyone will end up with the same thing."
There are two explanations for her reluctance to buy clothes on the market.
First, the clothes available there are not to her or her husband's tastes or needs
(work smocks, farm-work and walking shoes, and the like) and evoke dressing
habits quite removed from theirs; second, when, as Mme. Patio readily admits,
she sees clothes on the market that are identical on all points to the ones she
buys elsewhere, they seem different because they're displayed next to ones she
wouldn't buy. Mme. Patio would not think to buy underwear at the market, and
the way it's displayed—brassieres on opulent mannequin bosoms, panty hose
of all sizes thrown together—makes it easy for her to forget that in many cases
they are the exact same items she might buy tomorrow at Auchan or at a shop
in the Rue de la République.

The way stallholders select and display—"stage"—these ordinary products accentuates the sense that they are specific to the market. On the one hand
they carry articles that are hard to find elsewhere but continue to be sold on
the market; the circuit system is well adapted to the low markup–low turnover
characteristic of such products. Moreover, there is enough space on the market to display everything, including low-cost items. In the Place de la Mairie,
Georgeon unloads meters of buttons, fastenings, zippers, spools of thread of all
colors. Not far away from his stand is Mme. Arési's; she specializes in corsets,
girdles, long underwear, matched underwear sets, and other somewhat old-
fashioned lingerie items. It is as if the market put center stage precisely those
items that give people the sense of being at the market, in the same way that
shopkeepers choose "classy" items for their display windows.

Stallholders also use display to give a special look to ordinary products,
the ones everyone knows they can find elsewhere. This can be done at both
"catchall" stands and specialized ones. Espenon's extraordinary jumble and
Noël Cappo's savvily disorganized hardware and household products stall recall old village grocery store–cafés where you could ferret out the most unexpected items from a chaotic bric-à-brac. The close proximity of stalls selling
different types of wares—bedspreads next to garlic and melons, shoelaces one
stall over from bonbons—reinforces this effect.

Conversely, by displaying massive amounts of one specific mass-produced
article in a large stall—heavy cotton-synthetic mix shirts from Taiwan, slippers
from Portugal—one may create the illusion that the product is available only at
the market. Casanova sells ladies' aprons only, and the counter at Barnabé's is
carpeted with rows of overlapping caps—the only product. Other stallholders,

like Suzanne Neboit in the Rue de l'Evêché, sell only socks. Rows of saucepans in red or marbled enamel, aluminum kettles, buckets and basins of all sizes, teapots, cake and tart molds, spaghetti strainers, tea strainers, still other items take up twenty meters of sidewalk in the Place du Théâtre (though not every Friday). All of this can be found at Auchan, and yet all of it seems different at the market. The Morin family in the Rue de l'Evêché seems to know that displaying large quantities of unwrapped tea biscuits of all sorts in wooden trays next to candies, barley-sugar sticks, and multicolored lollipops is enough to make them look utterly different from the many rows of industrially made brand-name cookies at the supermarket.

Specialization of this sort makes good business sense since the circuit system multiplies sales outlets. But such stands also reinforce the idea that the market is still a place where you can find bargains or a rare and precious object. The synthetic socks that Mme. Neboit sells are totally ordinary; only the breadth of her selection is specific to the market. Nonetheless, when Henri Charvet returns to his Provençal manor in Saint-Didier, he has his friends admire the find of the morning: "Real *chasseur alpin* [mountain infantryman] socks!" Meanwhile his wife exhibits her set of *métis* [cotton-linen mix] dishcloths "of the sort you can't find anywhere anymore"; and Mme. Delavigne is sure she's bought "one of the last cast-iron frying pans to be manufactured in an iron forge in the Ain."[1]

Big specialized stalls with a vast and widely spread out selection evoke a time when people used the market differently. According to current, widespread representations, the market was a place where people bought a great variety of items in great quantities. "My mother used to buy twenty liters of olive oil at a time," recalls Doctor Brun. "We bought two years' worth of soap. We didn't go to 'look around,' open to temptation by the slightest little thing, to purchasing something we didn't really need. We went to put in supplies for the week, sometimes for the year, replenish the reserves of the entire household in biscuits, walnuts, garlic, potatoes . . . We waited until Friday to replace the worn-out overcoat or shoes, buy utensils or tools, seed, shot, other indispensable manufactured products." "My father used to tell me," says Mme. Favier, "that in his time people came to the market in the nut and garlic seasons to buy their provisions for the whole year. The same for onions and potatoes. People bought sacks of walnuts for the whole year—two fifty-kilo sacks, for the year's desserts." And "women went to buy dresses and fabric that they then took to the seamstress. We bought everything at the market, it was traditional. There were customs that aren't practiced anymore, like getting a whole new outfit for the Easter holidays and the feast of Our Lady, which corresponded to the beginning of July."

The profuse accumulations of caps, slippers, aprons, fabrics, oilcloths, candies, and cookies at the market are so many occasions for today's visitor to remember figures from another world, a world built out of childhood memories, *images d'Epinal*,[2] and firmly established stereotypes: the old peasant with his cane and cap, the good housewife at the oven in her smock and fichu, the peasant woman arrayed in her Sunday best for feast days, the gaggle of children in slippers and flannelette robes. The market seems to refer to or have as its backdrop an enduring mode of consumption perceived as rural and of another age: vast kitchens with arsenals of saucepans, rows of bottles and jars, tight-lidded boxes where soft caramels and Mont-Saint-Michel butter biscuits were preciously preserved for the children's mid-afternoon *goûter* [snack].

Once again, the particular selection of products and the way they are displayed give the impression that they are for a clientele that continues to entertain a traditional relation to the market. And it is in this that they are essential. Even if only a small proportion of customers buy them, they attest that this is an authentic market, rooted in local practices, not just part of some folkloric manifestation. In order for the market to appear a "real" market, people have to be able to believe that it is still the place where country people come to sell the fruits of their labor and lay in provisions of manufactured products; still the market of olden days where peasants go to "buy the indispensable iron plowshare, or obtain the money needed to pay their dues and taxes by selling a few eggs, a lump of butter, a few chickens or vegetables,"[3] the market Braudel described in the book the Parisians have taken along on their Lubéron vacation and are so pleasurably rereading now in the cool evening air.

No matter how unoriginal stallholders' products may be, they have to seem to be for local folk. It is crucial that the winemaker from Caromb buy his Pataugas [basic country walking shoes] on the market, the Saint-Didier road mender his balaclava, and that everyone see them do so, even if not many do the same. That way everyone can feel they have participated in that Friday morning's local-life event. Moreover, "foreigners" like the idea of buying market products precisely because they are perceived to be used by natives. Mme. Delavigne's daughter laughingly buys two pairs of long underwear "for skiing" precisely because she can imagine Mme. Arési selling the same item to the *rabassiers* who brave their way up the foothills of Mont Ventoux in winter. It would not have occurred to her to buy such an item in another context.

CHAPTER TEN

The market product appears different because it is ultimately in all actors' interests to believe it is. The whole thing works on the basis of a tacit shared understanding between stallholder and customer: the former stage-manages, the latter is perfectly content to be taken in; the stallholder is not trying to deceive, and the customer never really believes. Mme. Patio recounts: "I bought some roses. Maybe I could have bought them at Lemouel's for the same price. If you think about it, you realize that there's not really any competition because everything originally comes from the same place." But "thinking about it" as a reasoning customer does not prevent Mme. Patio from taking pleasure in the idea that one can "find finds" at the market, discover products that are not always the same as elsewhere—the roses from Les Platanes have a je ne sais quoi that makes them unlike those in buckets outside city florists': "One has the notion that these ones are better." This near-complicitous relation between stallholder and customer seems analogous to what Jean Baudrillard, referring to advertising, called "Santa Claus logic": "a logic of fables and adherence or fidelity. One does not believe in it, and yet one cares about it; it matters." It matters little whether the message is deceptive or accurate; one believes not in what is said but "in the advertisement that seeks to make us believe."[4] One can know full well that products on the market are identical to those in the stores and yet remain faithful to the idea that on the market everything is different. In my observation, this sort of belief, and what it can involve in the way of bad faith, is common to almost all market customers regardless of origin or social milieu. Foreigners from bigger cities and persons who have adopted and been adopted by the Comtat tend to bedeck what they buy at the market with all the virtues of tradition precisely because authenticity is what they have come in search of. But even the most in-the-know city housewives express their conviction that the quality of M. Hébrard's smocks is as good as that of bygone days, and that Andréoletty's socks in the Place du Palais wear better than the ones you can get at Auchan.

Market wares constitute an enchanted world within the festive market moment, the break from daily routine. One buys naturalness with the tomatoes, a bit of Comtat soil with the strawberries, Giono's Provence in the form of "little goat cheeses." One rediscovers ancestral savors with Delvaux's *caillettes*; the peasant soul thanks to old Jeanjean's sachets of seeds; one invents a *terroir d'origine* for oneself in choosing one's olives. With a crocheted bedspread or Provençal-stitched quilt people "buy a past for themselves, a genealogy of ancestors," as Martin puts it. "It's the same for secondhand goods," he says. "People make themselves an old attic." The charcutier's *croustillons*, like Morin's *sablés* [butter cookies], are not bought just for the pleasure of the eating, but satisfy other needs: the need to truly be from "here," the need for an image of oneself as a child again. Perdiguier's shoes or the small sachets of lavender that you slip into the linen closet answer and fuel a vague nostalgia for a lost world. What people consume on the market is quite different from what they buy.

But taking home a market product also means having a trace of what retrospectively appears an event. In the midst of other domestic objects, the most innocuous or unremarkable now has a label: it's "from the market." It acquires a special virtue from which all its value then derives. The succulent brie at dinner, the Pleyben *galettes* [round butter cookies] the children like so well, the crêpe pan, the galvanized aluminum bucket that will hold armfuls of wildflowers, the "real" metallic basket for shaking water off the lettuce leaves—any object one procures on the market is distinct from others of the same category; its origin and the memory one cherishes of its provenance give it a strong identity that ordinary consumption products do not ordinarily have. When the market purchase was made, an exchange relation that cannot be reduced to pure economic rationality was established that involved a thorough mise-en-scène in which, for a brief instant, the buyer was an actor in a collective spectacle. The market context transfigures the merchandise that comes from it in much the same way the richly dressed doorman, the attentiveness of the many whitejacketed waiters, the ceremonial air of the maître d'hôtel make a hake fish and mayonnaise into a exceptional dish from another world. When the garden rake that Henri Charvet found one September day at Allemand's stall is put away in the shed with his spades, shovels, hoes, and other tools, it gets baptized "the rake from the market." When Mme. Delavigne wears the bulky, loose-knit offwhite sweater she bought in the Place du Palais, her children always say, "So, you're wearing your sweater from the market."

It is surely the hawkers who know best how to play on this logic. What customers buy from a spieler is not so much what he's selling as how he sells it, the crowd he attracts, the spectacle he offers, the event he creates. "Come along, hurry up, children, today we're giving away the right foot, you only pay for the left. At that price I usually only give out two right feet! You can 'get a kick' out of things for five francs here. Size 39? Okay, here's the right foot, and here's the left—whose turn next?" The slippers you buy after such a speech are not just ordinary slippers. However common they may be, they are enveloped in a stream of words: the clownish rhetoric, the laughter it gets, the narrative one will work up of the scene, the memory one will keep of it. Similarly, articles bought at the secondhand clothing stall bear the market "mark" very distinctly: their value is indissociable from the event they serve to fix in memory. These are precisely the sort of impulse buys Avon speaks of, the temptation one succumbed to one day when one was open and relaxed enough to let oneself give in to the charms of "any old thing." As one is putting one's closet in order of a winter's evening, one suddenly comes upon a little lace camisole one had fairly forgotten. And into one's memory surges the joyous brouhaha on the steps of the Place du Théâtre, the ray of sun playing on the rich colors of the piled-up clothing, Martin's complicitous smile, and the jokes elicited from one's friends by this inhabitual purchase.

11. The Truffle Circle

Merchandise on the market seems different from merchandise available in city boutiques or lined up on Auchan shelves because of the illusion-creating game that stallholders and customers alike enjoy playing. Strictly speaking, there are no "market products"; their distinctness is a mere simulacrum.

One product does deserve the epithet "market," however: truffles. First, fresh truffles cannot be purchased anywhere else in the city. Supermarkets now carry other luxury foods—caviar, foie gras, smoked salmon—at least during the holiday season, but they never have truffles. Second, truffles are the only product whose naturalness and localness are not mere staging effects. The truffle does not receive its "market product" identity from the way it is sold or displayed; it requires no presentational artifices or verbal hype. The truffle *is* what it appears to be: a fragment of nature torn out of the wild slopes of Mont Ventoux and miraculously present on the market. The seller has a country look about him precisely because he is the very peasant who went to *caver* [excavate] the truffles the day before in his *lot* above Méthamis, not someone seeking to create the illusion of a direct relation between producer and seller of the sort that existed at markets of bygone days.[1] It matters little that truffles are displayed in orange plastic Auchan bags and not, as they used to be, rectangular wicker baskets called *toilettes*. Truffles are traded among experts who don't give a fig for appearances.

Carpentras is *the* truffle city. "France produces two-thirds of the world's truffles and Provence produces two-thirds of the truffles in France; the Vaucluse produces two-thirds of Provence's truffles, and two-thirds of the truffles on Vaucluse markets are on offer in Carpentras," as I am told repeatedly. These figures are imprecise and surely inflated, but it is true that the most prestigious variety of truffle—commonly called the black or Périgord truffle, but people in Carpentras affect to know it only by its scientific name, *Tuber melanosporum*—is found primarily in the southeast, particularly in the Comtat Venaissin and the Tricastin. Less than a third of French truffles come from the southwest today, and they are more likely to come from Quercy than Périgord.[2]

In contrast to Mistral's olives, which are "from these parts" not so much because of where they come from as how they are displayed—big quantities in big wooden buckets, their evocation of *la Provence éternelle*—in contrast to tomatoes grown under plastic which we would find perfectly ordinary if the vendor hadn't indicated that they come from Pernes, truffles are authentic local products. Not only are they from the region, but an experienced connoisseur can distinguish by appearance and odor those that were gathered in the pebbly soil of the slopes of Mont Lure or from under the mass of fallen rocks and earth on Mont Ventoux (often small and odd-shaped, with a particularly pungent, heady aroma) from those that grew in the sand next to Richerenche or Saumane: "extremely round, very little grit, few bumps," explains Baudoin. No need, then, to add with a knowing look that they are "from the Enclave," or to remind the buyer that on holidays in olden times they were served on Comtadine tables *en brouillade* [with scrambled eggs] or *à la serviette* [whole, raw, wrapped in a napkin]. Truffles are by nature "of these parts," if only because this is where they find the highly specific geologic and climatic conditions required for their development. The fact that local people hardly consume this luxury product, that the truffle clientele is ultimately cosmopolitan, does not keep it from being authentically local.

As traded on the market, the truffle is a nugget of raw nature—you need only see one to believe it. In shape and size a truffle resembles an old, gritty, warty potato; the pretty matte black of the peridium (the fine bark locally called the skin) is hardly visible beneath the earth or sand clinging to it. Even to the neophyte, the truffle's rustic appearance evokes the wilderness. Market customers of course have little chance of seeing truffles since they are traded out of sight, their presence betrayed only by the captivating, animal-like odor that suffuses the Place du Théâtre on Friday mornings. For people who know how to appreciate them, they are enough to evoke an entirely different, increasingly residual space, one that has not yet been subjected to the laws of our asepticized world.

The truffle is the "natural product" par excellence. It bears no relation to the calibrated, mass-produced fruits and vegetables from the Comtat plain. The truffles traded here are of highly variable size. A "good-sized" one weighs between sixty and seventy grams, but some are the size of a hazelnut, while others, exceptionally, reach five hundred grams. There is no need to guarantee that the product has not been "tampered with" through the use of fertilizers or pesticides: truffles cannot be grown at will. "It grew wild," they say. This is of course what makes it so rare; no seller has more than a kilo or two per market. Bunches of radishes and daffodil bouquets are just as scarce on Roux's stand, but that scarcity is an effect of artifice designed to hold at bay all images of industrial mass production. Truffle scarcity, in contrast, is due to the capricious parsimony with which nature delivers its treasures.

The truffle is a symbiotic fungus. It develops through mutual exchange with a host plant, usually a green or pubescent oak. In a propitious biochemical environment, fungal spores will germinate, throwing out long filaments called mycelia from which the truffle develops. For this to happen, mycorrhiza must occur: the mycelia have to link up with the tree rootlets (the root hairs or "beard"), an infinitely complex process dependent on a number of climatic and ecological factors.[3] Whereas farming is becoming increasingly dissociated from the rhythm of the seasons and uncertainties of the weather, the *rabassier* anxiously watches the sky every morning: "For this to work it has to rain before Bastille Day and again around August 15 [Assumption, a holiday in France], and we've got to have two or three good, soaking rains. After that it's too late." Not to mention the phases of the moon—decisive, it seems. The finest truffles are found at the new moon and during the first quarter: "We often get going on a moon with truffles the size of eggs and finish it with marble-size ones." In sum, the truffle seems to entertain precisely that relation with the weather that modern agriculture is becoming increasingly free of.

While one may gradually acquire intimate familiarity with nature, the idea is that it can never be fully controlled. The process by which truffles reproduce and grow was long a total mystery and the object of extremely unlikely prognostications. Today we have a fairly clear idea how it works, but it is still impossible to grow truffles; the currently used term *trufficulture* [truffle cultivation] is not strictly accurate. It has been possible to facilitate truffle reproduction and development through better knowledge of the ecosystem and by acting on the host tree. But even INRA's attempts to use mycorrhized plants—a procedure whose effectiveness is still hotly debated among *rabassiers* ("Artificial mycorrhization does neither good nor harm")—doesn't change the fact that the quantity of truffles a *truffière* or truffle ground will yield remains uncertain.[4] Though truffle grounds can now be created, the mystery remains: "You can have truffles on one parcel of land and none on the one right next to it." In fact, people of the *rabasse* world don't really believe it's possible to domesticate the truffle. It is considered in essence capricious, and even when modern techniques appear to work, their tendency is still to attribute this to magic or chance rather than agronomic science.

"Truffles are really nature, even if we coax them along a bit," and to *caver*, even on "planted" land, is a gathering activity closely associated with nature at its wildest: forest and mountain rather than cultivated fields, places where vegetation grows spontaneously following none but its own laws, "like in the jungle." "In our day, farming strictly speaking has become an industry. There're all the different ways of treating the land, it's a lot of work. With grapevines and cherry trees you have a pretty good idea what you're going to harvest. But truffles are like the bush, the only place where you're still in nature. There's no nature in the vineyards anymore," says Saulnier, who has been "digging" on the slopes of Mont Ventoux for years. For both country people and city dwellers of the region, truffles are the "peasant" product par excellence, the product of bygone times, when agriculture was not yet a heavily industrialized activity. They are the symbol of a lost world that people think of with nostalgia.

Like all gathering activities, truffling supposes an intimate familiarity with the natural environment, a type of familiarity more readily associated with a sense of vocation or destiny than acquisition: "I was born into truffles, that's really all my father did." Whoever sets out in pursuit of "the black diamond" has to know through esoteric and largely intuitive experience how to decipher the few signs that this secretive, rebellious bit of nature will give of itself. Truffles grow underground—a sort of invisible mushroom: "You don't know until the last minute what's going to come out of the ground. The farmer, viticulturalist, arboriculturalist can watch their crops grow, whereas with the truffle you only know about it when the dog's finished digging." One has to learn to track the slightest sign with unflagging attention.

Truffle formation affects the area around the tree quite strikingly. Herbaceous growth disappears; the soil appears naked; a circular, charred-looking zone forms called the "witch's" or "Virgin's" round. The soil "burns" or "smokes"; the tree "marks"; hence the term *brûlé* [burnt patch] used to designate an active truffle ground. "The *brûlé* for a good truffle is not the same as the *brûlé* for a bad one, the one we call 'dog nose,' which isn't worth a thing. For good truffles, the *brûlé* is tight and contrasts sharply with the part that hasn't been affected yet, whereas with a 'dog nose' the *brûlé* is vague, indecisive." One has to be familiar with not just the terrain but nearly every tree on it.

One "goes truffling" much the same way one goes hunting, setting out with one or more dogs for a day of adventure in the mountains far from cultivated land. One is engaged in a personal, solitary relation of combined "knowledge" of and confrontation with a stretch of nature that is both familiar (each *caveur* has little spots known only to him) and forever unpredictable. "Going after truffles is just as interesting and thrilling as going after game"—a passion sharpened by the wait (oak trees may not produce until the age of seven or eight), by the crucial role of chance, and kept alive by the repeated delight of discovery. "You never know where exactly the truffle's going to be, and when the dog marks the spot, you never know what's going to come out." On the way home, exhausted but content ("You can't go gathering truffles in ankle-high shoes or slippers—you've got to go up where the poisonous snakes are"), the truffler recounts and repeats the day's exploits to the point of satiation.

The expedition is a treasure hunt, and the sought gain justifies the *trufficulteur*'s speaking of it as work rather than play. Whereas after hunting in the mountains one may enjoy consuming the small birds one has brought down, here the pleasure of the quest is mingled with the lure of profit. "It doubles your excitement when you sense you've got five hundred or a thousand francs just beneath the tip of your pickaxe," admits Nouveau. "I don't confuse the two passions," says a seasoned *rabassier* who is also an accomplished hunter. "One is a sport that should be practiced as a dilettante, the other fills the wallet."

As an authentically local and natural product, not to be compared therefore to the foodstuffs available in city boutiques or supermarket display cases, the truffle is the only real "market product." Paradoxically, however, truffle trading does not involve any mise-en-scène. Though it takes place in one of the busiest sections of the stallholder market, the Place Aristide-Briand, it constitutes an aside. People who are neither market habitués nor familiar with the region can easily amble along the bustling city streets and even venture into the cluster of jeans stands and mobile shoe shops in the Place Aristide-Briand without ever suspecting that a few meters away the biggest truffle market in France is in

143

session. Mme. Patio of course takes a detour to breathe in the perfume, and another of my respondents makes sure to get a glimpse on his way to the bank on Fridays. But you cannot really see or participate in the truffle trade, essentially a professionals-only affair. Nothing is done to attract stallholder customers to come buy directly, though retail sale is not prohibited. Truffles are traded almost clandestinely like this throughout the region, often in the backroom of a café, as in Richerenche or Forcalquier.

This is especially surprising given that truffles are a major subject of Carpentras conversation—"A lot of them today, do you know?"; "They must've made about two thousand francs"—not to mention all the newspaper articles, complete with photos, that celebrate both "producer" and broker "heroes" of the truffle world. This uncommon product, associated with the city's patron saint—"Truffles get going at the Saint-Siffrein," as everyone in the region knows, in other words, the day of the big annual fair, November 27[5]—and the focus of numerous histories and legends trotted out by local scholars, fuels the sense of local particularism. Old Jeanjean is fully aware of this: "Whenever I see tourists, I tell them to go see the truffle market. Yesterday I saw two Swiss and I sent them there." The municipal authorities are more than willing to use truffles and the truffle market to highlight the city's age and its close ties to the rural world. The bureau of tourism even has an entire exhibition on the fungus, which includes a few well-worn *picholons* and *biasses*, *banastes* used in the nineteenth century when truffles were abundant, and some photos and old engravings of the market.[6] But there is no attempt to make a show of the truffle market itself.

At eight in the morning under the vast blue tent over the terrace of the Bar du Théâtre café,[7] a group of bundled-up women and men in bulky fur-lined jackets coalesces. Truffle buyers—brokers—are discernible by the leather bags they carry on their shoulder. Sellers hold small wicker baskets or plastic or canvas bags tightly against their chests. The truffle itself, subject of every utterance, remains invisible, its presence betrayed only by its captivating odor. A stone's throw away, in the early morning cold, the secondhand clothing dealers are setting up trestle tables, laying out old, worn clothes, hanging up "retro" shirts and jackets. The café is crowded. Stallholders and clothing dealers stand at the counter or sit at tables under wan neon lights, warming themselves with a small coffee, attentively watching the unfolding scene. The truffle world is the main attraction, and all eyes are on the participants. They in turn have eyes only for the *patronne*, first wife of the biggest truffle broker in the region—"a woman who knows truffles," says another broker respectfully. Her ex-husband is there too, Robert Panza, a man on whom *Le Provençal* often bestows the honor of its attention. Familiar and distant at once, the *patronne* jokes with truffle world people, busies herself with this and that, pays for a round of drinks, and teases the young waiters, content to find herself in this universe where she knows all the protagonists, the serious and not-so-serious customers. In the meantime the conversation gets going among the sellers, accustomed to seeing each other both here and at the fruit and vegetable market: "How much will they bring today?"

Slightly before nine, the truffle world—about sixty persons, more at Christmastime when demand is at its peak—gathers beneath the tent a ways off from curious onlookers. There are approximately twenty sellers, men and women, most of whom come from the surrounding area, primarily the flanks of Mont Ventoux and the Vaucluse plateau. They are often fruit and vegetable producers who use the free time they have in winter to *caver*. Most sell only on this market. Brokers generally go the rounds of the various markets in the region—Apt, Valréas, Richerende—in accordance with a calendar fixed more than a century ago. There are still a dozen of them in the Vaucluse, down from seventeen twenty years ago. Some work only for themselves, selling what they buy; others are paid a commission by specialized houses, usually processing plants in the Périgord. In the summer they deal in honey and lavender, occasionally fruits and vegetables. Some are *trufficulteurs* themselves. Local processors occasionally buy truffles at this market (the other markets are smaller and even more firmly closed to the public), and *charcutiers* and caterers occasionally come to buy before Christmas. But most truffle transactions are with brokers.

In a verbal hubbub where Provençal holds its own, the truffle *placier*—this market is not in Pascal's jurisdiction—busies himself collecting the regulation fifty-centimes-per-kilo dues and arranging the sellers in a circle, as is the custom here. The circle delimits the space in which transactions are to be made, though it does not preclude a certain confusion; it used to be much bigger and thus much more clearly drawn, as may be seen in the photos. Dealers set the week's harvest at their feet, fold back the white cloths—the truffle appears. A bell rings: buyers may now penetrate the circle and transactions begin. They pass back and forth in front of the *rabassiers* assessing their respective *lots*.

Outside the circle, professionals (producers with nothing to sell who want

145

to keep abreast; processors who want to see how the market will develop) comment nonstop on the proceedings. Quantities are sized up, with occasional nostalgic mention of the big trade of bygone days when the truffle market took up the whole of the Place Notre-Dame; quality is judged. Some express admiration for the round, regular black specimens one producer is displaying in a small wicker suitcase, upon which it is murmured that they are from "irrigated" truffle grounds—the eternal debate about new production techniques has been reopened. Information is requested on how much is on offer at other truffle markets, and prognoses pronounced on the ensuing "campaign."

Within the circle people speak very little and very low. Little of the proceedings filters out. "How much d'ya want?" asks a buyer tersely, displaying his readiness to move on, and the seller whispers a price. Quickly, discreetly, without bargaining or discussion, the broker opens a booklet of sales slips bearing the stamp of the *maison* he works for, jots down the agreed price, slips the paper into the seller's hand. The scene calls to my mind the "silent trade" I have observed at other latitudes. One by one the bags close; the circle begins to come apart. In a mere thirty minutes some two hundred kilos of truffles have changed hands.

Then comes the weighing and the paying up, most of which is done near the café tables at a slight remove from the sales space. This takes up the rest of the morning. It is a moment for letting go and bantering after the tension of the sale. The *rabassiers* slowly lay their truffles on the tables. *Lots* are always purchased whole. Before weighing one on a *briquet,* a Roman scale, the dealer empties it into his *filoche,* a regulation-specified linen net bag for shaking out soil and sand, though the increased use of plastic bags is putting an end to this practice. He palpates the contents with an expert hand, occasionally pulling out one or two, sniffing to make sure they aren't "musky"—a gesture propitious for jokes.[8] After the silent negotiations, this physical contact with the truffles opens the way for low-flying remarks and ritual joshing, and in this scene of professional camaraderie, each type of participant has a role. Buyers make a few observations for form's sake—"You left too much dirt on today!"—to which sellers respond with a light shoulder shrug, or retort, "You dropped one, I saw it roll away!" upon which everyone bends down and pretends to hunt for the runaway truffle.

Payment is in cash on the spot. Buyer pulls from his leather bag a pocketbook packed with unfolded bills and lays the agreed sum on seller's extended palm. This scene takes place where the truffles were weighed. Meanwhile, Panza's new wife is waiting inside the café next to the big cast-iron stove to settle up with each of the trufflers her husband has bought from. People readily gravitate around this young, smiling woman, her ample bosom somewhat exposed beneath a fur coat. The sight of banknotes circulating pleases the group that has formed around each seller, and the happy beneficiaries are profusely gibed. Meanwhile, under the tables, the big white or blue linen sacks are filling up with truffles—up to forty kilos per sack. This is the most animated moment of the morning; people will spend a good hour now talking and strolling in the immediate vicinity. Occasionally accompanied by a broker, "colleagues" go to the bar for a pastis to celebrate their transactions. Latecomers, generally women, bring their merchandise directly to Panza, who buys it at the day's going rate. This is also the moment he graciously sells two or three truffles to a few city residents. Gradually the group disperses. When Panza closes up his canvas bags the clocks have not yet struck noon. The truffle market is over for the week.

To all appearances, the same scene is replayed from one Friday to the next. The operation unfolds over the same series of moments with their varying moods and tones: prerequisite phase of mutual observation at the bar, silent tension during the brief negotiations, longer conclusion period, which everyone spends as they please while remaining in the same immediate area until morning's end. Behavior, gestures, and utterances are repeated so invariably that they seem to follow a well-established code. One has observed what seems more like a strange if not exotic ceremony than a commercial transaction.[9]

Such ritual formalism is of course partly an effect of the rules governing wholesale markets. Prices on such markets are supposedly determined by confrontation between supply and demand, so the market has to be transparent, implying unity of time and space: the market has to take place during a particular time span known to all; operations have to unfold within a clearly delimited space. As mentioned, the Carpentras market before World War I encompassed a multitude of specialized marketplaces of this type, where the face-to-face encounter was not between merchants and consumers but between regional farmers and wholesale buyer-sellers. These markets amounted to so many closed, clearly delimited worlds governed by municipal regulations such as the following decree (July 18, 1904): "In the interests of both sellers and buyers, it is necessary to have a fixed opening time for each market season and to prohibit sale of products and merchandise outside the space and places designated for holding of said markets."

But the truffle market today is in no way a "bourse" where prices are determined. It is more a means of delivering merchandise to those whose job is to purchase it—brokers and processors. Demand is always strong for this food product, as scarce as it is passionately sought after, and supply is never sufficient. In the last twenty years, the price of truffles has gone up by 30 percent a year.[10] The price on a given day, however, depends above all on the sum that the buyers, few in number and always the same, are willing to pay. The truffle market scene appears particularly ritualistic because there is little chance of its being shaken up by unexpected variation. This is a far cry from the *marché-gare*, where very strict selling protocol serves as a framework for multiple, uncertain economic micro-events from which some emerge victims and others beneficiaries.

Nothing in the way the truffle market works—sellers arranged in a circle, Roman scales on café tables—seems to follow the logic inherent in commercial transactions. There is no haggling over price, no intense negotiation, only near-immutable utterances, the eternal jokes on the art of "dressing up" the truffle or adding a few at the last minute without paying for them. And indeed, how could such an exceptional product be exchanged without ceremony? Every winter Friday, then, the actors play precisely the same roles in the same scene, repeat the same gestures and the same words, conform in sum to what seems an indispensable tradition. "You don't exchange truffles like you do apples or table grapes," insists Nouveau, producer of *chasselas* and "Alphonse Lavallée" grapes but also an accomplished *rabassier* in his Méthamis hills.

The truffle, result of an anachronistic gathering activity resistant to all agricultural domestication, is the product-of-the-wild par excellence. Introducing it into "consumption culture" is therefore no simple matter. Discovered at the end of an adventurous, solitary quest, the occasion for a thrilling escape to "the desert," the object of an untiring, seldom answered hope ("You need fifteen years to make a truffle ground, and you're never sure of the result. It's a state of mind from another time"), the truffle is an object of intense affective investment, and this precludes its having the status of merchandise. The only way the truffle could become merchandise would be to sever the relation of identification between the *rabassier* and the object of his passion. Every truffle is charged with implicit references to places, landscape features, events that have left their mark, moments of disappointment and delight, the experience and history of an individual or family. At the extreme, every truffle is unique, and the finders take pleasure in touching it and vaunting its shape. A *belle truffe* is one that is round and black at maturity. A truffle may be spoken of as a person; it is said to "be sick, get well, suffer, die in a drought." In order for the truffle to be merchandise, the near-personal relation by which it is linked to the *terroir* in which it developed and the person who dug it out would have to be abolished.

Trading truffles, then, is problematic. This is why conventions and formalities must be followed with regard to them, and an appropriate symbolic system used. Indeed, the market must do the work of mediating between two worlds sharply contrasted on all points: the slopes of Mont Ventoux or the Vaucluse plateau scrub land that the *rabassiers* roam over in search of the "black pearl of the Comtat"; the urban universe where the truffle will later circulate as a luxury product. The conditions of its production, the mystery, uncertainty, contingencies implied by those conditions, the fact that the truffle appears to be a product of wild nature that escapes human control—all these points give it a kind of sacred aura, implicitly recognized in the trading procedure. The rituality of the exchange, its structure as two moments, one hushed, secret, serious, the other public and joyous, constitute the truffle's "domestication." A small group of officiants closes in around gritty specimens as yet infused with "magic." Only after the mute, mysterious transactions have been concluded does the circle open up again and the truffle become "public." Only then can it be handled and moved, swapped for banknotes, as conversation starts up again and participants fire out commentaries on the day's dealings. At the end of the exchange, the truffle has not only changed hands but entered into the world of merchandise, a universe where objects are interchangeable. Though physically unchanged, it is not the same as before the process. When the brokers leave the scene with their bulging sacks, the truffle has begun its profane existence as a valuable bit of merchandise.

The actors have of course engaged in market exchange, but an exchange that follows a protocol that cannot be reduced to its strictly functional dimension, a special set of usages that seems required by the product's specificity. That the truffle, both near-miraculous gift of nature and object of great monetary value, should be "handled" by means of a fitting rite may seem the consequence of an inevitable metaphor. As Espenon, president of the *trufficulteurs* union, explains: "The truffle is exchanged somewhat religiously . . . The reason this market is more private than others, blanketed with a certain discretion, is that the truffle has become something rare. When you're at the diamond dealer's, for example, or a jeweler's, well, you know, things don't really happen in broad daylight, out in the street. And when the jeweler brings out rocks of great value, people speak almost religiously. In the presence of such beauties of nature, they speak in a whisper."

To exchange a singular object bearing a specific history and the traces of events and personal ties, that object has to be made to change states, it has to be "disenchanted," transformed into an ordinary object, a mere quantity of matter and value. The modes and procedures of market exchange are not generally analyzed in these terms. And yet the destiny of becoming merchandise, however ineluctable, cannot always be taken for granted. In this respect the truffle, pure product of nature, is comparable to an art object. Despite the fact that most art objects were created to be sold, their uniqueness and the relation linking them to the body of their creator or owner can make turning them into merchandise a risky enough proposition for it to be necessary to "respect certain proprieties." The vernissage ceremony, for instance, in which a selling event is disguised as an exhibition, could be seen as an example of what Pierre Bourdieu would call "collective bad faith in the good-faith economy."[11] Likewise, auction sales can be considered a profane rite for reducing the objects on offer to the state of merchandise. The matter-of-fact assembling of a series of objects of different origins and values in a single room, buyer anonymity, competition among buyers, the ups and downs of the process turn the auction into a public ceremony which effaces the identity of the object and facilitates its reappropriation more effectively than transactions among private partners.

Before becoming an ingredient in sophisticated dishes on prestigious tables throughout the world, the truffle is a local secret shared among initiates. It would be indecent to display this pure fragment of raw nature, this last vestige of otherwise lost authenticity, to the eyes of the crowd at the market stalls somewhere between "forced" tomatoes and melons harvested from under plastic tunnels kept at constant hygrometric temperatures. The truffle is an affair to be handled among "ourselves," sheltered from indiscreet onlookers. This explains why the little world of truffle lovers gathers to celebrate its cult in private. Farmers make nonnegligible extra revenue from truffles, of course, especially since their income may be low in winter, and the truffle trade is also highly profitable for brokers and processors. But these people are united not so much by interest as by a shared passion. Vestige of another world, an object bearing values alien to modern agriculture, the truffle is not a mere product to be sold. The logic operative here is not so much maximum individual profit as the weekly repeated affirmation of consensual ties engendered by adherence to the same "truffle culture." This explains the friendly relations observable during the market session, whereas outside the exchange scene the truffle often gives rise to conflict. As one *rabassier* describes it: "It's relaxed here, but underneath all this, you've got widespread swindling and tricks." Under the blue tent of the Bar du Théâtre a serene, hushed atmosphere reigns. We are far from the tense relations that can be felt, if under a façade of good humor, in other professional marketplaces.

The multiple meanings associated with the truffle confer a mediating role upon it. In the space and time of the market, the truffle unites all those who are involved with it for varying reasons. Both within and on the margins of the stallholder market, the truffle organizes a space of specific social relations: fraternal feelings among expert, devoted followers, a bond among those who possess the same more or less occult knowledge. Shared fascination with the truffle defines the boundary between those who are "in the game"—parties to the exchange, initiated observers, informed amateurs—and the masses excluded from it.

Hence the paradoxical position of the truffle market. Touted by tourist guides obsessed with local color and the source of much of the celebrity of the Carpentras market as a whole, the truffle trade should by all rights be one of the biggest draws. And yet very few people actually pay any attention to this small gathering of "extremely ordinary people" going about their business like a group of *pétanque* players on a Sunday morning in a village square.

PART FOUR

Pleasure of the Agora

As we have seen, the Carpentras stallholder market is not a mere means of doing business. More than other types of markets, it functions through enticement. Nor is it just one more link, if a picturesque one, in the national distribution chain. To think of it as such, to use the reductive language of administrative economics, would be to disregard what really goes on there, the fact that for a few hours, onlookers, customers, stallholders, and shopkeepers construct a distinct and separate world. It is to this world as a whole, not merely to the commercial arrangements involved in it, that the term "market" refers in local usage.

If one is even slightly familiar with daily habits in Carpentras and the surrounding towns, one need only visit the Auchan supermarket and mall on a Saturday to measure the degree to which the stallholder market constitutes a specific world. Virtually the same people move around in the supermarket aisles, but they behave in a very different way. This struck me from the beginning of my study, when I was not yet in a position to understand the reasons for it.

If any place in Carpentras competes with the market in terms of social life, it has to be the Auchan mall. Auchan has nothing in common with the charm and atmosphere of old-city streets on Fridays. Twenty kilometers out of town off the freeway to Avignon, Auchan is a long yellowish warehouse-like building adjoining an immense parking lot planted with tall streetlights. The outdoor reception area is done up like a village square—a circle of red plastic benches around a streetlight—and leads directly into a cafeteria. From here extend the "streets" of the mall with their rows of shops and services. The Auchan super-market, clearly delimited by a line of cash registers, occupies the whole back of the building.

In contrast to city supermarkets, Auchan is where people go for a carefully planned bit of entertainment or distraction. You go in the car, in a group; you stay there a good while; you bring a grandmother or guests on Saturday after the midday family meal. City and country inhabitants of all social milieus and ages stream into this major gathering place on Saturdays. In this neutral terrain ("You're not *chez* anyone there"), on the pretext of buying spare parts for the motorcycle or seeing what's new in stereo equipment, young people from all the surrounding towns and hamlets come together or rather, as they put it, "see each other." Groups and gangs identify each other, size each other up. The supermarket is closed on Sundays, but people come to have lunch at the Flunch cafeteria anyway. "Auchan is like an outing," Mme. Martinez notes bitterly—she runs the Mont Ventoux hotel and restaurant. In fact this consumption temple, a terrain for "supermodern" domestic adventures, is omnipresent in people's conversation—perhaps even more so than the market; everyone mentioned it in the accounts they gave me of their daily existence. Going to Auchan around 10 a.m. is just something you do, at least for the locals. You don't need to plan it in advance or have a family debate about it.

Auchan could almost be thought of as the "Saturday market." And yet despite the manager's obvious desire to make it a major gathering and entertainment spot (the mall was added on later), nothing is done there as at a "real" market. The most striking difference for an outside observer is that people don't talk to each other. As I learned myself in conducting interviews, it feels totally inappropriate to start up a conversation with strangers there: doing so elicits reactions of discomfort or distrust. In fact, apart from young people, who tend to think of the mall as where *they* meet, people seem unconsciously to use this space as a continuation of their private home. Coming up to them is seen as a kind of invasion of their space. Moreover, supermarket shopping is one of the situations (like car trips and vacations) in which family tensions are aggravated. The children are particularly obnoxious, the grandmother more demanding, the husband more of a burden, the wife more irritable. In this commercial space ideally aimed at reconciling rational distribution and market-type sociability, individuals and families are particularly self-enclosed. Actors coexist here; they do not really meet or interact. Why is this?

My questions elicited evasive answers. People do generally perceive that the quality of social contact is not the same as at the market: "Nothing happens between people." "You can meet people you know at Auchan too," remarks Mme. Patio, "but people are there with their carts, they're in a hurry, it's not at all the same. They don't stroll around [*flâner*]." And yet regardless of what she says—and the word *flâner* surely has a romantic connotation for her more in keeping with the somewhat outmoded charm of the old-city market—no one dashes out to shop at Auchan or dashes through the shopping once they're there, if only because it's so far away. In contrast to the quick daily purchases people make at Intermarché or Leclerc just outside the city gates, they take their time in the supermarket aisles and mall shops, and they have a good time. But because the pleasure they take is confusedly perceived as more ordinary and less valorizing, they prefer to say it is the others' pleasure and to justify their own use of the place in purely economic terms. There is a degree of bad faith in their emphasis on the functional side of supermarkets. It is often a way of distinguishing oneself from unconditional fans of this type of commercial space.

The difference in atmosphere, which everyone is aware of without being able to explain, is due in fact to the nature of these instituted spaces. The supermarket is a commercial arrangement open to all, but most customers, in Carpentras at least, use it privately. On the contrary, shopping at the market involves organizing a public space in the city streets every Friday morning. Those who visit the market engage in a multiform social activity analogous to what the Greeks called *agorazein*, to linger in the agora, sell or buy products while conversing freely, discussing political or social affairs—"life matters"—with fellow citizens.

The actor who behaves on the market like a "public person" (*agoraios* is the term that was used in Athens), a lover of interminable discussions or an inveterate stroller, not just a trader or customer, is, at Auchan, a mere consumer. At the market, which may be thought of as a politics- and orator-free forum—"I wonder if it's a market or a forum," says Mme. Patio—people amble and look around while buying lettuce or a can opener. At Auchan, between the detergent aisle and the refrigerated low-fat cheeses, up against an anonymous, all-powerful business, people retreat into their household cell, the basic cog in the national if not international economy. In accordance with the logic of mass consumption operative here, inequalities in fortune and taste come to the fore. In these imitation agoras where mood music and the voice of advertising dominate, people speak only to their own, extending the privacy of family life into

155

the commercial space. At the market, in the noisy jostling of that powerful moment of local life, the individual acquires the status of civic community member and participates, whether merchant or customer, in the enacting of a relation of equality with "the other" where differences in social position are temporarily blurred. As we shall see, everyone at the market practices a sort of "generalized friendship," superficial of course but capable of evoking the famous *philia* that Aristotle defined as the basis of the polis. This is why people on the market not only "run into" each other but interact.

What exactly is a public space? I do not have enough space to untangle the skein of meanings operative at some level in the multivalent use made of this term today. Just two remarks. First, our agoras are not places of debate, and even less of decision making and policy making. At best they are the occasion to stage a representation of a shared local identity. Though the circulation of merchandise never precludes that of news and rumors, the public space of the polis has been returned to what is perhaps its original function: the market. In contemporary nation-states (in contrast to the city-states of antiquity or the Renaissance), the relation of political equality among citizens is played out in a more abstract context: the "public sphere" and the various means by which it is actualized, such as elections, opinion polls, media activity. In the Place de la Mairie or the Rue de la République, then, it is more often a question of the freshness of the lettuce or the quality of the olives than the major political debates of the moment—though markets in France have remained one of the chosen places for political propaganda: all political candidates are obliged to be seen on the market pressing the flesh and exchanging a few affable words.

Furthermore, the fact that a place is open and common to all does not necessarily make it a public space. It must be defined as such by specific social relations. A place defined as common in legal and functional terms—that is, "nonprivate"—can be a public space or not, depending on the moment or context, depending on what is played out there, the position that actors assume in relation to each other.

Given that people enter into relation at each market stall and in their chance encounters at the market, it can be said that the common space of the polis of Carpentras is being used publicly. On the other days of the week, the streets of the old city are no more than a thoroughfare used to get from one place to another.[1] People run into each other, catch sight of each other, greet each other with conventional signs. On Fridays, this same place, transfigured by the presence of the market, is no longer merely a space of coexistence.

PART FOUR

Because of the formal equality and relative effacement of social statuses and hierarchies that the market induces, market exchange as it occurs in what is legally speaking a part of the public domain, freely accessible to all, reinstitutes a real community for a few hours every Friday. Not only do people share a common activity, "doing the market," but it is appropriate for people to recognize each other as alike and to treat each other as fellow citizens, in a way that is independent of private friendships or status ties. People are *entre nous* at the market, even if some ignore the others' identities. The situation of relative anonymity, the fact of engaging in relations of equality, and the practice of fictive interacquaintance are to my mind what characterize and define the publicness of this type of social space.

12. Equality of Opportunity

For the space of an enchanted morning, a utopian microsociety develops around the innocuous domestic activity of doing the marketing. An old founding myth is staged. For a few hours, the classical model of civil society is realized, the ideal of a place in which free and formally equal wills confront each other. In the face-to-face encounter between buyers and sellers there are no personal obligations or external constraints. This is open competition; one stallholder is worth another; the one who offers a better product or price wins the sale. Though one group is there to make a profit and the other to spend its income, everyone acts as if any and all players in the exchange game could win. A market is in its very principle an egalitarian arrangement.

This is true first and foremost because the market is produced by what is understood to be a fair allocation of public space. The market space is distributed every week among all merchants who request a spot; the common space of the street works to mediate among the various particular interests.

For a Carpentras habitué, the spatial organization of the market is fundamentally the same from week to week—above and beyond seasonal variations, of course: burgeoning in summer, reduced to its fundamental armature in winter. Perdiguier is always in the Place du Théâtre, the two fishmongers are invariably at the Porte d'Orange, and Jacky Thevet can be found nearly every Friday in the Rue de la République. This relative stability, without which it would be very hard to find one's way, is due to the considerable number of "subscriber" stallholders who regularly occupy the same spots, and to the fact that sedentary merchants also participate, displaying goods in the public space in front of their shops.

Described this way, the market might pass for a sort of weekly mall. But that would be to disregard the fact that it results from how the selling space is shared out in response to a set of merchant requests that differs from one Friday to the next. The proportion of permanent, acquired places is such that equality of opportunity for sellers can only be imperfect. Nonetheless, the market is in principle open to all who want to sell there, on condition that certain legal requirements are met—sellers have to be registered with the chamber of commerce, although Gypsies, among others, benefit from a certain tolerant goodwill on this point—and within the limits of available space, since city territory must remain a place of free and open competition that city residents may benefit from. Space is allocated in Carpentras in accordance with two rules: accommodate the greatest number of merchants possible, and distribute spots through a deliberately egalitarian procedure wherein all candidates are considered equal.

It is not yet 7 a.m. when Pascal the *placier* sits down at a table in the back of the Rich'Bar at the entrance to the Rue de la République, the main way to the market. A few customers are already leaning against the counter. Pascal has a large blank sheet of paper spread out before him; people enter alone or in small groups and head immediately in his direction. These are "passing" merchants (called "fliers" on other markets) who want to obtain a place for the day. Among them are habitués without a fixed spot, some of whom have been on the permanent-spot waiting list for many years; a few "market men" ("homeless" stallholders); professional merchants who have "come down" to the Midi for a summer vacation; occasional sellers, amateurs, marginal young people, and of course the Africans.

Everyone gives the *placier* the document certifying registration with the chamber of commerce. He notes down the names. After a coffee or *petit blanc* at the bar, it is already 8 a.m., time to draw spots. The table scrapes against the tile flooring as Pascal rises weightily to leave the café. The "passing" merchants flock around him. In winter, in the rain, in the mistral wind their numbers are few, but in the peak of the summer season there can be more than eighty. Pascal reads out the names on the list; when a seller's name is called he or she draws a slip of paper out of a hat and announces the number on it. As the *placier* notes the numbers down, people let their comments fly. "Ah," says one, "those *nègres*!

Always the lucky ones!" "I'm leaving," says another, "don't feel like going fishing." As everyone there knows, the lowest numbers correspond to the best spots. Pascal begins his tour of the city with the most lively streets. Sellers with numbers over 40 on a July Friday often give up, but in late August even with a high number one has a decent chance, since many stallholders are on vacation.

As soon as this operation is over, Pascal starts his walk down the Rue de la République followed by a troop of "passing" vendors, some already carrying trestle tables or canvas tarps on their shoulders. Though he is extremely familiar with the permanent stallholders' habits, he does not know at the outset the exact number of available spots; rather he deduces it by walking through the market, checking density with an expert eye. In general, the available spots are those that have been left by subscribers, but he sometimes adds a bit of pavement as he goes by. He stops at every span of blank space, measures it with ample strides, then calls the next number, asking the "passing" in question what product he "does" and how many meters he'd like. If the spot suits the seller, Pascal hands him a paper with his name, the surface area, and the spot designation. If it's too small or there's a problem of incompatibility with neighboring stalls, he goes directly to the next number. As he pursues his peregrination through the Place du Palais and along the Rue d'Inguimbert, members of his cortège drop off. The size of the procession has greatly diminished when he reaches the northern sector of the city. By the time he gets to the Porte de Mazan and the bird market, many have given up, discouraged by the distance and the advancing clock. At the end of his itinerary, covered in nearly an hour, there are still a few sellers who have not been placed. They can either give up and go home or settle for the small market at Courthezon, fifteen or so kilometers northwest, which has been growing in recent times, in large part owing to sellers turned away from Carpentras.

Pascal's tour through the city after the spot drawing may be thought of as the act that opens the market. Once he's done, the market is complete and ready to function within its assigned limits. A temporary community has been instated on the basis of two distinct categories of stallholder, regulars and spot drawers; a community made up of all the various merchants who have or have just obtained a spot. All of them, from the Paris-region lingerie salesman who's driven down in his truck to spend the summer in the sun to the egg lady from Sarrians or Althen-les-Paluds, are full-fledged members of that day's group of market traders. Furthermore, the *placier*'s progress seems a means of officially introducing the day's "passing" sellers to subscriber stallholders. Bonnet, a shoe salesman in the Rue de la République, may not be overjoyed to see a demonstrator of cleaning products set up next to him, but he accepts it because he knows that this neighbor is only temporary, imposed on him by the incontestable authority of chance and the *placier*.

Once Pascal has finished his turn through the city, he leaves the two woman fee collectors to go the rounds and heads toward the youth center, though on his way he does check length and alignment of counters here and there, ensures that places allocated have been occupied as specified, and informs those who have "unloaded" behind his back on their own initiative that "it's okay this time" but he doesn't want to see them again next week. In comparison with what *placiers* at other markets do, Pascal's duties may seem rather limited. At many markets *placiers* are in charge of managing the waiting list and allocating fixed spots when they become free.[1] But Pascal's role is decisive. He's the one who shares out of the public domain among merchants every Friday, an essential competition regulation activity, since to do good business on the market one needs a good spot.

Everyone in Carpentras knows who Pascal is and that he runs the youth center; they readily acknowledge how influential he is. He himself considers his role as *placier*, which of course occupies him only one morning a week, not as a mere administrative task but as a mission. When I go to visit him at the magnificent eighteenth-century manor in the Rue des Pénitents-Blancs where he organizes leisure and cultural activities for the city's young people, he makes a point of telling me that he distributes market spots "as a service," free of charge ("I do it willingly, but it would be nice if . . ."). He says he found himself "catapulted into the post of *placier* by chance," though in reality he spent many years assisting the retired gendarme in charge, who "taught me the work." In addition to his official function, he takes it upon himself to advise young people who are thinking of setting up as stallholders, and also works to defuse potential conflicts, such as the racism of the disappointed "passing" seller, which is rumbling just beneath the surface, and the repeated recriminations of subscribers concerned with respectability and worried that some adventurer will set up next to them, buy up the stock of an old shop that has fallen into bankruptcy, cheat everyone, then disappear. In fact Pascal's role is due more to his personality and status in the city than to his *placier* function.

The spot-drawing ritual is only one possible method of handling a perpetual problem: how to contain an increasing number of stallholders within a limited amount of space without threatening safety and public order, disturbing inhabitants' peace, or threatening the interests of sedentary trade. One need only skim city council decrees to see that this irresolvable debate is as old as the market itself. Despite its apparent archaism, the allocation procedure is not at all traditional. Pascal himself introduced it a mere fifteen years ago, and explains that it is used only at a few Provence markets, in Nîmes, for example, and more recently in Martigues. In most cities, the preferred criteria for determining spot allocation are seniority on the waiting list and arrival time.[2]

In Pascal's mind, spot drawing, i.e., chance, is the best means of ensuring equality of opportunity, at least among sellers without a fixed spot. "Spot drawing is tedious, but it's the fairest way, the most legal. It means I don't have any cronies. If my brother came, he'd have to draw a spot like everybody else. People often say, 'Listen, I know a stallholder who's not coming this morning—can I have his place?' 'Absolutely not,' I say. You've got markets where people say, 'You're from Carpentras? Here, take the best spot. You're from Mazan? Here you go.' When I worked with the ex-gendarme, they didn't do spot drawing. He said, 'What are you in, Monsieur? So you'd like three meters? Here's three meters.'" This kind of innocent, trusting arbitration, acceptable at a time when there was less demand, is precisely what Pascal believed had to be changed.

For him, the market is a place for practicing equity. He purports to organize it with reference to an ideal of fairness and the classic model of perfect competition specific to the liberal representation of the Market. Not only does he give each "passing" seller an opportunity to have a "good market" that day, but in the name of the same principle of equality he makes an effort to minimize the number of spot-less sellers each Friday, to "fit in" the maximum number of merchants, in accordance with his maxim: "Everyone's got to be able to work." And he carefully pressures city hall to open new streets for market use. But Pascal's personal concern for fairness actually dovetails well with city hall's concern to ensure that the market is as fully patronized as possible and to make it a showcase for the social peace understood to reign in this city.

Among sellers, Carpentras has a reputation as a "good market," not only because "you can do a good day's work there" but also thanks to this egalitarian mode of allocating vacant spots. The publicness of the procedure is reassuring, and they know it serves no purpose to blame chance. The other selection methods (by arrival time, for instance) open up the possibility of *placier* arbitrariness, favoritism, all sorts of cheating. "At other markets," an occasional seller of small mechanical toys assures me, "they decide on the basis of what a guy looks like—it's the jungle." Moreover, the thought that one has at least a

163

chance of getting a good spot that day makes it easier to accept the inequality between "passing" and "subscriber" stallholders and helps attenuate conflicts between them.

In fact, as everyone is well aware, spot drawing is not a purely transparent process. The *placier* gives priority to sellers of perishables, for example, and discounters, hawkers, and *posticheurs* are granted spots independently of the drawing procedure, in accordance with the *placier*'s judgment about how best to organize the market in the general interest. Moreover, certain stallholders find a way of skewing the rules in their favor. The Senegalese—there can be as many as sixty of them—all sign up with the *placier* as soon as they arrive from Marseille, but after the spot drawing they cluster together on the good spots that some of them have drawn. This is what gives the other traders the impression that the Africans always get low numbers, a strange phenomenon that Pascal prefers to explain in terms of the power of their *grigris* [amulets, fetishes]: "These people are really lucky, no? Often—I don't hear anything, mind you, but there are some breaches of regulation. The French say: 'Aren't you the lucky ones!' and you can feel that there's an atmosphere . . . some tension." Lastly, many marginal sellers make arrangements directly with sedentary traders to "spread" in front of their shops, or they try to occupy a bit of sidewalk without going through the spot-drawing procedure. The Gypsies with their wicker baskets and lemons do this every Friday, winter and summer. Pascal lets them get away with it because scattered as they are throughout the market, they bring a touch of local color everywhere, somewhat like the olive merchants. This is also sometimes the case with the Africans, but he doesn't really see it as a challenge to his authority: "These people think, 'No one will say anything to me because I'm a foreigner.'" He would be more severe with a professional stallholder who set up surreptitiously in the spot of a "colleague" thought to be aware of the maneuver. If someone "marks out" a spot, lays out trestle tables and unloads wares without prior authorization, "then I'm fairly firm. But really, when a young guy arrives at ten with, say, ten francs' worth of necklaces, I turn a blind eye." Rule bending of this sort is generally quite minor and doesn't elicit protest. Spot drawing remains the primary means of access to vacancies, and Pascal's tolerance with regard to most rule breakers is in a way part of the same ideal: everyone on the market, big traders and small traders alike, has to have a chance. "You can't prevent them from working!" says Pascal.

By the time the crowd of customers has flooded the market, the *placier* has finished his turn through the city and the whole arrangement is ready to function. Most customers, including the early risers who watched Pascal and his troop make their way through the streets, have no idea what procedure was used; the spot drawing was carried out on the side, among the initiated. The operation is nonetheless essential to the "effect" the market produces, the perception people have of it. Not only is the market different from one Friday to the next and potentially a source of surprise despite its stable armature of fixed stallholders (people often cite the market's ever-renewed diversity as a source of the pleasure they take in being there), but this mode of allocating places gives an image of the market as a space open to all, as if one could just come and sell there whenever and however one liked. On the margins or in the interstices between fixed shops and permanent stallholders, there is opportunity for everyone, because the poorest seller is not necessarily the one with the worst place, nor do the richest necessarily have the best, contrary to the situation for city boutiques and the Auchan mall. Manu's little peanut cart—Manu is a former "*zonard*" [marginal, dropout] who now lives near Barroux—stands right next to Cilichini's superb mobile shop, and a vendor of raw wool lords it in the center of the Place de l'Horloge. Taken together, the minimal weekly variations half noticed in passing work to create the impression that the market is a world of freedom and equality; a latent, blurred sense that cannot readily be developed into a fully political representation but is nonetheless constitutive of the market experience. If there were nothing to create or bolster that impression, one would not feel one was at a "real" market.

In this space of competition instituted and regulated by public authority in the interests of all—authority in this instance incarnated by Pascal, a respected and appreciated mediator—the customer moves from stall to stall with the surely highly illusory image of being in a place where bargains are within arm's reach if only one knows how to take advantage of the opportunity. Because it aligns face-to-face a series of independent sellers, the market offers everyone, big and small, the opportunity to play the role of an economic actor sovereignly exercising his or her free, rational will, as if reality were suddenly identical to the classic liberal model of a universe of equivalent wills whose divergent interests all manage to adjust to each other by the market's "grace."

The sign par excellence of this ideal world where equal opportunity reigns is the practice of bargaining. This is decidedly not Auchan or Leclerc. Here buying still means negotiating price face-to-face with the seller. "The word *marché* means *marchander* [bargain]," I was told innumerable times, by stallholders and customers alike. "At the market you can make deals, it's always possible to bargain," declares Mme. Renaud, a retired elementary schoolteacher. "It's not like in a store, you can always discuss the price," claims Mme. Rouve, member of an old family of fabric dealers. Or else people recount what the others do, like the owner of the Bar du Marché, who affirms: "I don't haggle because I know what's what. I know how to assess the quality of things. But everybody else tries to haggle."

In fact, there is no longer any real bargaining, if by that word is meant a negotiation between buyer and seller to conjointly determine price. The idea that one can still bargain is above all an imaginative projection of the bygone market onto present-day reality. It functions through implicit reference to the "traditional market," a representation fueled in turn by the speaker's own memories of travels and texts: the souks of Marrakech, the kilim bargained for at the Istanbul bazaar. Carpentras market regulars, both stallholders and customers, know full well that people don't bargain as they did in olden times. Instead, the accounts of that period help create an image of the market that everyone is eager to find a more or less fictive trace of in today's practices. "In my father's time," recounts old Perdiguier, "there was a great deal more bargaining than now. Bargaining is a little like the guy who sold *canadiennes* [fur-lined jackets]: he always put a banknote in the pocket. The first thing people do when they try on a coat is put their hands in the pockets. So when they felt the bill they said, 'Okay, I'll take it.' Today people hardly bargain anymore, except the clientele from North Africa a little. We have lots of Algerians and Moroccans who buy from us, but they don't insist. They've acquired the French habits and don't try to bargain anymore. They understand that it isn't worth it, that the prices are fixed, like in a shop. Bargaining is their tradition—what can you do. In North Africa—I saw this on vacation—they've still got traditional markets, the souks, and there you really bargain a lot."

People preserve the memory of a time when transactions were more open and the market more entertaining because every purchase took on the feel of a personalized confrontation where the only rule was "May the best haggler win!" "It wasn't ultimately to get more," explains Mme. Sorel. "It was a game that seller and buyer got absorbed in. It was fascinating. The prize went to the one who had the last word. There was a special vocabulary, plays on words." Likewise M. Favier, a former postman, remarks: "*Marché* really does mean *marchander,* but today that kind of market is over and done with. Things are thus and such price, you can't change it by bargaining. The real market used to be bargaining. In Castres there are only small producers and you can bargain, but here there are nothing but traders. On city fair days, or right before the market closes, when sellers want to liquidate, then you can bargain a little, but it's exceptional." "In the old days there was competition between merchants," adds his wife. "Everyone offered their best prices, prices were not imposed. Small merchants sold cheaper than elsewhere. It was more personal. Women buyers bargained—it was a way of making conversation, and it ended up being a game. The women, the housewives, considered it a point of honor to pay the lowest possible price, while for the merchants the point was not to give in. It was so very lively!"

In those times everyone made use of his or her bargaining talents, a savoir-faire often learned in childhood. "It was a skill, because at the time there was no advertising," continues Mme. Favier. "Sellers had to talk up their wares, know their merchandise, know how to sell, talk to customers, reel them in. Sellers cried out to customers, they cut prices—three cauliflowers for the price of two. And customers bargained, there were no set prices, it was entirely different. There's also the fact that in those days people had to sell their produce before the morning was out because with their carts they didn't have any refrigeration. It was a point of honor not to bring anything back, to sell it all."

Until World War I, as mentioned, professional retailers worked side by side at the market with craftspeople and peasants who for their part came to sell their products as much to retailers as to private individuals. It was of course at the market that prices were determined. And it goes without saying that transactions with traders in those times were heated. Bargaining was a decisive, time-consuming process governed by a complex protocol where everyone took care not to let his own interests get trampled and not to lose face. The spatial and temporal commingling of quite distinct functions, retail and wholesale, made bargaining a fully recognized, if not generalized, practice.

But the "iron and broom" market has not been held on the Place du Théâtre for a long time. At Espenon's mobile shop people now buy screws and brushes of unknown provenance that Espenon himself procured at the wholesale center and whose price is therefore no longer up for discussion. As for fruits and vegetables, in the 1960s Carpentrassians could still get provisions directly from producers at Les Platanes in the half hour preceding the flag lifting that signaled the opening of the wholesale market. But the wholesale market as we know has been moved to the outskirts of town, and the city market is now only for retail sales. In this it has indeed become one link among others in the major distribution circuits. Already fixed "upstream," prices can no longer really be negotiated.

It therefore makes no sense to expect slashed prices and incredible "deals." This explains people's nostalgic memories of a time when a bargain was waiting for you at every turn on a market worthy of the name. "There used to be sellers who only had cabbages or pears, and they had to liquidate all of it on Friday morning," explains Mme. Favier. "They lowered their prices, and women bought what they needed for the whole week." A good housewife was practiced in the art of rooting out a good product at the best price. "What bargains we used to get! You can't find merchants anymore who will sell to you by the batch." Loyal to the ideals of the *gauche populaire*, Mme. Favier believes the market should give the underprivileged a chance to get by for less money.[3] "The market used to be for the poor," she continues. "There used to be merchants who sold off stock from a store—a boon for poor women. The women who buy old clothes at the secondhand dealers' now are all snobs."

There are only a few, highly particularized segments of the market where transactions still involve real bargaining. One turns out to be secondhand clothes. On the steps leading down into the Place du Théâtre, Martin is fully engaged in conversation with passing friends. As we know, he generally stands back a bit from the space in which his fur coats, leather jackets, taffeta dresses, and other luxury items are carefully hung. When a customer manifests pointed interest in a blouse in crêpe de Chine with an embroidered collar, for instance; when she looks at the price tag and seems disposed to try it on, he calls from a distance, "That one I can give you for 350 [€ 55]." It's a way to open trading and at the same time make clear that this is not a mass-produced article but a unique object whose value cannot be calculated exactly. The price will thus represent a compromise between seller's goodwill and buyer's desire. Here we are on different ground than rational distribution and reasonable purchasing; we are in a world of unique objects and shared feeling, where merchant is necessarily sensitive to customer's sudden fancy. Customer, for her part, doesn't answer but continues to examine the blouse, holding it up to herself in the mirror, asking vendor's opinion with her eyes.

"Just right," he says, "and you know, I can't find them anymore. It's all synthetic now."

"It does look good, doesn't it. How much will you give it to me for?"

"You have to realize, it's really perfect. You'll never find crêpe de Chine at that price."

"I'll give you 300 for it."

"Three twenty and it's yours."

Everyone seems to know that the price of secondhand clothes, like that of most crafts sold by "students" in the Passage Boyer as well as farm produce sold directly by small producers (honey and royal jelly, goat cheese), cannot be calculated and may even not be known to the seller. Like craftspeople and small producers, what the secondhand clothes dealer is selling first and foremost is his or her own labor—in this case the time spent mending, bleaching, ironing, and starching—together with his or her fashion sense, art of making clothing finds, discovering the rare pearl. This is why the price seems more open to negotiation than when the trader is only retailing an item.

Since it is advisable for sellers to make customers believe they are selling the fruits of their garden, some customers may imagine that they are facing a producer and can bargain. If they do so, however, they seriously risk getting the cold shoulder. At Les Platanes, where retailers sell cut flowers bought at the Hyères wholesale auction market, a "fine upstanding" lady lingers for a moment in front of a stall, then asks, "How much if I take two bunches?" This incurs a mocking retort—"And at the butcher's you ask for a discount if you buy two steaks?"—and remarks to the gallery: "They're incredible! They think they can do whatever they like when they come here!" Conversely, charging an exorbitant price that will make bargaining inevitable, like the Senegalese do with their fake ivory knickknacks and bush hats, is a way of making a product pass for genuinely handcrafted.

The practice of bargaining is limited to a few specific types of trade, but however marginal these may be, they work to give an image of the market as a land of adventure where everyone can find just the thing that will make them happy. In all other segments, what is called bargaining is a pale imitation. People are not really negotiating prices, but rather requesting (and perhaps obtaining) a symbolic reduction. The stallholder charges a "good price" or gives "good weight"; he "pulls it down a bit" or insists on not taking the pennies over a round sum ("Don't bother rummaging for it, you'll give it to me next week"). It's a way of playing out throughout the market what can occur only in a few atypical transactions or in very particular circumstances—at the tail end of the market morning, for example, when some traders, usually occasionals without a regular circuit, are obliged to sell off perishables.

169

Sometimes it's the stallholder who offers the discount. This may involve either price—"Listen, today's my birthday. I'll give you the two baskets ten francs!"—or quantity: "Ah, it's heavier than usual today. I'll do you a favor," comments the *crémier* [dairyman] as he weighs the block of butter he's just wire-sliced from the mound. "Sometimes," recounts Delvaux, the *charcutier* at the Porte d'Orange, "when I'm offering a deal on pig's feet, tails, all that, if it's a regular customer, I don't lower my price, but I say, 'Okay, that's a kilo and a half, so listen, I'll take off two francs.' When she hears that, she's really happy, she's delighted." Pseudobargaining of this sort can also be initiated by the customer, who generally begins by "knocking" the merchandise, as in this exchange overheard one day at Venturi's stall in the Place de la Mairie:

"Your green beans don't look good."

"How's that, they don't look good?"

"They're too thick."

"Of course they're thick—they're *mange-tout*."

"Maybe, but they're too thick . . . So you'll give me a deal, right?"

In fact, neither buyer nor seller really believes price is negotiable. Instead they play out a script understood to reflect the intense bargaining of a "real" market, transposing for the occasion a negotiation model that in other contexts determines the outcome of truly decisive transactions. It was by decrying producers' wares that shippers opened exchange with them that very morning: "Have you even looked at your tomatoes? Tomorrow you'll be taking them to the canning factory!" Though the words may be the same and the warp of the dialogue formally identical, the situation is nonetheless radically different: in one case the tension is a game; in the other, it is very real.

The slight reduction that customer requests and stallholder concedes is a parody of bargaining. A situation where supply and demand confront each other and create the implied antagonism has here become merely a game, though one that gives the market its particular style. Instead of concluding the transaction quickly on the quiet, the actors pretend to engage in a debate that everyone knows is vain. They make "a big deal" out of it, a micro-event in which other customers too feel implicated. Even the brief amount of time people devote to clarifying the price point is enough to indicate that here we are far from Auchan checkout counters, products with electronically read bar codes.

The "gift" sought and received is above all "symbolic": it initiates or perpetuates an alliance. The reduction, however minimal, creates a debt, and the transaction is thereby inscribed in a span of time that stretches beyond that morning's market. Seller is not trying to draw customer in by selling him goods for less, but rather to oblige him morally to return. The appeal is less to customer's economic interest than to her sense of reciprocity. Competition among the traders present at the market is in no way a price fight. The point is to develop customer loyalty, as they say in the world of marketing, or as the stall-holders say, to "acquire regulars." And customers readily comply with this business tactic. In requesting a discount, they are really asking for special treatment. In obtaining that minimal privilege, they feel they have been recognized as a "good customer" in the eyes of their fellows, regardless of how much or how little they buy. In fact, one is buying both thirteen eggs to the dozen and a precious mark of friendship that distinguishes one from the passing tourist and the just-settled-in Parisian.

When Mme. Delavigne, who belongs to an important industrial bourgeoisie family and inhabits a fine estate on the banks of the Ouvèze which her husband inherited, asks one of Boyac's *commis* [shop clerks] to give her three heads of lettuce for the price of two or requests a discount on apricots at Venturi's— "Give me the ripest, it's for the jam. And you can give me a discount too!"—she is playing the thrifty, provident housewife who spends her Saturdays putting up preserves for the winter. Likewise when Boyac, whose two fruit and vegetable groceries are among the most prosperous in the city, hotly defends his lettuce to the last centime, he is playing the small stallholder afraid to be "out of pocket" at the end of the business day.

Each thus publicly plays a sort of average-representative role, adopting a low-profile position not at all related to what he or she is in ordinary, extra-market social life. This is a means of staging the principle of equality specific to the market exchange relation. They are not bargaining but acting as if price were negotiable in a confrontation between partners where nothing is settled in advance. In fact, Boyac will apply his "markup" and Mme. Delavigne very much wants those lovely Bergeron apricots. But both play their parts, thereby providing a representation of the paradigm of the market as a locus of freely negotiated transactions. By ostensibly engaging in a dialogue that looks every bit a negotiation to the audience of waiting customers, they are "playing market." If Mme. Delavigne did the same in the *parfumerie* in the Rue de la République, the salesgirl would think she was really asking for a bargain— utterly inappropriate behavior. The market, however, is a public space. Here persons can create an image of their sovereign autonomy: I don't really need all that is for sale here, this vast display of heterogeneous products in the streets of the city, and if I buy, it's purely an effect of my goodwill. One has neither obligation nor commitment to these strangers come from nearly everywhere, and every transaction is an occasion to make this manifest. One is there as a free citizen who, in total independence, is making a contract in the public eye. At least this is the impression one should give, by engaging if only for the briefest of moments in a semblance of price negotiation.

Clearly for most products price variation on the market is subject to national and international determination, and up against this hard reality, stallholder and customer alike can only feel entirely impotent. They cannot of course perceive the infinitesimal effect of their transaction on the general state of the Market. But taking the time to bargain means assimilating the face-to-face encounter with the stallholder to one of those exchange situations where each participant may measure the influence of his intervention on price determination, e.g., buying a dresser at the Avignon auction house or a neighbor's old Peugeot. The fact that the price of strawberries comes down in May reflects an overall economic context that Boyer and his customer Mme. Ayme can only note passively. But the fact that that day Mme. Ayme obtains three punnets for the price of two (after a small demonstration of affection and further proof of her loyalty) is a micro-event, economically negligible of course, but that has the advantage of placing both of them in the position of equal partners who can freely negotiate a contract. By angling for a small reduction—"Ah, the *daurade* [sea bream] is expensive today!"—one acts as if prices were determined at Bachini's fish stall, and one experiences, if only for an instant, a pleasure that consumers are generally deprived of today, that of playing the decisive economic actor.

In the supermarket aisles, where most domestic provisioning is done today, up against impersonal, nonnegotiable machinery that leaves one only the choice of product and brand, one is at best a consumer-master of one's tastes—if one doesn't fall for the five-pack of juniper-flavored pâté, that is, the bargain of the day at a "knocked down" price. In the dual relation with each stallholder, one can always hope to modify the terms of the contract after a skillful bit of negotiation, though in reality the prices are just as fully predetermined as in the preceding case. At least during the short time of the transaction, and however small the stakes, each can act as if the situation he or she is experiencing were dissociable from the overall economic context.

CHAPTER TWELVE

This is to some degree the same illusion that governs events in the *marché-gare*. And it explains producers' persistent attachment to this wholesaling mode, despite its many inconveniences (time-consuming, danger of being left with produce on one's hands, and so on). Prices *are* determined there of course. As soon as the market is over, Nicolas's employees, who have gone through the truck rows noting down quantities and prices, gather in the offices of the "Château" and "set up" the market price list that will be displayed an hour later and sent by telex to Avignon, where similar information from markets throughout the region is being received. The price for "Carpentras strawberries" this May Monday thus results from a series of mutually independent face-to-face transactions between producers and shippers. In front of each truck a brief man-to-man confrontation has taken place that either has or hasn't led to a compromise. The game is rigged, however, because one of the players has to sell locally. The best Belin can do is sell off the rest of his strawberries on the Perne or Monteux satellite markets—whereas the shipper makes his offer on the basis of the overall Strawberry Market and data enabling him to anticipate daily rates at Rungis or Cologne.[4] Still, it may well seem to Belin that his action that day, his tactic for getting a better rate from Boyer or his refusal to sell at such a low price to Pao, was decisive, like that of each of his "colleagues." This would not be the case if he had signed a contract for direct delivery at the outset of the "campaign."

The small rebates and other instances of "good weight" that customers wangle or win out of merchants in the joyous bustle and confusion of a Friday morning market are a parody of the tight, nervous negotiation between professionals on the cement parking lot of the *marché-gare*. The same illusion is repeated in each, though in ironic mode in one, and it was by moving back and forth between these two sharply different worlds that I understood the principle of fictive equality which the actors are most likely unconscious of but which nonetheless defines the warp and woof of relations around the stallholder's stall. In allowing themselves to get drawn into the exchange game, the market partners can always imagine that the relation between them is independent of external constraints, particularly macroeconomic ones. At Venturi's stand, Mme. Ripert can "imagine" she is Demand, just as Belin, standing in front of his truck full of strawberries, can "think" he is Supply—as if the Carpentras market had by enchantment identified itself with the Market. Here actors play out the utopia of a founding relation between free and equal individuals that is the very principle of the classic liberal representation of society. Like

173

Ricardo's primitive hunter and fisherman who, according to Marx, traded fish for game and game for fish without being aware that their transaction, elementary though it was, presupposed the London stock exchange, actors on the Carpentras market replay the first market exchanges, of a time before there was such a thing as a *cours des Halles.*[5]

CHAPTER TWELVE

13. All at the Market, All in the Same Boat

In a good agora at peak hour, people jostle each other and mix, rubbing shoulders both physically and socially. Though the Friday morning crowd is not always as thick as it is in August, it is always socially varied. Going to market means using the city differently, experiencing it as a "melting pot." Here for a few hours social groups that are different from each other in every way—place of residence, behavior, the culture each identifies itself with—and that rarely come in contact with each other mingle and commingle. A big, socially mixed, ephemeral crowd is the indispensable construction material as it were of the specific social space of the market. Carpentras is a small city where people all know each other more or less, at least within the narrow limits they keep to on ordinary days, i.e., their *quartier* [neighborhood] and the area around their place of work. But to venture into the flow of people at the market on Fridays is to enter a social environment where the proportion of strangers has suddenly become enormous.[1] A situation of relative anonymity is thence created where actors interact with each other as "public" persons; that is, independently of their personal social identities and private relations.

Market crowds are not necessarily socially heterogeneous. The probability that the head of a local business or the solicitor's wife will rub shoulders around the same stall with a farmworker or the postwoman is not the same on all markets. Social statuses do not vary greatly at neighborhood markets in the Paris suburbs, for example, or at the small rural markets I studied in the region around Carpentras, such as Monteux, Pernes, and Saint-Didier, where customers are likely to be local, though in summertime there are generally more foreigners.[2]

The Carpentras market, however, draws from a wide circumference. The Comtat capital is geographically central, as may be seen from the layout of the freeway network, and therefore attracts people from all the small neighboring towns. Moreover, during the four summer months the region is a highly prized resort area, a vast vacation land that stretches from Gordes to Bédoin for a wide swath of Parisians ranging from the intelligentsia to "show biz," as well as a required stop on the road to the Midi and all tourist itineraries. Moreover, the population of the city is itself highly diverse. Most of its inhabitants are employed in small businesses, the liberal professions, and office work, but there is also, as mentioned, a high proportion of immigrants, the vast majority from North Africa, most employed on the surrounding farms.[3]

On Fridays, then, the city is full of people who aren't usually there. Country people temporarily abandon their fields; summer residents leave their rented country houses; "neo-rurals" living on the margins of established occupations also go to market, in addition to members of the usual market networks. A group of young people from Lyon, for example, who have a house near Saint-Didier and make their living rebottoming chairs, come to offer their services in the Place de la Mairie. Pierre Barenne, who lives near Sault, sets up his trestle table in the Rue des Halles to sell goat cheese. This is his sole contact with the city.

As for the Carpentras residents, regardless of whether they follow a clearly laid out itinerary of familiar stalls or simply their fancy, most of them take what is for them an inhabitual path on Fridays, leading them into neighborhoods where they otherwise have no occasion to go. The North Africans of the Cité des Amandiers in the northern part of the city or the small neighborhood known as Saintes-Maries near the Porte d'Orange go to Les Platanes on Fridays to buy cassettes of Oriental music and are likely to linger there, talking in small groups. This is the only time Muslim women are seen in the city center. On other days they don't leave their neighborhoods, except very occasionally to go to the Association Islamique in the Rue du Collège (opened in 1984). Mme. Sorel, who descends from an old local family, rarely leaves her fine house in the Rue Moricelly at her age, but on Fridays, whatever the weather, she walks all the way to the Porte d'Orange to buy a few red mullet. Because the market runs all through the city, oblivious to marks of social status or identity, and because, for a few hours, the use made of the urban space is less functional and therefore more erratic, more conducive to ambling and whim, the city space becomes somehow porous; neighborhoods flow into each other and internal boundaries, invisible yet known to all, are temporarily abolished.

The very morphology of the Carpentras market accentuates social commingling. The sinuous, seemingly muddled yet ultimately continuous course of the market affects individuals' paths while giving each the feeling that they are choosing and inventing their trajectory. Since the market is not strictly organized by product sector, and since even with a shopping list in hand or a precise purchase in mind, people always also stroll and take a look around, everyone is in fact coaxed to proceed through the market from end to end in both directions. (Buses pull in at either Les Platanes or the Porte d'Orange.)

Though many urban markets in the region are of comparable size, they do not have the same physiognomy. In Sorgues, for example, the market is made up of two sharply distinct zones. In one, secondhand clothing and Arab music are sold. This section is for all intents and purposes reserved to North Africans, all the more likely to come as it takes place on Sundays. In the other zone I found several Carpentras stallholders. Visitors here are almost entirely city residents; tourists are rare. The spatial arrangement of the market at L'Isle-sur-la-Sorgue is not conducive to social mixing either. The clientele for the antique dealers grouped along the banks of the river is composed of retailers, Parisians looking for objects to decorate their Provence *bastide* or *presbytère*,[4] and souvenir-hunting tourists, none of whom are likely to visit the rest of the market.

A market like that of Carpentras, on the other hand, is a sort of apparatus for producing equality out of highly diverse social material. The mere fact of being part of a mass of people works to this end: "A head is a head, an arm is an arm," wrote Elias Canetti. "All demands for justice and all theories of equality ultimately derive their energy from the actual experience of equality familiar to anyone who has been part of a crowd."[5] Moreover, the physical proximity imposed by crowd density tends in itself to reduce social distance. But at the market a social space is constituted that breaks with the relations of domination which govern the rest of society. The active principle in this space is equalizing of conditions. In direct contrast to "real" democracy, where those in last place never really come first, every customer at the stallholder market is worth another, regardless of whether they have come from the elegant villas of La Lègue, preferred spot of young executives and other dynamic entrepreneurs, or the public housing projects in the north. No one is privileged here; there is no socially determined order of precedence. People do not come to the market to make a show of who they are or gain recognition for the place they occupy or aspire to on the social ladder. Rather they take pleasure in letting such differences blur, recognizing each other as equals, even if that means appearing to be what one is not. Each person turns the principle of formal equality into a rule governing his or her behavior, and the market becomes a fictive world composed of like individuals where differences in social status and fortune are temporarily obliterated, a sort of concrete image, visible in social interactions, of the abstract public space "peopled" by equal, rights-endowed subjects.

The market is not where to go if one is thinking to use one's respectability or prestige to be better served. "We don't have any more rights than the next person there," says Mme. Patio. "It's not like in a shop." It will get one nowhere to make it clear that the authentic San Daniele one is demanding for the *melon-jambon* is to be served to the deputy mayor or an important doctor. Nor does one obtain different treatment by mentioning one's meager retirement pension or other misfortunes. "Give me two nice grapefruit, I'm taking them to the hospital," calls out a customer. "Hospital or no hospital," retorts Lacaze, "everyone here is in the same boat." The relations that come into being as customers stop at this or that stall to make their purchases cannot be based on their intimation or affirmation of a position or status external to the trading situation.

In this respect, the market contrasts with all spaces in which social hierarchies are enacted: offices, businesses, residential and other spaces. Gérard Althabe has shown how behavior in housing blocks on the outskirts of Nantes, for example, follows identity-related strategies whose logic can be reconstituted in minute detail.[6] Actors in such spaces are captive to issues and concerns that may seem minimal but on which their social existence nonetheless seems tragically to depend. They need to distinguish themselves at all costs from the welfare-collecting family on the third floor or the immigrants in the next housing block over, and it is with reference to these third parties that they establish solidarity ties among "ourselves." At the market, on the contrary, people accept a temporary suspension of hierarchical differences, even if the signs of them remain manifest. The logic implicit in behavior here is to hold at bay all that makes perceptible the inegalitarian structure of the social order, and the mode of doing so is not so much dissimulation as an ironic wink or amused denial. As at certain other moments in social life—commemorative holidays, the aperitif at the corner café, or the "fiction that social distinctions did not exist" characteristic of early-eighteenth-century coffeehouses, where, according to Richard Sennett, "when a man entered the door. . . . distinctions of rank were temporarily suspended; anyone sitting in the coffeehouse had a right to talk to anyone else, to enter into any conversation, whether he knew the other people or not, whether he was bidden to speak or not. It was bad form even to touch on the social origins of other persons when talking to them in the coffeehouse, because the free flow of talk might then be impeded"—people at the market act (more or less effectively) in such a way as to make themselves all seem alike.[7]

The clearest manifestation of this equality game is speaking familiarly to each other. From the gentle word to the ribald joke, affected negligence to out-and-out rudeness, familiarity is the rule for dialogue between stallholder and customer. When the *charcutier* in the Rue des Halles hands Mme. Coste her sausage—Mme. Coste is a little lady "of a certain age" dressed all in gray and bent under the weight of her thick plastic shopping bag from which protrude the floppy green ends of a few leeks—he invariably says, "Here you are, my pretty!" One might think it a sign of recognition; that he is making an ironic comment on her lost attractiveness, perhaps a discreet allusion to a time when he knew her to be more appealing. In reality, as I observed, the *charcutier* speaks to all women this way, whether he knows them or not, and one cannot even say that his affectionate teasing is reserved for "good customers." To cry "Here you are, my pretty!" to Mme. Coste is above all to show her publicly the same attention as the pretty girl next to her, the spruce Béatrice, who has left her secondhand clothing stand for a moment to do the shopping and who, a minute later, will be addressed in exactly the same terms.

Familiarity of this sort is also a way of not recognizing the differences in social position that may be inferred from style of dress, overall appearance, and other signs that any stallholder deserving of the name picks up instantly— ignoring such differences in the name of the charm assumed to characterize the female sex as a whole. When the fishmonger at the Porte d'Orange hands Mme. Delavigne her red mullet with the words "Here you go, dear, and let me know how you liked them!" this is a way not merely of ignoring but of publicly denying her obvious membership in the chic, country-house-owning bourgeoisie of the surrounding area by including her in the set of *personnes du sexe* who are, by definition, all desirable. In virtue of the same logic by which all women are called "my beauty" or "my pretty," all male customers around Lagarde's mobile shop are gratified with "And what will it be for the young gentleman?"

A few steps further on, at the bonbon and tea biscuit shop in the Rue de l'Evêché, the same Mme. Coste is addressed not as "my pretty" but with the question "What will it be for grandma?" At one stall, then, her age is ironically denied; at another it is deliberately stressed. But in both cases she is given a circumstantial identity that makes it possible to disregard what she is otherwise. To be the "biscuit" grandmother in the eyes of all is temporarily to cease being the hardworking erstwhile grocer of the Porte de Monteux who not so long ago headed for Les Platanes as early as 6 a.m. to buy her fruits and vegetables for less. Affectionately or teasingly defining the other in terms of age effaces the features that would categorize him or her in socioeconomic or occupational terms.

In apparently the opposite way, the stallholder may just as readily under-score—with a touch of humor—the most obvious signs of a customer's wealth. When a rather too elegantly dressed woman approaches Noël Cappo's mobile shop (you don't put on your Sunday best to go to the market these days; you try instead to be "like everybody else"), he is quick to seize the occasion: "Whose turn is it? The grandma over there in her fur coat? Nice, that. What kind of fur? Must keep a body warm!" When Rouvre's daughter-in-law lets Raveau know he's weighed her out a hundred grams too many strawberries, he is ready with the retort: "With a nice jacket like that, don't tell me you've got your eye on a hundred grams!" Distinctive signs of social success are pointed out mockingly, to deny any effect they might have on trade relations. At the market, such signs are simultaneously exposed and canceled.

For the stallholder this is a deliberate business tactic. "It's completely differ-ent than in a shop," explains Delvaux. "In a shop it's everyone in their place. On the market it's not at all the same. Sometimes you joke around just to make sure the (female) customers don't leave, because when you're working by yourself, you know, you've got to hold onto them—the customer gets impatient quick! You've got to skewer one on while joking with another. There's always one in the lot you can joke with, so you joke with her while rushing around serving another. You bring out the funny stories, make everyone laugh—that works well. It means finding ruses—you've got to calculate, and that's what I like. At home I never say a thing, I don't talk. And my wife, you know, she says, 'What's the matter with you?' I don't say a thing. But here I'd gladly go on all day."

The joking is what gives the market exchange relation its specific form, turn-ing the series of disparate customers into a small society of equals. This is why customers do not find it unseemly. The market would not be what it is without the jokes and teasing. People would be very much surprised if the *charcutier* weren't "macho" and the fishmonger rude. Customers tend to play along, often delighted. "Thank goodness for Rey," Mme. Coste once told me. "He's the only one who says things to me like that anymore." With a knowing smile the customers accept the attribute the stallholder saddles them with and are often ready with a reply to show they're in the game too. "And what might the pretty lady be wanting?" cries Mme. Pincevent to Laure, busy "digging around" in the former's mound of socks in the Place du Palais. "She'd be wanting thin white cotton ankle socks," answers Martin's girlfriend, as if for the space of an instant this ardent reader of Proust and Bourdieu had taken on the typical role of the "pretty lady" doing her marketing.

It happens that the teasing or tender call-outs give way to risqué jokes along the order of "Take the hot, spicy olives—good for husbands," or lines constructed speedily from a more or less daring *sous-entendu*:

"Are they good, your cherries?"

"Have one! You can taste everything here, including the vendor if that's your fancy!"

Another way of creating a fictively homogeneous world for the occasion is around a "love knows no social barriers" script:

"Did you remember me?" a woman customer asks Delvaux.

"I've been doing nothing but," he answers, handing her the two fine *caillettes* he's put aside for her.

When Mme. Arnoux, well known in the region (her husband co-runs the cooperative wine cellar in Caromb), and her friend Mme. Garcia appear hesitant to buy *rillettes* [potted meat] "because it's fattening," Bonens, who knows whereof he speaks, hastens to reassure them: "The fatter you are, the prettier!" The tone of the elicited reply is similar: "Ah, I'd take a fat man like you any day!" Mme. Arnoux and Mme. Garcia are both contented wives and attentive mothers who also know how to boss North African workers at harvest time when they think they have to. But they enjoy surrendering their respectability for the duration of a Friday market, playing liberated women unafraid to challenge convention.

Still, the stallholder has to know how to strike the right balance in the taking of verbal liberties. It would not do to go overboard, as Delvaux is well aware: "You can tell immediately which women customers you can joke with, which ones you even have to joke with, and which customer you better not say a thing to. It can be an older woman, a young one—you can see it. In my opinion it's not something that can be learned, there's no school that'll teach you. There's a psychological aspect to it: you've got to see the customer come up to know whether or not you can joke with them. There are some who would like nothing better, even if the jokes are kind of bad. If you don't make them, they feel like something's missing. It's really a kind of gift. We learn how to weigh, how to slice, but how to sense that sort of thing about someone—I don't think you can learn that."

The question arises of the implicit rules and conditions for this kind of familiarity or nonrespect. It cannot be observed at all stalls and does not seem linked with type of product, though it does occur more frequently in food stalls. Certain stallholders abstain primarily because they have no talent for it. Sexually connoted jokes are not pushed very far in Carpentras and may be barely decodable. When, in reply to the question, "What've you got that's good today?" the stallholder answers, "Everything's good here, you know that," only a ribald tone would permit one to think he is touting anything other than his wares. At Paris markets the jokes are much cruder. Beyond a certain limit this kind of behavior is commercially possible only on condition of near-perfect anonymity, and this is hard to come by in a small city. It is significant too that the North African stallholders I observed on neighboring markets (Pernes, Monteux), though skillful users of humor, never said anything with a sexual connotation, as if the community created by this means, however fictional, had implicit ethnic limits.

The market customer does not expect to be treated with any particular deference. What would elsewhere be perceived as an unseemly attitude is here just part of the game. "You're not going to mess up all my merchandise now—you're not at Auchan!" cries Mme. Arnaud to a lady whose reserved manner hardly invites such familiarity. Then comes what seems like a tirade of indignation: "With Auchan and their like, they've gotten used to touching everything, they think they can make themselves at home anywhere. They have no respect for the merchandise anymore or for people who work. They come touch the merchandise even with their hands all greasy after a hamburger—they think that's just fine!" Then she looks the customer directly in the eye: "So, are you going to take it or not, that shirt?" The target of this angry outburst is none other than Mme. Chavance, honorable wife and mother whom no one in the city would dream of treating this way. She just opened a speech-therapy office in the Rue de la Sous-Préfecture, the street where the most renowned doctors are located, and her husband just took over the biggest insurance company in

Carpentras. Yet she doesn't seem offended. On the contrary, she thoroughly enjoys replying, playing on the sympathy of the other customers around her: "I certainly hope it won't shrink, your shirt, because at Auchan at least . . ." Slightly further on, an old countrywoman is just as unshaken when the plant seller in the Rue de la Porte-d'Orange whom she has just asked to save her some basil until the end of the market replies: "If you think that's the only damn thing I have to worry about!"

The stallholder's art lies in giving the impression that he's roughing everyone up a bit to show that everyone's in the same case. In reality, he modulates this faked aggressiveness by trading partner. The criterion here is not so much customer's age or what can be perceived of his or her social status as whether he or she looks up to playing the game. The stallholder must be both disrespectful *enough* (or this would not feel like the market) and *opportunely* disrespectful. As we have seen, Delvaux is fully aware of the subtlety required: "There are women customers who you've got to shake up a bit. There are others who you have speak to with white gloves. And there are still others who you have to tease, make them laugh or ask them how the cat's doing—it's curious. I like the atmosphere of a market better than a store. In the store you've got to watch your step, whereas at the market you can allow yourself to do certain things you wouldn't do in a store. I've got a customer here, she comes up, she asks me for three slices of ham. I know they're a family of five so I say, 'What are you going to do with three? I'm going to give you five!' and I cut her five slices. So then she says, 'Well, add two more—it looks good!' She does it to me every time. But if I don't say anything and cut her three, she says, 'What's the matter with you today? Is something wrong? You don't feel well? You're sick?' It always goes that way with her—you've got to shake her up."

These forms of apparent aggressivity should not be taken literally, though that is what people who study the "speech situation" rather than the market as a specific social space tend to do. If one does not go beyond the "mode by which utterances are sequenced" and their "formal properties within the dyadic relation between merchant and customer"—the focus of a number of sociolinguistic analyses modeled on studies by Dell Hymes and John Gumperz—this sort of speech event might seem to establish a genuinely unequal relation in which "the customer has to show patience and submission" in response to the merchant's authority.[8]

Mme. Chavance does seem to have been put in her place by the unpleasant vendor, but the vendor's attitude acquires its real meaning only when we understand that it's a bit of playacting, and this is precisely how Mme. Chavance took it. "Poking fun at the customer" is a way of indicating that one is not really a merchant, of ensuring that nothing in market exchange evokes the de rigueur conventional courtesy practiced in shops. The same is true of exaggerated stallholder politeness. At one stall the customer gets roughed up, whereas a bit further on the stallholder is very nearly obsequious, letting the customer know, complete with bowing and scraping gestures, that he is "at her service," as if to pervert from the inside out the sacrosanct business law that proclaims the customer king by applying it to the point of absurdity. As he lays a floorcloth or a bag of cat litter in a customer's basket, Noël Cappo asks grandiloquently, "Is Madame satisfied? Would Madame like anything more?" Just as everyone knows that a stallholder may call out "Who's next?" or "What will it be for the little lady?" so when he says "Would Monsieur like one more sausage?" everyone understands he is poking fun.

The script can be reversed from one stallholder to the next. This one playacts the perfect salesman providing more than the service expected of him, making a show of his zeal to serve. Another, choosing to act a surly character or a bad mood, blatantly mistreats his customers. Both the constant switch in the tone the exchange is staged in and the fact that this is independent of the customer's status or identity are specific to the market. In contrast to stores, where beneath superficial courtesy and amiableness the merchant always finds a way of letting the customers know she knows who she's dealing with, the market gives itself the appearance of a world of chance where one meets, from one stall to the next, as in a fairy tale and without knowing why, here a prince, there a churl.

CHAPTER THIRTEEN

14. In Full View

Because market exchange holds social statuses and their hierarchical arrangement at bay, a microsociety develops at the market, particularly around a given
stall, where actors not only coexist as in a crowd but also relate to each other.
What makes the market a public space is the combination of anonymity and
interaction among subjects who recognize each other as equals.

What looks from the outside like a crowd may correspond to a set of extremely diverse types of social interaction. The Carpentras market is not the
Gare Saint-Lazare.[1] Though most actors at the market do not know each other,
relations among them are not of the same kind as what Ulf Hannerz calls "traffic
roles and relationships," the "result of a crowding of large numbers of people
in a limited space," the sort "managed" by "avoiding sidewalk collisions." As
Hannerz judiciously remarks, such interactions are "a pure form of meetings
among strangers" and are at "the borderline of being relationships at all." Indeed, people in this situation "may not even be aware that they are 'taking each
other into account.' "[2] "To study traffic relationships," writes Hannerz, "is often to study how people deal with one another while they are doing something
else."[3] The vague concern one has about others while rushing to work, the
mutual indifference of people who, each busy with his or her own affairs, pass
each other in a neutral space that is the means rather than the end of their movement, are completely alien to the forms of active co-presence that develop at
the market.

Nor is there the sense of a mass of unified persons like that produced by a sporting or theater event, where all eyes converge on a common, mediating object which spontaneously organizes communication among people who are both in close physical proximity and strangers to each other. The market is a spatially segmented arrangement; people are looking in many directions rather than all at the same thing, so it can never be reduced to spectacle or show. And though one can always mentally, internally drop out of the game to consider it in its entirety as an object of curiosity, one nonetheless remains an actor in it. Even a tourist who chooses to assume the position of observer of an event external to her is, if unconsciously, an integral part of the thing, not to mention the fact that he is continuously exposed to the risk of succumbing to a spontaneous desire to purchase something. What would the market be, at least in summer, without Germans in shorts and cotton sun hats with heavy camera bags strapped across their chests? Everyone "does" the market as he or she pleases, of course. Some come to stroll through, breathe in the ambiance, desiring nothing more than to give themselves up to the moment; others have particular purchases in mind; one fellow is taking his habitual turn through the city to say hello to his *connaissances*. But everybody is doing what they're doing together, in a way, and together they create a collective event.

Pursuing this type of description of the market means working to recapture the multiple, fleeting relations that develop in it, both around particular stalls and in the course of unplanned itineraries through the space. The market space is subject to the Brownian principle of indetermination. It is a unique overall event, the sum and combination of an incalculable number of micro-events of the type "X meets Y," each one the result of chance intersections between and among the innumerable trajectories of individuals who have come from different places for different purposes. Actors often pay little or no attention to these barely limned, futureless "encounters," but without them the market would not be what it is. The actors do not have sufficient distance on their own practices to necessarily be aware that multiple interactions are taking place in this situation of anonymity, interactions without which the public aspect of the event would disappear. But this is indeed what is missing from Auchan supermarket aisles; it is what people experience there negatively, by its absence.

To follow individual trajectories and thereby restore the actual social field both presupposed and constituted by the multiple operations that everyone performs without thinking and that taken together are called "doing the market," it therefore seems to me preferable to be situated "on the ground," rather than up in the sky engaging in aerial or statistical observation of shopper flows. A rigorous description of the phenomenon would require noting all the singular trajectories followed by actors in a given day and the innumerable intersections of their paths. Clearly the market is not a mappable phenomenon. Only the skeleton—the market structure—can be traced, not its actual physiognomy. The market is not just an organized sequence of stands and shops. It is the social field that the actors bring into being by the combination of their many unpredictable encounters.

I therefore had to try to note these short-lived interactions as closely as possible. One way to do this was to accompany Mme. Patio to the market several times. I met this passionate marketgoer through her nephew, a Paris academic, eminent Joyce specialist, and a friend of mine. M. Patio, retired director of the local branch of the Crédit Lyonnais bank, belongs to a family that settled in Carpentras several generations ago. The couple live in the Résidence du Mont-Ventoux, a well-maintained little building with neatly mown lawns on an avenue that extends to the east amid *garrigues* and gardens toward the hills of La Lègue and the fine villas that dominate the city. Mme. Patio hardly ever goes into the town center, though it is only ten or so minutes from her house. The Patios usually do their daily shopping "a stones' throw from here" or, occasionally, at Auchan. But except for the few weeks a year they spend in Juan-les-Pins, they never miss the market. Around ten in the morning, as soon as M. Patio comes home—"We go to the market separately rather than at the same time, we like to relay each other"—Mme. Patio walks down to Le Quinconce, beginning a trajectory that is almost identical from one week to the next, a long crossing punctuated by various purchases, though her alibi for this is often (as she willingly admits) one or two items she could get any other day. "My pharmacy is at the other end—we used to live in the Place du Théâtre and I got used to that pharmacy—so I often go to the pharmacy on Fridays to be able to cross through the market. And sometimes we go to the bank on Fridays because it's closed on Saturdays. The bank is in the Place du Théâtre, so you see, going that way takes us all the way there."

She goes up the Rue de la Porte-de-Mazan to the Rue des Halles, past the bird market ("a place where country people gather") to see if her friend from Caromb has come to sell snails or a few mushrooms. She then proceeds to *les petites halles* [the little food hall] at the corner, where she buys vegetables at Martinez's or Llorca's ("They don't come specially for the market, they're there all week"). I see her pass by Mme. Chalon without realizing it. Mme. Chalon once ran a seed shop near the Porte de Mazan, as she recounts in her memoirs. Her son writes novels and a society column for *Le Figaro*.

Mme. Patio continues her turn through the market by way of the Place d'Inguimbert, where she lets herself get "caught up" by a hawker-demonstrator loudly declaiming to a very mixed group of spectators including North Africans and tourists. "When there are things for making mayonnaise or cutting *frites*, for example—you don't see that kind of thing very often. They have such things in the stores, but they're not on view, you can't see how they work," says Mme. Patio. She is, however, not particularly interested in the clothes. "Our family is rather special. My daughter works for Cacharel, she's a marketing executive so she often gives me things. I don't really trust market clothes. The way they're put out on the market makes you think that everyone will end up wearing the same thing. Though really, it's quite the same with Cacharel!"

When she reaches the Place du Palais she waves to old Jeanjean, who is sitting on the tailgate of his minivan behind his folding table, surrounded as always by a court of habitués, most of whom she knows only by sight. *Le père* Pécavan is there too, a retired farm producer living with his children in the city. His weekly conversations with the seed vendor enable him to maintain a tie to the land. Reynaud and his wife have stopped for a minute to discuss the new seeds; they grow melons and tomatoes south of the city and went by Perdiguier's earlier to "take back some work shoes we bought last week—we hadn't tried them on." There are also some of Jeanjean's "vacationer" clients, namely, Jean-Paul Lefrançois, a Paris journalist who fixed up an old Provençal manor house near Saint-Didier and has been coming for years to buy seeds for his garden. And this is where I've often run into Mme. Arnoux. Her husband lets her off in the Place du Théâtre, and while he goes to find his "colleagues" at the wood and vine market, she takes a thorough turn through the market, regularly buying *charcuterie* and vegetables—in contrast to the Paris journalist, she has no time to tend a vegetable garden—and never failing to take a look at the fabric displays. On an itinerary that is nearly always the same, she goes by the seed shop that Mme. Laborel took over from her mother, Mme. Chalon. But she wouldn't dream of buying nasturtium or lawn grass seeds from anyone but Jeanjean.

A bit further on, in front of Saint-Siffrein, Mme. Patio stops to take a look at Jojo Spinelli's vast display, checking to see if by chance Mme. Arnaud is not there buying a few remnants. "I don't buy fabric because I don't know how to sew," she says, "but I have many friends who buy at Jojo Spinelli's." She doesn't know Mme. Favier, who at that very moment is moving around the heavy bolts of printed cotton in search of a remnant. Mme. Favier is an old-time Comtadine originally from the small, steep village of Le Barroux, a few kilometers from Beaumes-de-Venise. She has repeatedly told me that she doesn't go to the market anymore "because it's not at all like what it used to be, it no longer has any raison d'être." This is invariably followed by a long nostalgic account of the market of olden days, when her stallholder grandmother crisscrossed the region in a cart or she herself accompanied her father: "In summer he was a *primeurs* dealer going from client to client and in winter a stallholder-merchant." The market of that time, with its tooth pullers and public entertainers, "wasn't monotonous like now." And yet every Friday, I come upon her frail, black-clad figure, always in a different place. She is always carrying a heavy shopping bag. She sets out on the stroke of ten from the public housing development of Pous-du-Plan where she lives with her husband and slips like a shadow from one stall to another, exploring the slightest nooks and crannies of the market.

As Mme. Patio heads back up the Rue de la République, she glances with amusement at a big family with a gaggle of chattering children who have got their little hands on everything. They're here from Lille on vacation and staying at the Monteux trailer camp. Usually they get provisions from itinerant peddlers, and at Auchan every three or four days. They have never been to Carpentras and are here today to buy fresh fruit. In the midst of a group of laughing teenagers in front of Daspas's stall—Daspas sells traditional shoes and also has a shop—she notices a neighbor's daughter buying clear plastic sandals, an item that has been "followed" here for a long time, but this year become "hyperfun" and a "must." "A lot of young people come here," she makes a point of telling me. "They're interested in the market too."

At the bank in the Place du Théâtre she runs into Doctor Brun, the renowned scholar of the locale, "the one who knows everything about Carpentras," to whom she introduced me as soon as I arrived. I also see Grossage, the former tailor who once sold on the market, engaged in animated conversation with Perdiguier *père*. He has just made his "little turn through the market to say hello" to his former "colleagues"; he is not there to buy. In Carpentras, as Rousseau explained to me, "men don't run errands." It is therefore Mme. Grossage who has come to do the shopping in the Place de la Mairie, where she has her *fromager* and her *charcutier* (who "makes sausage this way, not that way," as her daughter-in-law likes to say teasingly), two stalls that are heavily

189

patronized by city merchants. Lastly, Mme. Patio "goes back down" through Les Platanes (one "descends" from south to north). "I go to the market above all for the flowers," she tells me, though this will not be the last stop on her long tour. Without a clear idea of what she wants, she takes the time to see what there is and compare prices. She moves from one stall to the next, retracing her steps several times before choosing.

It is clear that if I asked Mme. Patio to relate her trip to the market afterward, she would mention only the encounters with people she knows, i.e., those she exchanged words with (anything from "bonjour" to a prolonged conversation) and those she knows but avoided or pretended not to see. But I have noted everyone she crossed paths or rubbed shoulders with—a much higher number. She may remember having caught a glimpse of people she knows by sight or by name but is not obliged to treat like *connaissances*; she may have let it be known to a third party or in one of those brief exchanges customers sometimes have among themselves that she knows full well who those persons are. But all the strangers with whom she coexisted for an instant in the same space, around the same stall, for example, fall into the limbo of what for her does not have the status of an event, the infranarrative, though she may well have been led to exchange a few "market utterances" with them about the rising price of melon, how hard it is these days to find real peasant blood sausage.

The fact remains, however, that what actually happens on the market, what it is my job to describe, is due to how these variable sorts of "encounters," from the conversation she had with her neighbor across the landing at home to the knowing smile exchanged with a stranger while they both listened to Jacky Thévet's spiel, come together. The sketchy interactions that come into existence in this situation of anonymity, interactions, that is, with "whomever," do not appear to the actors as real social relations, and yet they are constitutive—without their knowing it and for the greater pleasure of all—of the type of public space a market is.

The market crowd, i.e., the necessary co-presence of a multitude of individuals ignorant of each other's identity, is not merely an element of the setting, not merely a framework or backdrop for market relations. Most specialized analyses concentrate on the buyer-seller relation, relegating the situation of being "elbow to elbow" and the pleasure of "mingling in the crowd" to the relatively uninteresting status of "context." This is to neglect the fact that the direct relation between merchant and customer is only autonomous and therefore only legitimately isolatable in quite a different sales context, namely the shop, where each customer is served separately and discreetly (even when there is a waiting line), off to the side and perhaps even in a hushed voice, in an ostentatiously attentive type of interaction where all other persons are held and hold themselves at a distance.

At the market, on the other hand, there is a kind of implicit contract whereby everyone accepts to expose his or her private purchases to public curiosity. The crowd, the massive presence of an anonymous Other, is thus a feature *internal* to the market relation, not merely a contextual one, a kind of surrounding atmosphere. It is impossible to buy individually and discreetly at the market. The customer's order, even if spoken in a low voice, is instantly repeated and amplified by the stallholder: "And a kilo of tomatoes for Madame!"; "Pass me the *parme* [prosciutto] for the demoiselle!" This is of course to allow the customer to modify the order if desired, but the booming repetition functions above all to transform a private transaction into a public show for the people in line. The stallholder has only to use the occasion, as she often does, to tout the quality of her wares by adding a comment—"And a kilo of turnips for the lady—pretty turnips, I must say!" or "Five slices of ham, and nice ham it is, too! We take the customer seriously here!"—and your order is promoted to the status of exemplary purchase for all the potential customers pressing or milling about behind you.

All stallholder behavior is aimed at developing a "show" in which customers waiting their turn will become implicated in spite of themselves as both audience and actors. This explains the stallholder's theatrical gestures, the emphatic air he takes moving around behind the counter, the ostentatious attentiveness with which he chooses the vegetables, weighs them, lays them with his own hands in the housewife's basket. His movements call to mind Sartre's café waiter.[4] If only to help his customers wait patiently, he turns to the next one without having quite finished with the last. While Delvaux is weighing pork chops for one, he's calling out to the next, "So your little girl isn't with you today?" Then he turns back to the first: "That'll be twenty-four francs for the chops, and with them you'll have . . . ?" Or he handles orders coming in from several people at once, thereby creating a situation of embedded interchanges of the sort that Erving Goffman remarks are frequent in public places.[5] Stallholders also know how to break off a one-to-one relation with a buyer to create a discussion in which all who are present may speak. When Mme. Ayme asks,

"It isn't too bland, your *tomme?*" Taillefer responds by passing round a sliver to everyone there.[6]

For hawkers, turning each sale into a collective event is a deliberate, systematic technique. From the outset they call out to their audience at large: "When you've got a mess like this at home to clean up—and you had to work to make a mess like this—personally, I'd advise you to . . ." Another invents an imaginary interlocutor: "If there's a doctor among you, he can't possibly disagree with me." Then he selects one of his listeners—"I heard one of you say . . . you, the young man over there"—whom he makes into his special interlocutor, offering him as consenting victim to the view of the amused, complicitous crowd. "Look, ladies, watch this and you'll understand. You push down your button, your thread goes through the needle eye, you hold onto your thread so it doesn't get away—got that? If you didn't understand, you can invite me to lunch and we'll see to it over dessert. Did you understand, Madame, back there? No, so let's show her. Of course she's intimidated. If she doesn't know how to do this at her age, what a disgrace! Look, Madame, when you get home, you take this great tool and you . . ."

Shopping on the market thus means exposing oneself to the gaze of others— a virtually unavoidable observation activity that everyone engages in while standing in line, almost without realizing it and surely without thinking of it in those terms. Such observation can inform the observer ("I'm not going to get any of that today, it's too expensive!"), offer inspiration for what to make for dinner ("Hmm, I could make eggplant"), but more often than not is a source of gratuitous pleasure, a kind of innocent voyeurism: the unfortunate object of our floating attention, all caught up in making his or her purchase, gives us so much to look at! One idly draws conclusions about her living standards or lifestyle ("She's buying strawberries in the middle of winter," "He's buying a single chicken for seven people"), about his eating practices and tastes ("Buying *olivette* tomatoes for a salad—what an idea!"), how much she knows about produce ("I'd wait another week before buying asparagus") and prices ("He'd do better to buy hake, the whiting is so expensive today").

The very social mix and commingling engendered by the market makes the spectacle of market exchange one of the most likely places for ethnic stereotypes to be fueled or confirmed (remarks heard on the market: "Those Arabs! As soon as they've got a few *centimes* they spend them"; "Only Parisians would buy old shirts at such prices"). But people also identify customer personality traits: openness to impulse buying; improvised shopping or list and pencil in hand;

passive timidity or bossy authority. The habitué holds out his basket himself, asks for basil when none is visible because she knows it has to be kept underneath the stall where it's cool. Then there is the man who, clearly somewhat ill at ease, perhaps because he doesn't often do the shopping, lets the vendor "slip him" a wedge of brie that's been around too long. It's easy to see that those people over there in a group are campers, that those others are only taking a look around, trying to figure out what they could buy, that the relationship of that pair over there must be rather complicated given the way they have to consult with each other before purchasing a mere head of lettuce, and so on. While standing in line in front of a stand, one seeks almost involuntarily, in a continuous internal monologue, to draw a plausible sketch of one's neighbors. Having details of domestic and even intimate personal life offered up as spectacle this way no doubt accounts in large part for the pleasure most of us take in going to the market, as well as the repulsion of some—agoraphobes, and so unconditional supermarket shoppers.

Not only are you observed at the market, but people don't hesitate to meddle in your affairs. In contrast to a store, it is not considered unseemly to intervene in a verbal exchange between a stallholder and her customer ("I'd get a goat cheese in oil instead") or a family discussion among one's neighbors in line ("We've got a whole garden of green beans, too, and my husband is sick of them!"). The transaction under way, supposedly a private relation between customer and seller, tends on the market to be transformed into a public debate involving all actors present, called upon to confirm, bear witness, give their opinion—like the woman trying on a hat with lace veil at Martin's stand who shyly seeks out the approval of surrounding onlookers. "Forty-nine francs, your asparagus!" sighs one of Boyac's customers, as if the speaker were saying to anyone within hearing, "Doesn't he have a nerve!" and thereby trying to transform her refusal to buy a product too dear for her particular purse into collective recognition that the vendor is charging an abusively high price. The stallholder himself may ask for audience recognition of the quality of his wares ("Aren't they gorgeous, my tomatoes?"), in which case audience silence amounts to consensual consent. The slightest hesitation on the part of a potential buyer can be used to make an appeal to the audience at large: "Aren't you usually well served here?" or "Don't force yourself, there're plenty who like it." The face-to-face relation particular to shops is replaced here by a microgroup in which information, commentary, and knowing winks can be made to circulate. Among actors who do not know each other and very likely belong to highly diverse social milieus, an ephemeral, circumstantial, surface community is formed.

But it cannot be taken for granted that communication will be established among people who do not know anything about each other. There has to be matter for recreating a world on the basis of this elbow-to-elbow anonymity. Here again the stallholder plays the crucial role of stage manager, with his art of conferring a minimum of identity on the customer he's serving or whom he recognizes in line, providing the company with a few indications that allow for recognition without saying anyone's name, as this is almost never done at the market (though it is common practice in city boutiques). Ollivier, a grape grower and *rabassier* when he has the time, is greeted with, "How are things in Bédoin?" The Parisian seen every summer gets a "So vacation's finally here, eh? Lots of people in Saint-Didier!" Likewise Llorca, busy as he is behind his pile of lettuce heads, calls out to Mme. Patio, "You're back then! Must've been hot at Juan-les-Pins."

194

Stallholders may also make a few allusions to a customer's private life: "How's your husband doing? Out of the hospital now?"; "So when is Mireille getting married? They'll surely get married one of these days!" Showing friendly interest like this is a good way for the merchant to distinguish himself from occasional stallholders, make it clear to buyers waiting in line that, like shop owners, he has his regular clientele. In fact they are scraps of information—the kind that neighbors or inhabitants of the same village often share—fed to an anonymous audience. By means of such inconsequential indiscretions, a few features of customers' family lives are made public, just enough to give some substance to their respective "characters."

It might be thought that by announcing what he knows of the customer, the stallholder changes their relation into one of interacquaintanceship. Yet none of those in attendance conclude that a customer so addressed has any kind of private tie to the stallholder. Greeting Ollivier with "How are things in Bédoin?" is a way not of shedding anonymity but of making Ollivier "exist" in the public eye. The utterance cannot be understood if we ignore the fact that it is really made for the next customers, whom the stallholder is trying to hold onto by capturing their attention. It would be particularly misguided to think that his question manifests a relationship external to the market. If the stallholder asked, "So how did the game of *boules* end last night?" he would produce the opposite effect. By mentioning if only allusively an event that he and the customer have both experienced, he would exclude all the others instead of encompassing them. Moreover, when stallholder and customer do indeed have a personal relation, reference is generally not made to it, except in an aside once the exchange is over ("Are you coming over tonight?"), since they can engage in longer conversation only when there are no other customers waiting.

The stallholder's art lies in providing a few personal traits likely to endow the customer with a face and some semblance of identity without anyone's thinking these bits of information have any source other than the market itself. In fact, such information attests only that the relation obtaining between these particular market partners is old, habitual. In no way does it allow listeners to suppose it has originated or developed outside this public time and space. Moreover, because the stallholder is sketching a character for a more or less heterogeneous audience, he has to choose identity features that will mean something to everyone waiting. Even Parisians know where Bédoin is and associate a certain image with the name, that of a scraggly village at the foot of Mont Ventoux. When the owner of the hunting and fishing shop in the Place du Théâtre says to Pons, "So, will your Saint-Didier cherries be ripe soon?" only people who live in the area understand that he is alluding to that dreadful moment of the year when everybody is enlisted to help gather cherries and the market undergoes a dramatic slump in "attendance." But it is also a way of making him into "a local peasant" in the eyes of strangers to these parts.

In the case of a customer about whom the stallholder knows strictly nothing, he still has several means of constructing a fictive but concrete tie within the formally anonymous relation of the exchange. Recourse to a number of stereotypical formulas works to personalize the relation—"It's our turn now," for example, said to distinguish a customer from the collective third party represented by all other people in line—and generates the following type of subtly pragmatic utterance: "And what does *my* little customer want?"; "That'll be twenty-six francs fifty for *us*." The stallholder's ostentatious familiarity means not that he knows the customer, but rather that he attributes to him, accurately or not, the quality of market habitué. The stallholder may also evoke a world that the customer is understood to share with him ("The children are really tan, I see. We went to Costa Brava too") or find a means to relate the customer to his or her domestic life ("Now be sure to start the cutlets in a cold pan. My wife always cooks veal and white meats in a cold pan or oven. That way they stay tender"). The very idea that customer and stallholder could run into each other on the beach at Palafrugell or that their wives could exchange recipes enables a stallholder who has no more detailed information to give a semblance of existence to the customer or at least move him to join in the game: "No, this year we went to Palavas," clarifies a customer. Though the stallholder generally initiates the transformation of the exchange relation into a microsociety, the customers contribute greatly. Often without being invited, a customer offers a few indications that make it possible to place him: "Where did you get your apricots? We don't have any yet in Beaumes," or "Give me five pairs of leather laces—I can never find them in Paris!"

It is never the stallholder's intention to identify the actors, but rather to flesh out characters around which a microscript can be "written." A woman of indeterminate age hesitating before she buys is worked up into a penny-pinching *mémé* [grandma]. The "distinguished gentleman" clearly perplexed in the face of so many different types of lettuce—"So, will it be mesclun, arugula, radicchio, or oakleaf?"—quickly becomes an abandoned husband. If the stallholder is given half a chance to suggest he's a perfect lover ("I've got just what you need, my sweet!"), his lady customer may just be ready to play the woman of easy virtue saddled with the eternal jealous mate. Around a few clichés intelligible to all and using very few words, stallholder and customers improvise a little "boulevard" theater scene for the gallery.

The game has to be played at the least possible cost. People don't tell about themselves; they slip on the mask of an archetypal role. It is appropriate to be brief, as amusement in the waiting-line quickly turns into irritation if the scene drags on. We know the stallholder has to have humor and a light touch, and not go overboard; anyone who does so is swiftly sanctioned. There's nothing inappropriate in a customer's playing the seducer, complimenting the seller on her "beautiful eyes," for example. But if he continues in the same vein when she takes his order ("Have you been told that before, that you've got beautiful eyes?"), the audience groans impatiently: "Hasn't he finished his circus?" The idea that strangers or newcomers have of the supposedly warm, good-natured behavior at a Provençal market often makes them go too far. In trying too hard to follow the tacit rules, they fail to grasp them at all.

When several people go marketing together, they readily expose their little problems publicly, staging family life. "So which do you want," says an exasperated mother, "the one with Zorro or the one with Astérix? Hurry up, you can see everyone's waiting, the gentleman has other things to do!" "Give him a minute to decide, will you? Don't push him like that!" intervenes the commiserating father. When Arnoux, a personality at the *marché-gare*, accompanies his wife on Fridays to the Jardins du Comtat, he never fails to call the vendor to bear witness to his trials and tribulations: "I get zucchini every day—she insists I lose weight!" Faucon, a young, energetic farmer and union leader, plays the martyr husband whose wife drags him along to market to carry the baskets—as he lets the vendor know at every stall they stop at. The North African husband collapsing under piles of Jacky Thevet's linens and apparently resigned to his wife's rash purchases is playing somewhat the same role. In this way, everyone with whom one temporarily coexists in a given space or within hearing becomes the spectator of one's personal misfortunes. But these are actually false confidences. One is showing only a more or less conventional image of self constructed for the circumstances. And no one really believes that the scene is authentic. Conversely, a real domestic quarrel ("I'm sick of the whole family!"; "Listen, if you keep on like that, I'm leaving!") is judged unseemly: "Where do those people think they are? Can't they settle their personal affairs elsewhere?"

The market is thus the occasion for numerous little plays and comedies that people act out for themselves under others' eyes. Buisson, who grows melons near Pernes using state-of-the-art techniques, is only too happy to act the peasant setting foot in the city for perhaps the first time, oohing and aahing over everything in delighted amazement, while his neighbor, from Paris of course but of country origins and fully familiar with the practices of the region, enjoys playing ignorant city boy hungry for explanations: "Oh really? That's a different variety of tomato? How is it different?" People take pleasure in inventing a circumstantial identity for themselves. The Saint-Jaillets, terrorized by their children, overwhelmed with domestic tasks, not to mention the garden, the rain that won't come, and the cherry trees that need trimming, offer a remake of *La Famille Fenouillard* or Tati's *Mister Hulot's Holiday*.[7] In reality they are media figures, always between two flights, and when you go to visit them in their Provençal country house near Saumane, the children are playing well-behavedly in the swimming pool under the watchful eye of "their" *jeune fille au pair*, cool drinks are being served, and the table setting and meal are impeccable. Likewise Pierre Julian, who dines every evening with the celebrated political biographer Jean Lacouture, the novelist and member of the Académie Française Pierre-Jean Rémy, and other Paris-in-the-Lubéron personalities, plays the part of a hermit dug in at the farthest reaches of the Vaucluse plateau who has just come down from his retreat to ensure his survival: "Give me that sausage, it'll last me the week."

Some market habitués visibly enjoy changing roles from one stall to the next, whether those roles are imposed on them or freely chosen. Mme. Levasseur asks Bourget, a "Paris articles" and knickknacks man who regularly sets up in Le Quinconce, if he doesn't have something less expensive: "I just want a little something, it's for a small present," she says—one might almost think she was in financial difficulty. In fact, she wants the vendor to understand she's got her eye on price. Further on, at Bressy's big olive stall, she asks for "volos" or "kalamatas" like a regular connoisseur. At one stall she's the wary housewife; at the next she surrenders all authority, appearing a know-nothing city girl when asking for a "chicken that's not too tough." "The ladies want chicken," comments Milhaud, "but they don't know what a real chicken is, a chicken that runs around. They think they like it, but in fact they don't." She can also play a woman attentive to the tastes of the day who, in a conversation with Annick Ceret, the Indian skirt and dress dealer in the Place aux Oies, deplores city women's lack of imagination: "You can't get them to budge in Carpentras. They've got to have brand names. They go for Marie-France, or pay two thousand francs for Chacok and leave feeling pleased and reassured." At Havart's in the Place de la Mairie, she becomes the self-assured wife and mother: "Give me a ripe saint-marcellin for my husband, for the children I'll take a Caprice des Dieux." Each one of these roles is more or less a part of herself, but the diversity of the circumstantial, public characters obscures her real identity, that of a Parisian who left the capital some years ago to settle in the region and has opened a public letter writer's office, less out of a concern to make a living, she says, than for the pleasure of contact with the "ever so nice people here."

All her roles correspond to typical characters that cannot be identified with any particular social milieu and that everyone immediately recognizes, roles that can be played effortlessly without any "specific habitus." They are just so many rudimentary scripts of the eternal human comedy, which everyone, regardless of milieu, knows how to improvise: the scrupulous female manager of the family budget (the "ant") and the spendthrift coquette ("grasshopper"), the jealous husband, the bullied husband, the unfaithful wife, the city dweller in the country, the submissive spouse, the attentive mother, the kind soul always ready to listen to an account of others' misfortunes, the hardened single man, the "*femme savante*," the disoriented intellectual, the country bumpkin . . . Slight differences between people are stressed and enhanced almost to the point of absurdity, so as to bring to ephemeral life stereotypical figures in whom everyone present can recognize themselves. The logic of this masquerade is never to exclude or pigeonhole, nor to lay claim to a given status or quality. By caricaturing all the little inconveniences in the lives of average human beings, what people are in fact making manifest is how "we are all alike." They stage for themselves a society—a fictive one, of course—composed, or so we are invited to believe, of individuals who are all of a kind.

15. Generalized Friendship

People participate unthinkingly, as a matter of course, in multiple interactions with strangers that allow for the momentary limning of a microsociety around each stall. And when they evoke the "ambiance" of the market, as characteristic as it is undefinable, they are activating a vague memory of those microsocieties. But the pleasure of mingling in the crowd is not a recognized motivation. You don't think you go to the market to enjoy rubbing shoulders with people you don't know anything about and to whom you are indifferent. On the contrary, people say they go there to meet people they know. "There's a physical attraction in going to the market," claims Rousseau. "It's for the joy of meeting up with each other." People always stress this purpose, this end.

"You know in advance you're going to run into people you know," explains Mme. Patio. The city is really not that big and neither is the market. Today she "saw" her sister-in-law there ("Her children are coming to see her this weekend and she's doing a big shopping") and talked for half an hour with a woman friend of hers, principal of the lycée in Brazzaville (Congo): "She's here on vacation and wouldn't miss the market for all the tea in China! When she's in Monteux, it reminds her of her young years, our young years." In this respect, the market does seem to compensate for a certain lack of social life in Carpentras; there are few other occasions or places to keep up relations with people who are outside the circle of family and close friends. And in general I observed a withdrawal into the family circle that stands in contrast to the desire everyone expresses to stand as a model of the famous "Provençal sociability" underscored by historians of the region and promoted to the rank of national value.[1] "We are people of the Midi, open and warm," insists Rousseau.

Here, in contrast to Aix, Avignon, and Apt, there are no big cafés with terraces where everyone gathers as soon as there's any sun. Market and café go together in the standard image foreigners have of a Midi market and Provençal *dolce vita* in the shade of plane trees. In Carpentras, in fact, the *"apéro"* is not a required component of the stroll through the market, not even for men. The city does have a number of small bistros, but each has a clearly defined clientele: *boule* players gather at the *bar-tabac* on Le Quinconce,[2] young people at the Bar de l'Univers or the Rich'Bar in the Place du Théâtre, construction men at the Hôtel du Mont-Ventoux. To these may be added locales for collective leisure activities (tennis club, municipal swimming pool, *boulodrome*); lotto games, organized during the month of December in schools and cafés; and, in another style, the Lions or Rotary Club, where the pharmacist, solicitor, and their friends meet. In the nineteenth century, Carpentras undoubtedly had more gathering places of this sort than now. In 1871 there were more than thirty *cercles*, most of which met in cafés.[3] A few were markedly political; a number of others were for gambling. Some recruited among the working class; "going to the *cercle*" was not reserved for notables.[4]

Customary city festivities (the Saint-Siffrein, the July city fair, and so forth) tend to get moved to the outskirts these days and therefore no longer play the same role in public life. "The Corso [parade], which takes place on the Saturday before Bastille Day, draws lots of people. It's beautiful, but it doesn't come through the city anymore, so everything is closed, completely shut up, and the whole fair takes place outside the city in the Allées Jean-Jaurès, Le Quinconce, Les Platanes," notes Mme. Martinez.

But it should not be concluded from people's retrospective accounts that the Friday market is a sort of open-air social club where everyone goes to meet friends and relatives. It is possible and even likely that one will run into people from one or the other of those categories around Venturi's stall, but this is just as true of the Place de la Mairie on any other weekday, or Auchan on Saturdays. The market is not an occasion for maintaining private-sphere ties, which in any case have no need of such a ceremony. On the contrary, what is specific to the market in my observation is that one treats an old childhood friend and the anonymous person buying leeks ahead of one in line pretty much the same way: in a tone of overt, superficial conviviality.

CHAPTER FIFTEEN

"Running into" a friend on the market does not imply an obligation to reproduce your usual relations. Once you have shown the required marks of affection, you can leave him or her standing there and move on. Nearly every Friday around eleven, when Mme. Patio passes by Saint-Siffrein cathedral, Mme. Arnoud is nearby examining Jojo Spinelli's new stock. Though the relation between the two is one of friendship, Mme. Patio may well do no more than tap her on the shoulder, saying for anyone within hearing, "I'm in a hurry today!" And if a conversation does develop, it is characterized by a freedom of tone it would not have in another context. Mme. Patio may launch into a detailed account of the family news: her daughter Mireille, the one who works for Cacharel, is arriving Sunday from Paris where she had dinner with her cousin, "you know, the one who works at the university. He just got back from Ireland, he often goes for his work . . ." Mme. Arnoud may well cut her off: "By the way, have you seen Mme. Ducros? I haven't seen her in a long time. And her husband? Is he doing better? Is he back teaching *collège* [middle school]?" There follows a long monologue on her own grandchildren's study difficulties, which Mme. Patio abruptly breaks into: "Yes, it's hard these days. Now I've really got to go!" Apparent lack of concern for the other has no consequences here. In any case, the ladies are not there to chat; they have other things to do. They've come to take care of a daily-life obligation, and these "good reasons" are recognized by both. Moreover, however likely it may be for them to run into each other here every week—given their shared habits, the chances are quite high—the meeting was quite unplanned. Because the exchange might very well not have taken place, and nothing obliged them to engage in it, nothing obliges them to conduct it in accordance with convention. They move easily from one subject to another, interrupt each other—even mid-sentence. This behavior is completely different from the way they act when they come together over a cup of tea at Jouvaud's.

Just as one can limit contact with a lifelong friend to a merry tap on the back and three trifling sentences, so one can for an instant establish an apparently intimate relation with someone one doesn't know from Adam. In this case the verbal exchange does not reflect a preexisting tie but establishes one performatively: the fact that I speak to my neighbor in line in front of Mistral's counter makes him or her, quite temporarily, a *connaissance*. People readily open conversations with strangers at the market, or with people they remember having noticed one day at this or that stall. Here people can become familiar immediately, dispense with the preliminaries, as if they already knew each other or were picking up the thread of a conversation interrupted the week before. Elsewhere this would be considered extremely impolite behavior. "The market is familiar," notes Espenon. "People end up knowing each other. They see each other every Friday and they end up talking to each other."

When one shops at the market one is in fact conducting a domestic activity in a public place. Through their purchases and the commentary they elicit everyone exhibits a bit of their *chez soi* to others: "It's true there will be six of us. Give me two more, then." This interpenetration of private and public is both the principle and matter of the familiarity that people show, introducing references to the home world into relations alien to it. The stallholders and various *connaissances* one sees around the stalls have in common the fact that they are outside one's closest circle, but being at the market implies having conversations with them that may well suggest the opposite. This explains the stallholder's perpetual joking intimations that his customers' homes are wide open to him: "The sausage? You'll tell me how it is. I'll come over for the *apéro* this evening!" or "What—you don't like it? Well I'll come over later and ask your husband how he likes it."

Such paradoxical behavior—treating close friends or relatives lightly and strangers as familiars—is characteristic of the market. The same principle is operative in both cases: market relations follow their own rules and give rise to a homogeneous field of interacquaintanceship in which the distinction between one's own kin or set and others becomes blurred. Conversation may be engaged with anyone about virtually anything, while for one's sister-in-law a vague hand sign is enough. It is in this way that a crowd becomes an agora, a market a public social space.

We see what it means, then, to "meet people" at the market. Hidden beneath the vagueness of the expression is a highly characteristic practice, though one the actors would have a hard time defining; a sort of generalized "market friendship," in the warmth of which relations normally kept distinct are temporarily combined. "Meeting people" at the market is not so much maintaining otherwise well-established relations as "meeting *lots* of people" ("I go to meet people, you know, whomever—because I never know who I'm going to meet," says Mme. Patio); it involves the instating of a kind of energetic, omnidirectional sociability for a few hours and within given spatial limits. People start or continue a market relation with a highly disparate set of *connaissances* ranging from dearest or close friends and family to total strangers and including persons one knows only by sight, by name, by hearsay and with whom one would ordinarily exchange nothing more than a quick meeting of the eyes or head movement. The point is to greet the highest possible number of persons, and each encounter is an opportunity for evoking all those that might take place; that is, asking each "friend" for news of all the others. In this connection the stallholders play an important role—all the more willingly because it's good business strategy. One can ask a stallholder for news of all the people one hasn't seen that day, thus enabling him or her to perpetuate multiple bundles of once-a-week relations, though this may involve including people one knows only from having glimpsed them at the stand several Fridays in a row, as if being customers of the same stallholder created as strong a tie as playing soccer together or having spent several months guarding the same peak in the Aurès mountains.[5]

Friendship at the market is not only broadly extended but ostentatious and effusive. Every encounter is the occasion for warm exclamations, affective overflow in the form of loud cries, explosions of joy or surprise ("How do you like that!"). Words are accompanied with gestures: shoulder slaps, arm grabbing, hugging of children, and so on. People hail each other from a distance, across the street over the heads of the crowd in voices loud enough to be heard above the bustle, or across the space of the stall. "These people haven't seen each other for a week," explains Espenon; "then all of a sudden, boom, they meet each other. That gets them talking—let me tell you! They ask for news of the children, the grandma, everyone." The conversation is carried out in voices so loud that the people nearby are implicitly invited to follow, willingly or not, the news of a bedridden grandfather or the most recent addition to someone's family. And a listener who joined in would not be frowned on. Friendship is publicly exhibited at the market. On the contrary, it would be unseemly to seem to be protecting oneself against others' indiscretion or intrusion, as if one had a secret.

This demonstrativeness is not meant to distinguish true friends from others but rather to treat with equal familiarity one's sister-in-law, the gas station attendant, the winemaker from Flassan from whom one buys one's rosé once a year; i.e., to bring together relations of extremely different statuses under an avalanche of equivalent signs of affection. Effusive greetings at the market therefore do not reflect relations as established outside it. They are self-referential; they signify "the market"; the fact that one is at the market and behaving as one should by establishing "market relations" with "a pile of people," relations that are not actualized elsewhere, or not in the same way. The market authorizes a broader, blurrier sort of sociability, one that overflows the private sphere. Nearly every week one "sees" people there that one would not have to one's house. For wives it is the occasion to maintain relations independently of husbands, relations sometimes external to the social milieu in which the couple usually moves. "I have a whole bunch of friends here," says Mme. Ayme, "but I wouldn't see them at the house. I see them outside, and often I meet them at the market. I say to myself, well, why not go to the market for a bit, and I meet a whole bunch of people." Likewise Mme. Patio readily presents Mme. Arnoud and that woman who's come from Caromb to sell a few snails, mushrooms, and other "little things" as "friends"; in fact, she sees them almost exclusively at the market, though on listening to what she says in situ one might believe there was real closeness.

It is significant that the Patios, like Rousseau and his wife, prefer going to the market separately. Each one has his/her own network of *connaissances*, as independent of spouse's sympathies as they are of the social proprieties, networks without any necessary extension beyond the market. For Rousseau the former canner, well known in Carpentras, the market is the opportunity to run into "produce brokers. They come around the market in winter, because in the high season they don't have time," but also to maintain still looser ties with farmers of the region, his former suppliers. The simple fact of encountering them in the street, sometimes without speaking—"I meet people I know. I don't necessarily stop, but I know them"—is a way of maintaining bridges and keeping alive the possibility of renewing relations at some later time.

The specific nature of a "market encounter" is that it commits one to nothing. This is because it is both fortuitous—no date or appointment was made—and likely: there is a good chance it will happen again the following Friday. (In the case of its being utterly unexpected, it will have to be celebrated one way or another, which creates an obligation that is either accepted immediately—"Let's celebrate this!"—or deferred: "We'll call each other.") But the noncommittal nature, the extraordinary freedom enjoyed by partners to such a relation, also consists in each one's knowing that it is not to be continued outside the present context. Relations of apparent friendship can be established with people whom in other circumstances one would hardly greet. Mme. Roux, for example, sees her neighbor Mme. Vincent every day. When they run into each other in the entrance or corridors of their apartment building or its immediate surroundings, they throw out a few words in passing, the minimal signs of mutual recognition that politeness requires. But when they see each other at the market they hurry toward each other and commence a real conversation—which in turn will not prevent them from greeting each other with a mere nod on the landing or at the bakery the next day. The market is an opportunity to treat a relation that is otherwise more distant or formal in a mode of "warm affability," without actually transforming it. What happens in this "world apart" has no future. The hugs and busses of a Friday morning do not preclude people's limiting themselves to a distant *petit bonjour* in the Auchan aisles on Saturday.

By the same logic, one can temporarily transform into an apparently personal tie a relation that is in fact institutional or professional. One exchanges courtesies with the "little one's" teacher, congratulates the plumber on his many children ("So they're all yours!"). Waiting one's turn at the Jardins du Comtat, one jokes with the car mechanic's wife, but doesn't forget to call out in parting, "Tell your husband not to forget me!" Likewise, one may use an unexpected encounter at the market ("When you've no need to meet a particular person, there's always a good chance you'll meet them there!") to make a request, which appears less pressing precisely because in this informal context no commitments need be made. "We'll wait until Friday to see my friend from Caromb," suggests Mme. Patio. "That way we can ask her to introduce you to the truffle-hunting lady."

The principle of these market encounters is the gratuitousness of the conversations, by which I mean that most of them are without real object and have no other end but the pleasure of conversing.[6] When Mme. Ayme slips out of her place of work, the Bibliothèque Inguimbertine, at ten o'clock of a Friday morning, she regularly exchanges a few words with all the "market friends" she meets on her way through. In the company of Mme. Lacoste, a history teacher at the Monteux middle school who is often at the library working on her thesis on votive plaques in the Comtat, she frets about "the children," who are "worrying these days." Stopping two minutes to say hello to Mme. Maury, the pharmacist, she deplores the fact that in our times "there are no longer any seasons" and "one doesn't know how to dress." To Mme. Miège, who runs the *tabac* near the bird market, she says, "Will you be leaving soon? One has to take a bit of a break, a vacation. Last year we went to . . ."

At the market one speaks of everything and nothing, the weather, the rain, which is late arriving, the rheumatism that comes too soon, the quality of artichokes this year, and so on. Georg Simmel showed how, in situations of "purely sociable conversation," "this objective element is brought in not for the sake of its content but in the interest of sociability."[7] Speaking can be an end in itself, but what is said must also work to maintain the tie. This is the special value of banalities, clichés, fixed expressions, all those utterances whose content has "no weight in itself" and is therefore likely to be common to all. They make it possible to establish an ephemeral relation of unconstrained sociability with a high number of actors "known" to very different degrees.

Though communication may first be established on a meteorological basis (X: "There certainly are a lot of people today." Y: "Not surprising given the weather!") or a culinary one (X: "Is it the roma [tomatoes] that are good in a salad?" Y: "Oh no, I always use the *marmande*"), it quickly takes a more personal turn. What works to make relations with the post office clerk or little Paul's mother, whom one sees only when school lets out, and even with the Parisian whom one stands next to for five minutes at Mme. Bressy's olive stand, comparable to longstanding relations is the fact that we all apparently have no secrets from each other. From the commonplaces that have been used to open dialogue, one slips quickly to half confidences. This may be done on the basis of what is observable of the other ("Your children look like they've just gotten off the ski slopes!"), though in that case one must be ready to produce one's own story right away ("My kid couldn't go, he had the mumps"). Or you may take the first step, showing that you and your interlocutor are *entre nous* by communicating a detail of your private life without divulging anything important, in a way that elicits same from her or him.

In this potlatch of confidences, the tone must remain "not too serious." People speak of themselves so readily only because nothing important is being revealed. The tragic becomes trivial if mentioned while you are trying to decide between the hake and the coalfish or between two different pairs of shoes at Perdiguier's. The daughter's divorce and the brother-in-law's bankruptcy, alluded to in front of Gardiol's and his display of thrush and pheasant, momentarily lose their status of private disasters and join the common lot of earthly misfortunes and local human-interest stories.

The regime of pseudoconfidences is such that none of the partners expects the other to be really interested. When another's misfortune is mentioned, therefore, one does not feel obligated to manifest much emotion. A readymade expression levels the event, subjects it to the verdict of the wisdom of nations, and suffices to express the requisite compassion: "What can you do? One can only accept these things"; "Life isn't always a bowl of cherries"; "Ah, how little we amount to!" and so on. I was struck with how frequently such remarks may be heard on the market. They are appropriate to situations in which private-sphere events are mentioned when there is no real closeness, and in this they are characteristic of the language of sellers, who must show sympathy without prolonging the other customers' wait.

Exclusive use of banalities and clichés can of course become a means of establishing "distanced communication," to use Gérard Althabe's term. This is the case in common spaces (apartment buildings or workplace stairways, cloak-rooms, and so on), where it is fitting to be friendly without engaging in an exchange that could have any effect on people's sense of their official statuses. In my observation, this does not hold in situations such as markets or cafés. One is never really obliged to speak to anyone in those places; the multiple relations are engaged in voluntarily. People are there to act as if they had something in common, if only the same shared, public space.

By confining themselves to commonplaces, people delimit an area of understanding in which social distinctions become secondary. Faced with the small worries of daily life or the uncertainties of the weather, a momentary identification with the other is possible, one that transcends social milieu and usual lifestyle distinctions. Remaining at the level of commonsense generalities means people need not note the fact that the situations they are referring to are strongly dissimilar. Mme. Delavigne, for example, whose son is at the Lycée Louis-le-Grand in Paris studying mathematics to prepare for admission to a *grande école*, agrees with Mme. Fratini, wife of a fairly modest produce shipper, that "the *concours* period is really hard!"[8] "Mine too is looking pale," answers the latter mother about her son, candidate at the Avignon Ecole de fruits et de légumes. A bit further on, at Avétant's, Mme. Delavigne says to Arthur, officially apprenticed to the grocer and living in his boss's attic:

"I didn't see you last week. Were you sick?"

"I was doing some work in the house, I'm insulating the attic."

"Really? What are you putting in? You don't want to use the wrong thing. It's true that those things cost money, but it's worth it. We're going to have to think about it for our house, too."

Health, the garden or the house, cooking, household chores, children—all are fitting subjects for acting as if you were speaking of the same thing. The eggplant gratin at Venturi's stall, for example, is an object of discussion and debate ("So you sauté them first! I always salt and drain them") in which Mme. Saint-Jaillet speaks as one expert housewife among others ("At home we like them best in ratatouille"), though she is in fact quite dependent on the talents of the Portuguese woman who has been cooking at her house for years. Likewise, rising prices and the cost of living elicit comments from consumers who are equally vigilant if unequally fortunate.

If we pay attention to their content, what all these market conversations have in common is the fact of being both banalities and a series of pseudoconfidences. Everyone speaks of their private world, which the market seems a continuation of, but they limit themselves to commonplaces, those components of personal experience that can be shared by all and therefore neither exclude anyone nor point to hierarchical situation. While seeming to reveal things about one's private life to the other, one in fact communicates only partial, selected information in such a way as to give him or her the impression that what happens at "my house" is identical to what happens at his or hers. The behavioral logic at issue here is not as Goffman describes in *The Presentation of Self in Everyday Life*. Elements entirely unrelated to the scene under way are introduced here not to modify the self-image one gives the other, but rather to create a common ground on which limited, repeated identifications can be established. The pseudoconfidence regime fictively abolishes the boundaries of the private sphere. Since what happens *chez soi* is so similar to what happens *chez l'autre*, we must all be very similar. For a few hours, we constitute a world of the alike.

PART FIVE

Identity on Offer

For habitué actors, "going to market" does not merely mean filling one's shopping bag while glancing with amusement at the knickknacks the Senegalese are selling or listening for a moment to Jacky Thevet's imperturbable patter. As we have seen, it also means behaving in a certain way. The social form of market exchange involves manifesting equal familiarity with all those one meets in the tiny worlds that ephemerally come into being at each stall, where each exhibits to all something of his or her domestic life. It goes without saying that differences in social position are not effaced or forgotten. Peasants, bourgeois, immigrants remain who they are, each "doing the market" in their own way. No one really believes they are among equals, but behaving "as if" is a way of affirming that we are "among ourselves." And the reason people are willing to ignore each other's social identities is that each expects the other to recognize his or her *local* identity.

Everybody Mme. Ripert meets while buying her red mullet at the Porte d'Orange or her vegetables in the Place de la Mairie participates with her in the unfolding of this weekly municipal and regional ceremony. It is because of this, and by implicit convention, that she agrees not to take into account everything that makes them different from her: social status, cultural milieu, occupation, lifestyle, tastes. Just as at an exceptional family gathering (wedding, burial, and so on) people pretend in the name of a sort of circumstantial kinship to be just as interested in the old alcoholic uncle buried in debt as in the brother-in-law who has "been so successful in marketing" and was just honored with a long article in the weekly magazine *L'Express*, so at the market Mme. Ripert seems to pay as much friendly attention to the mechanic at the garage on the highway to Avignon as to the radiologist in the Rue de la Sous-Préfecture. The "generalized friendship" particular to the market is both conditioned by and gives rise to an affirmation, at least for the occasion, of shared membership in *place*.

Such mutual recognition, by which everyone present is encompassed in the category "people from here," establishes a neutral space in which hierarchies can be playfully reversed—the worker invites his boss for a drink—or people can affect to ignore them: the road repairman appears to be a close friend of the solicitor. One can also, thanks to ambivalent, ambiguous signs, reaffirm these hierarchies in denying them. When Rousseau, descendant of one of the city's most illustrious families, takes his turn through the market near the end of the morning, he stops for a moment to greet the stallholders he knows. But by extending his *left* hand over the counter, a sign of distant familiarity, he effects a subtle compromise between the usual handshake and market custom, which is not to shake hands at all. Limits may even be transgressed here that could not be anywhere else. Mohammed has been working for five years at Raybaud's in Caromb. Raybaud provides housing for two laborers, both North African, in a building close to his house, maintaining cordial but distant relations with them, conscious of a cultural difference between them, which he enjoys evoking with his "colleagues" from the *marché-gare*: "You can imagine how mine, with their Ramadan business . . ." Whereas ordinarily everyone keeps to their own living space and relations are limited to work, on market day everything changes. When Mohammed and his boss run into each other at the market they greet each other effusively, and to celebrate the event, Mohammed invites Raybaud for an aperitif at the Bar du Théâtre. On market day, Mohammed and Raybaud become cousins well met, treating each other to a round.

16. "Do you still make those little *caillettes* of yours?"

The market is the local event of the week. Regardless of how much or little one enjoys it, and despite the fact that, as we know, the prices are not particularly attractive, the market is like a religious service that one really must not miss. "It's the Friday religion," as the mayor of Mollans, a hamlet north of Mont Ventoux, explained to me. Unthinkable not to go, if only to purchase two tiny goat cheeses—the week would lose its meaning if one didn't go, if one hadn't been there. The market is therefore much more than a business arrangement. Auchan enables a massive, diversified population to gather regularly, but the reason people come from all over on Saturdays to this soulless warehouse on the edge of an interminable parking lot is only that they are at leisure to do their shopping that day. Auchan crowds are the result of a series of independent, individual decisions in which "rational" consumer interest ("You can find everything there for less") combines with the desire for a family outing.

The market, on the other hand, is not only a collective provisioning post but a powerful experience around which everyone's life to some degree revolves, a real public institution. In the case of rural inhabitants this is hardly surprising; the market in the neighboring city has traditionally occupied an essential place in country life. "My parents went to the Friday market at Carpentras all their lives," relates Espenon. "When they didn't go because somehow they didn't have time or it was harvest time, we heard about it all week: 'We don't know what day it is, we didn't go to Carpentras Friday!'; 'I don't know if it's Sunday or Monday, I don't know what I'm doing anymore.' We got ready for it the day before. You had the list of stops to make: we have to go to this one to buy that, to the other one to buy this. When I was a kid, I remember, there weren't many cars in the region. My father had one, the schoolteacher had one, there were four or five cars in the village and they carried almost the whole village to market. People would come looking for us the day before: 'Are you going to the market tomorrow? Will you have room for me?' 'No, I'm full, but go see Mouras, he's probably got room.' Nine times out of ten they all worked on Sundays, but on Fridays a bomb could drop—we were going to the market!" Growers hardly have time to stroll through the market in summer now, and the important moment of their social life is more likely to be the exclusively male, extradomestic, near-daily gathering on the asphalt square of the *marché-gare*. But some family member is always available to go to market.

The Friday ceremony also structures the week of the pseudo-country folk who take up summer quarters in the old houses outside the city. Marketgoing is a moment of intense activity in their idle daily lives. Starting in June, visitors to the market are to a large degree "internal foreigners." Concerned to follow local practices, they understand regular market attendance to be the duty of a good Comtadine. At Mme. Delavigne's in Pierrelongue, on the other side of Mont Ventoux, "we spend our time doing nothing," as she herself puts it. The days slip by peacefully in the huge house looking out onto the Ouvèze river where the family gathers for vacation. One does *point de croix* embroidery, discovers fabric stenciling, patches up Moustier faience plates, restores *restanques* [drystone walls], and tends to the medicinal plants in the garden. Apart from a weekly visit to the supermarket at Vaison, food shopping is done at the village grocery. But on Friday mornings there's to be none of the usual lingering at the breakfast table in the shade of the lime trees over big bowls of Leroux chicory drink and those thick slices of bread spread with the neighbor's honey that the children find so hard to get down—we mustn't be late to the market. In the general rush, the passing guest is told how important this event is. Before 9 a.m. the old station wagon full of adults and children is heading down the driveway.

As for the people of Carpentras, they readily tell you that "the others"—"vacationers" or inhabitants of the surrounding villages—are the real market loyalists. In reality, however, it is rare for city dwellers not to go at all, whatever their age or social milieu. M. Patio explains: "For the peasants, it's an ancestral way. They automatically get into the car and come from all around the city to take a turn through the market." But his wife confides that her husband never misses his Friday "promenade," the eternal excuse for which, as we know, is to purchase olives in the Place de la Mairie.

"One does wonder why a customer comes five or six kilometers to buy two frankfurters from us," remarks the *charcutier* at the Porte d'Orange, clearly stumped by my questions. The enthusiasm cannot be explained, as in the case of Auchan, by the convenience of the shopping arrangement. The distance between market and parking should itself be dissuasive. The fact is that on Friday mornings in the streets of the old city, people come together to participate in one and the same event, and each person, by his or her action—buying leeks, browsing at the secondhand clothing stands, exchanging three words with the mail carrier or the deputy mayor—helps constitute the event as such, whereas at Auchan people are brought together by pure statistical determinism, like vacationers stuck at the tollbooth on the freeway to Montélimar on the first of August. Instead of mere coexistence among actors concurrently engaged in the same activity, what develops here resembles an agora, the combining in a specific space and time of a surface sense of equality and a collective identity. The Friday fête, self-celebration of a circumstantial community, breaks up domestic and occupational routines, suspends statuses and rules, bringing a throng of citizens, temporarily detached from their private worlds and freed from ordinary social hierarchies, into the street for a few hours.

It goes without saying that one has to be part of this regular, exceptional moment that punctuates the public time of the polis. For the space of a morning, the market brings a single community into existence, a tiny *patrie* made up of market regulars all assumed to be of the city or its environs. On that day there are nothing but (real or fake) Comtadines doing their marketing. The market is the place where the public body of "people from these parts," with its blurred contours but strong identity, represents itself to itself. At the market people prove to themselves and demonstrate to others that they are indeed "from here."

While most of the sorts of behavior I have heretofore described create a specific social space, they are also a way for the actors to let each other know that they are "of the area" or claim to be. Market conversations, with their stream of commonplaces and pseudoconfidences, are also laden with references purporting to attest to close familiarity with the place and its traditions, shared experience of the "small true facts" out of which daily collective life is woven—authentic rootedness. First there is the accent, which, though not particular to Carpentras, is an immediately recognizable minimal sign. At the market, people who don't ordinarily have the *accent du Midi* (or have lost it) exhibit at least a touch of it. People also enjoy liberally dotting their conversation with idiomatic expressions more or less perceived as such—"Well, I'll let you go, leave you to *bader* [Provençal: admire or gape] at your ease"; "Shall I *plie* [fold] your eggs for you?"—or apparently banal or familiar phrases followed by the words "as we say *chez nous*": "That one wears his heart on his hand, as we say *chez nous*."

Places may be designated in such a way as to create the same effect. A monument that no longer exists serves as a reference point (Perdiguier is said to be at "Porte Notre-Dame") as may a declining sector of the market ("Let's meet at the bird market") or a sector that is no more ("You'll find that near the *marché aux vendanges*"). Instead of street name, people give the name of a well-known shop on the street: "You can get tea biscuits near Coissard's" (the photographer in the Rue de la Porte-d'Orange); "The cap seller is on the Place de Vallabrègue" (the speaker thereby substituting a fabric merchant for Bishop d'Inguimbert). Any conversation is an excuse to put forward shared knowledge of regional geography: "You ask if they're good, my cherries? How could they not be—they're from Saint-Didier!" (where there's a cherry market); "Don't tell me you don't have any more—I've come all the way from Murs to get some from you!"

People readily situate themselves in local time. "Plenty of *posticheurs* today—you'd think it was the Saint-Siffrein!" cries Doctor Brun in passing. "I used to buy flowers at the market when they were still at the Mairie," says Mme. Martinez, who considers Les Platanes too far away. People date past events or memories in reference to other events that only local folk could know of: "The last time I had thrush?" answers Mme. Coste at Gardiol's. "Well, that's easy, it was right when Charretier was elected." Lamenting the ills of the present, which Carpentrassians readily do, is also a means of evoking bygone practices: "There's not enough time today just to not do anything," says Mme. Barrau at Venturi's stall. "People eat differently than before. They don't eat chard or spinach anymore—chard and spinach take too long to sort. They don't even make *fritado* [ratatouille]." The eternal comments on the weather are also an occasion to mention old local customs: "We've got to have some rain if we're to put one or two in the Christmas turkey" (only real Comtadines know the reference is to truffles). These allusions, difficult for a stranger to decipher, function like passwords; people use them to let each other know they are indeed "*entre soi*."

"Internal strangers," i.e., neo-Comtadines who have settled in Provençal country houses in the region (and who in some cases have been there a long while), Lubéron Parisians or Ventoux Britons in search of an identity, also use these self-identification tactics, though often they are more laborious about it, multiplying allusions that let it be understood that they "know" as much "about that" as an old-time Comtadine. They don't want apricots, but Beaumes apricots; they decline asparagus that is not from Velleron; and potatoes should be from Barbentane if possible. When one's neighbor in line cannot decide between several varieties of olive, a neo-Comtadine hurries forward to advise: "I always take the *cassés* [cracked ones], they're the best." If need be, one unloads on one's interlocutor the recipe for *tapenade* that one has just read in "the Reboul," the bible of Provençal cooking. [1]

It is of course not easy to show one is "in everyone's good graces here" when the natives don't really know you. But it is out of the question to look like an anonymous consumer. People have to recognize you. A good tactic if you've nothing better is simply to act as if you were already known. "Keep three of them for me, as usual," cries a customer striding by a goat cheese vendor, who can only answer politely, "Which ones do you like again? The dry ones?" A famous variety show host insists that the olive merchant use the familiar form with him, as if the two had worn out their breeches together on a school bench in Saint-Saturnin or Entraigues. Or else people play at being regulars, saying to the stallholder, "You weren't here last week!" or asking the *charcutier*, "Do you still make those little *caillettes* of yours?" By laboring to look like a well-known customer, you ultimately become one.

In sum, one says whatever might let the company know that one is from these parts, or nearly so—it's only the accent you lack—so as to persuade oneself of the fact through the illusion created for others. People go to the market to endow themselves with ties to the locale, to the local—to give themselves roots. These days, when everyone is somewhat from all over, doesn't one need to be from somewhere in order to be someone? Given that for locals of whatever duration the market is the heart of local life, going there is the best way of manufacturing yourself a bit of Comtadine genealogy.

Every Friday, Jean-Michel Duval, ill shaven and wearing an old straw hat, comes down in his SUV from his retreat above Venasque, accompanied by his spaniel, his wife in a wide woolen skirt and white ankle socks, and their brood, raised as true Comtadines, to whom the village school owes its survival. All wear rough, heavy canvas jackets; their complexions have been burnished by the healthy mountain air. Duval, once a star reporter, is now a self-countrified writer who has shaped himself into a specialist of little-known features of Provence and the virtues of life close to nature. He teaches his readers what nettle and wild leeks can be used for, what to do with bedraggled lilies or overripe peaches. Thanks to the local grocer's husband, who is also the fire chief, Duval found and purchased an old sheep stable overgrown with brambles at the end of an utterly impracticable road. Working with his "chum" the village mason, "a superb *rabassier*," he has patiently rehabilitated it, reconstructing collapsed *bories* [drystone shepherd shelters] and restoring vaulted chambers. Today he and his family live the rough life of the peasants of old, cooking in the hearth, perpetually chasing chickens out of the kitchen, harvesting big, bitter radishes and Jerusalem artichokes from their vegetable garden, putting up jars of tomatoes and eggplant for the winter. And he never misses the *pastis* hour. In sum, today he feels himself a native of the land.

Duval relates how, when he first settled here over twenty years ago—in a blessed age when the Vaucluse plateau was still nearly empty, when bread was baked in wood-burning ovens and people made their own honey and wild plum brandy, cured their own meats, were relatively self-sufficient—an old peasant driving a small swaying van took him down to the market one day. On that day he felt he had been adopted. Old César has since died, but the market remains one of those places where Duval can feel he has become a native. In the midst of his solitary hectares, within the whitewashed walls of his drystone house, surrounded by his time-patined wooden furniture, he cultivates an aesthete's existence, dividing his time between writing and performing household tasks as if they were so many works of art. A far cry from the busy peasants of today bolting down dishes from the Auchan frozen food section in their formica kitchens and planning a vacation in the Canary Islands with a financial advisor from the Crédit Agricole. And on Fridays he can at last lead the life that local people lead. More than the local café, the game of *boules*, or all the other places where he could only be considered a stranger trying to look as if he knows what's what, the market, typical, regular manifestation of Comtadine life, is for him the occasion to fuse with the place, to be at last a full-fledged actor.

At the market he is in his element. Here he has mastered operations, knows from experience exactly how to behave. Just as at home he's the one who chooses the menu, who knows that sage goes better with pork than thyme, who turns over the *daube* meat in the marinade and bastes it every hour and goes out to the straw-carpeted rack in the shed to select a few perfectly ripened figs for the meal, so at the market he knows exactly where to buy his smoked lard, what onions will go best with the tomatoes ("Give me *cébettes*" [variety of green onion]), and that it's too late in the season for squash. Though his purchases this Friday are for a particular dish—he has promised his publisher to make *farcis,* an assortment of vegetables, zucchini, eggplant, tomatoes, and red peppers, stuffed with a ground pork filling—he never misses the chance to stop at Reynaud's for a few sausages ("The smoked ones are for the fava bean soup") and say a few words to Jeanjean, whether or not he needs seeds for the vegetable garden. "Let's go say hello to Monsieur Jeanjean," he says to the children, as if to inculcate one of the discreet rituals that distinguish authentic people "from here."

Every Friday Duval goes to buy a few dry beans from Mme. Bressy and show himself a loyal customer. "Your chickpeas were a bit hard last time," he tells her, "though come to think of it, that may be due to our water." His words indicate to anyone who knows how to interpret them that he has made the regional culinary traditions his own: pulse vegetables were the basic food of Comtat peasants a century ago, before the canal was constructed and irrigation practiced. Likewise he never forgets to buy a little "grating cheese"—"for the *aigo boulido* [garlic soup with bread]," he specifies, recalling thereby that this rather forgotten soup is regularly made in his house—together with almonds and walnuts: "a feast in the evening by the fire." In the Place de l'Horloge he purchases a few anchovies for a salad dressing of the sort made in the country while recounting to the general audience that he would never buy the butter lettuce or romaine you see at the market these days: highly preferable are the purslane and chicory he gathers beside country paths by the rising moon.

Duval makes it known at every turn that not just the market but the area as a whole no longer hold any secrets for him. He asks the melon merchant if "they're hillside grown yet" and specifies he wants "split ones." At the herb and spice stand he buys cinnamon sticks for the mulled wine (the herbs, of course, he picks on his solitary hikes), while engaging the merchant in a conversation reserved for the initiated: "So your lime-blossom tea comes from the market in Buis! I haven't been there in years. I remember a big bald fellow who always brought in an enormous quantity—you probably know him . . ."

The only people entirely precluded from using the market this way are ab-solute strangers—i.e., passing tourists, who are not so much market actors as curious observers. The distance implied by their position precludes their identifying themselves with the place. At best, those who are sensitive to its picturesque features represent the market as the emblem of Carpentras, like

Carnival in Rio or the Palio in Siena, an event to be added to their set of memory-souvenirs. "There are fewer things here than at Vintimille last year," invariably notes the camper staying at Pernes-Plage (a manmade swimming pond), or "It's more expensive than Auchan." The slightly more knowledgeable tourist, whose itinerary includes Senanque, the Vasarely Foundation in Gordes, and Sade's châteaux, will, like all good ethnographers, find the spectacle of the market inimitably unique without being able to define it by other means than a series of comparative statements; e.g., "There's not the same ambiance in Vaison." He may try to gather a fuller impression of the place by participating in the market game, diligently, somewhat clumsily. He may try to capture a whiff of the city's spirit by buying hard candies or scrupulously taking down the recipe for *morue en raito* [fried cod in red wine sauce] as dictated by the "local products" merchant in the Rue de l'Evêché.

CHAPTER SIXTEEN

17. In the Forebears' Footsteps

People go to market as natives, then, or because they would like to be taken for such. They are there neither by chance nor by necessity. They make it a duty to go, a bit as they might feel obligated to attend a distant cousin's wedding: not going would be like renouncing a certain identity. By buying salsify at Venturi's and a screwdriver at Espenon's mobile shop, they prove to themselves and others that they have roots, that they are not merely a "consumer of mass produced goods" who buys the same products at Auchan, the same as may be found in Bordeaux or Lille.

For the people of Carpentras, but also for the most thoroughly initiated strangers, going to the market means situating oneself within a local history, laying claim to a tradition that one feels oneself to be the repository of. This is why people recount their trips to the market with such passion or lyricism, transfiguring the institution of daily life into a genuine monument. I was surprised by the enthusiasm my curiosity elicited. I had only to begin a conversation with the question, "Do you go to the market on Fridays?" for people to respond with a constructed argument on the importance of the event, as if everyone considered it their citizen's duty to initiate me into what they held to be an essential moment of local culture.

Rousseau more than any other seemed to feel invested with this mission. I met him at the very beginning of my stay. I had just started explaining to a secondhand dealer in the neighborhood known as the Observance that I was beginning a study of the Carpentras markets when a man about fifty, with white hair, dark complexion, small moustache, and a blue suit, hurried up and declared, "I'm the person you need. No one here knows the market better than me." It was so. In addition to being a Carpentras market faithful like everyone else, he had regularly attended all the many markets in the region as part of his profession.

If only because he belongs to a very old family, Rousseau is a worshiper of tradition. He immediately took me on a scholarly tour of Saint-Siffrein, then to see the now fairly dilapidated home his forebears had lived in until the nineteenth century. In passing he showed me where the ghetto and the Porte Juive had been: "One of my forefathers did a painting of it—it's in the museum." I went to see him several times in his huge house on Le Quinconce, just beyond the heavy city gates, where he has lived since he was born. For our interviews he opened the capacious, usually shuttered salon on the ground floor, where no object has been moved since his parents' death. Sitting in a Louis XIV armchair upholstered in slightly faded damask and nibbling cookies from a plate on a small table, I listened to his detailed, carefully prepared accounts of developments in packing techniques, canning procedures, and the history of measuring systems. But the conversation often took a more personal turn, as when Rousseau evoked his great-grandfather Casimir, founder of the family canning plant, or his cousins from Apt—"We've been marrying at Apt for generations in our family, and in the summer we organize an afternoon tea attended some years by more than a hundred fifty persons"—and his great-great-uncle Auguste, the first in the region to have had the idea of planting truffle oaks; at the World's Fair he presented the finest specimens "grown" on their estate at Pous-du-Plan. The estate is just two kilometers from the city center; today the municipal swimming pool is on it. With the arrival of the warm weather, the entire household moves there, still transporting silverware and linens with them as in olden days. In his piously preserved memories of this *domaine*, which has been in the family for three centuries, the entire history of the radical changes in farming and their effects on the Comtat landscape is brought back to life.

Rousseau also related to me the major upset in his life. Ten years earlier the family business had declined so dramatically that he had to close it. Today he leases the space—just beneath his windows—to the Intermarché supermarket. Their canning factory was among the oldest and best known in the city, and virtually everyone had worked "*chez Rousseau*": "As soon as the season came, the women would stay home waiting to be called. No more than twenty-five or thirty years before, the town crier was still sent through the city to recruit personnel. 'Women needed at Rousseau's!' was the announcement. Our female personnel were very attached to us. They wouldn't have dreamed of working for another concern."

Late on Friday mornings, after receiving a number of country people, Rousseau takes his turn through the market. He is not shopping; he is walking in the footsteps of his forebears, performing a genuine ceremony whose structure is as elaborate as his account of it.

> The Friday market is a very old institution. It was decided by the pope several centuries ago, and it was very active. All the people from the countryside came, from neighboring *communes* [cities, villages, hamlets] and even remote ones. Some brought their own products, essence of lavender, cheeses. People came from Sault, Murs—fairly far away—to sell their products. Others, farmers, winemakers, came to Carpentras on Fridays even if they didn't have anything in particular to do there. In olden days the flower market was in the Place d'Inguimbert. Curiously, this square was nicknamed Place aux Oies [geese] because of the two fountains with swans on them. Today it takes place here, at Les Platanes. It's very lively and colorful, very nice . . . After that I generally go along the Rue de la Porte-de-Mazan. I very rarely buy any food. I don't buy anything in fact—my wife does the shopping. As for me, on Friday mornings I stay out late—it's an old habit. I mostly go out and about the city, to stroll, breathe in the bustle—this city is so pleasant and lively. After the Rue de la Porte-de-Mazan, I usually take a turn through the Place de la Mairie; there are always a few fishmongers, cheese and olive sellers, food vendors mostly, all the way to Les Petites Halles. At the Porte d'Orange, there are two or three fishmongers full of courage and constancy, there in the draft, selling their fish in freezing weather when the mistral blows hard and cold. On the Place du Palais, it's a profusion of clothes. This is where the four main streets of Carpentras intersect; this is where you meet up with the city's important figures and notables. If you continue toward the southern exit, you run into the Africans selling jewelry, and a few young men and girls selling knickknacks and nice but utterly nondescript jewelry. Then you move into the Rue de la République as far as the Place de l'Hôpital and you run into the pastor who sells Bibles and a hawker selling textiles. He's been coming for around twenty years, a very talented salesman—he could sell anything. I always stop a minute to appreciate his talent. After that, if need be, I go by the Société Générale [bank], and I'm back home as noon strikes or a quarter of an hour later. On Friday mornings, as I told you, the city is always in a state of jubilation, and it's been that way for centuries. The market is always attractive here, even in this age of cosmonauts, supersonic airplanes, what have you. There's always activity and human warmth in this old city market.

Rousseau of course occupies a very particular position in the city. On the one hand he considers himself a notable, and important figures readily make an appearance at the market in Carpentras, a thing not done in all small cities. It is an ordinary occurrence to meet up with the solicitor or a high town magistrate, and market habitués would consider it odd not to see Rousseau making his rounds. On the other hand, as mentioned, he uses the market to perpetuate a network of relations that can no longer be maintained by means of professional life. Still, while Rousseau's account is linked to his personality, his sense of mise-en-scène, and his taste for rhetoric, his attitude toward the market it is in no way exceptional. For every Carpentras citizen, though to diverse degrees, the Friday market is an occasion for symbolically reappropriating a strongly characterized social space where everything makes sense, and affirming the specificity of where one lives, precisely because it involves taking a turn through the city streets and meeting up with familiar or known persons. At Auchan the people of the city are also among themselves in a way, since all of Carpentras gathers there on Saturday afternoons. But the place does not confer identity. In that showcase of mass consumption, one has no particular identity. At the market, on the contrary, one experiences a feeling of solidarity with local collective life; one is both the author of one's performance and the proud enactor of it. In "doing the market" one also takes "the owner's tour," checking that nothing is missing from the feast, as if one felt invested with the task of preserving the order of things, a duty of scrupulous loyalty to these particular traditions, since this weekly event is also the commemoration of all that have preceded it.

Everything at the market is done in such a way as to enable each person to entertain the illusion that he or she is perpetuating a custom, rediscovering and repracticing the gestures of a bygone time, being the repository of a heritage. Anything and everything serves the purpose of inscribing each observable practice in a tradition going back to time immemorial, making what is often only a modern imitation of superseded behavior appear a dusty old survival. The market owes it to all its visitors to be an institution that has come to us out of the depths of time, gratefully transmitted from generation to generation. The valuing of particularisms is so internalized that going shopping at the market almost becomes a kind of cultural act, a weekly attestation that one does indeed adhere to or enact the spirit of the place. This is what produces the impression that going regularly to the market and behaving as one should there are enough to make you a true Provençal, despite the fact that you were born near Hyde Park Corner or in Saint-Germain des Prés or Washington Square. Going to market thus restores—fictively, at least—an "old style" identity of the sort that is no longer current given that other types of identification pre-dominate in today's social worlds. This kind of identity involves being rooted in the soil of a locale, attached to a place that has a name, belonging to a local culture—all the qualities that make one "someone from here."

Identity of this kind, furnished by membership in a local community, could once be taken for granted. In our day it has become an object of intense desire, desire that cities and towns labor to satisfy. Freeway bypasses and other major infrastructure projects are no longer in fashion; the aim now is to loudly com-memorate the major events and activities of local life. Under these conditions, in this spirit, a market is a major advantage as long as it is old or seems so, because in contrast to other manifestations, a market is not pure representation or spectacle. You still go to the market to buy something, a little goat cheese, a pair of shoelaces, and marketing continues to figure among the mundane, nec-essary activities of ordinary life, in striking contrast to summer festivals and other sorts of festivities that cities and towns create out of whole cloth. This is why Mme. Delavigne and Mme. Patio, who don't bother to attend the Corso parade on the Fourteenth of July, never miss the Friday morning ceremony.

In contrast to vestiges exhumed for the duration of an exhibition or collo-quium, the market appears to be a piece of the past still active in the present. This impression is particularly strong given how ill adjusted the market is to the constraints of modern life. The norm now is the full workweek, and peo-ple are unlikely to be able to organize that week around Friday mornings. In the period between the two world wars, says Rousseau, you couldn't rely on women personnel to work on Fridays. Maintaining Friday morning as market time is an economic aberration of which everyone is fully aware. But loyalty to the tradition is one of the conditions for the market's success and increasing prosperity. This is what gives the market an authentic legitimacy that distin-guishes it from all pseudotraditional manifestations aimed to rope in tourists. In this connection, it is also extremely important that the market continues to function all year round, however meager business volume may be in winter when "the wind blows in from the Ventoux." This is what gives the market its credibility, its "honorability," and distinguishes it from secondhand goods fairs held only in the fair-weather season.

Those who visit the Carpentras market are indeed justified in feeling they are in a historic place. For centuries it has been held on the same day in nearly the same spot. "Quod . . . ab antiquis temporibus fuit et adhuc est," as is written in the Charter of 1155.[1] First set up in the cemetery at the foot of Saint-Siffrein, the market gradually spread into the streets of the city center. Thanks to the municipal archives and scholarly monographs, I was able to reconstitute the layout of 1890 and can attest that it was almost the same when I began my study.

Moreover, as many of the documents I consulted at the Bibliothèque Inguimbertine indicate, the market was indeed a major event in regional life. "Carpentras offers neither luxuries nor pleasures," wrote the Abbé de Pazzis in the report commissioned from him by the prefect of the Vaucluse around 1808: "The city is entirely given over to commerce and industry. And yet this seems perceptible but once a week. That day, indeed, the commerce is astounding, appearing quite out of proportion to the city's size. Carpentras must be considered the center of a population of 80,000 to 100,000 souls, for quite this number come to buy what they need there and, in exchange, bring all they can. . . . The inhabitants of towns, villages, hamlets, and the countryside for several *myriametres* across the highlands all recognize Carpentras as their metropolis. . . . It is here that all this numerous population labors every Friday to bring the diverse products of their industry or the land, together with excess foodstuffs."[2]

In a poem written in Provençal, Jean-François Field (1727–1811) celebrates the market's vast drawing power (though with greater precision than literary talent):

> From Velleron and also Thor,
> Saint-Didier and Malemort,
> Apt, Gordes, Murs, and Méthamis,
> Blouvac, La Roque, Lagnes, and Lauris
> Vaucluse as well as Cavaillon,
> They come bearing their portion . . . [3]

In nearby Mazan, as people still recount, "every Friday morning the city was deserted by nearly all its male inhabitants, accompanied perhaps by their spouses and always by donkeys or mules loaded down with the week's harvest of products. They left to sell skeins of silk from emptied cocoons and their famous iron lamps or '*calèu*.' And hanging in bunches against the donkeys' flanks were cages of calling birds for the bird market."[4]

In many of my interlocutors' childhood memories, the Friday market was an event that upset the routine of daily life. "In those days," relates Doctor Brun, the scholarly dentist, "people hitched up the *jardinière*—they would leave around six in the morning. They'd unhitch the horses and settle them in the stables; the *jardinières* were left standing there, arms in the air, in the Place du Vieil Hôpital. Throughout the city were huge inns like the Auberge de la Marotte, which already existed at the time of the Revolution. People went to lunch there at noon, or else they put up at city relatives'—it was a tradition. In exchange, the Carpentrassians would visit their country cousins. The shops stayed open at noon. People left for home in the *jardinière* at nightfall, after going to market with their families, and they didn't return until the following Friday." Adds Mme. Barrau: "Sometimes the peasants slept at the hotel. The restaurants never emptied. On the day before market day, they had to hire personnel for the stables, for everything—the entire city was packed with people." "My father made a huge bouillabaisse in a cauldron that held at least a hundred liters," remembers old Gardiol. "The stallholders all came with their bowls and my father filled them with a ladle. They went back on the four or five o' clock train."

Though for many the market no longer has the same weight in the region's economy or social life, it can never be dissociated from their wonder-filled evocations of its former self; every present-day Friday is for them a repetition of the market of old. In its current form, however, as we have seen, the Carpentras market resulted from changes linked to the upsets to the Comtadine economy in the last quarter of the nineteenth century.[5] The development of market gardening made possible by the newly constructed Carpentras canal, together with the gradual concentration of farming on three major products— strawberries, tomatoes, melons—worked to distinguish and isolate wholesale trade in fruits and vegetables and push it out of the city center. Meanwhile, the various specialized markets, the soul of the market before World War I, where peasants and craftspeople came to sell their products to brokers and traders, gradually disappeared. Today's market is therefore "historical" only in that it has been reconstructed along historically documented lines through preservation and rehabilitation operations aimed at carefully conserving anything that can be taken for a trace of the past, and through the many accounts that selective memory activates as it falls in line with present-day sensibilities. These accounts celebrate the market of bygone days, often nostalgically, and it is in their terms that the market is being reinterpreted today.

To varying degrees, the vanished specialized markets continue to leave their mark on local popular and scholarly memory of market spaces. Mme. Chalon still remembers the sheep market ("It was on the Place Notre-Dame, where the Square de Champville is now. There was a fountain for the sheep to drink at. Another part of the market was set up in front of the Hôtel de la Marotte"), and old Gardiol remembers cocoons being sold by weight in huge sacks at the silk-worm market in the Place Saint-Jean. People describe with wonder the "Marché aux vendanges" on the Boulevard du Nord where they went to buy grapes to make their house wine. But their images of pigs cramped in pens at the foot of the Eglise de l'Observance not far from the potato market undoubtedly owe much to Denis Bonnet's engravings. As for the "garlic and wood charcoal" market in the Place du Tracadou, the "iron, broom, hardware, and notions" market in the Place du Théâtre, the "mulberry leaf" market at the Porte de Mazan, the "silks and colonial foodstuffs" market in the Place de l'Horloge, the "sorghum, tree, and American grapevine" market, and others, I found traces of them only in the archives.

There used to be a wholesale market for "grains and pulse vegetables" in the Place du Palais, with sacks lined up to display a sample of each product: "That's where the seed market was," recounts Mme. Chalon. "There was not as much market gardening as there is now, so after the harvest, people with grain to sell brought 'the showpiece,' a sack each of their wheat, oats, barley. They'd set themselves up and the commissioners would come purchase from them. Business was done right there." Today this area is occupied by fabrics, clothing, and household items bazaars. But old Jeanjean, selling bean and nasturtium seeds to amateur gardeners rather than grain to traders, old Jeanjean with his cap and tunic, his small bags on his garden table, his old-fashioned scale and set of weights, his litany of advice lightly, felicitously peppered with Provençal expressions, is a last wink at this tradition.

Indeed, he likes to present himself—with a touch of irony because, as we know, he heads an important business—as the last vestige of this once flour-ishing grain market. "The day I stop coming, there will be no one. I'm unique, the others have all been pushed back to Les Platanes. Shortly before the war there were seventeen of us seed sellers; at Les Platanes now there can only be three or four. You can no longer keep yourself fed and clothed selling seeds, so you've got to sell all kinds of things besides: flowers, vases, seedlings. But they've only got company-produced things. They're retailers, really."

Similarly, in the Rue Guillaubert you often see a few elderly persons and their grandsons selling two or three thrush, the cold bodies of the birds lined up on the sidewalk. It is as if it were necessary at all costs to commemorate the "bird market," a picturesque activity which, from what old Gardiol says, was the heart of the market of olden days. (The fact that people imagine it as much older than it was is an inherent part of the pleasure they take in it today.)

228

And at the local *bar-tabac* they do still sell reproductions of old postcards of the bird market (for want of anything more authentic). "In the old days," comments Mme. Chalon, "it was very lively—all the cheeping, singing. It gave an extraordinary animation to the place, it was chock-full of people. Everyone did their little transactions. They'd gone hunting during the week with bird lime and nets, they put their [live] takings in cages and brought them to sell on Fridays. Or they used them as calling birds to help them kill the others. It began in October, when the *chasse au poste* opened.[6] Then when that kind of hunting was outlawed, the hunters would bring pheasant, rabbit, hare—always to the same place."

Until it was transferred to Les Platanes in 1889, there was also a "fruit, herb and fresh vegetable, acorn, potato, and chestnut" market in the Place de la Mairie. This is where today's city authorities, with their concern for authenticity, would like to concentrate the food trade, and in this they are faithfully following the old practice of grouping the same products on the same spot, though today this is done not to ensure optimal price-setting conditions for different "markets" but merely to "do things as they used to be done."[7] Yet what do mobile shops overflowing with sausages and cheeses or the subtly arranged displays at the Jardins du Comtat have in common with the anarchic outpouring of wares from *banastes* directly onto the ground to display them to wary traders? Similarly, the idea of situating the flower section in the old market space of Les Platanes, where farmers of the region used to come with their *jardinières* to sell vegetables and *primeurs* before the *marché-gare* was created, was to reinstate old practices, though today there are more retailers than producers selling seedlings directly.

Furthermore, Gardiol *fils* has made a point of turning his boutique at the entrance to the square into a genuine "realm of memory." The walls are decorated with photographs of the store in the 1900s wherein the entire family pose with their employees amidst rows of carefully aligned hare and partridge. "I thought it would be good to show that we've been here for a long time. This photo dates from 1908, and here's one from around 1930; the others are from 1950. We intend to have some made of the present period, to show people we've been here for three generations. They like getting their provisions from someone who's been here a long time." "In the 1908 photo," adds his father, once known for the singing talents he exercised at the region's balls, "I was eight years old. I was already working with my father in the store but I wasn't selling yet—I helped pluck chickens. I started plucking at seven and a half. I didn't go to school long. My father knew I had a passion for animals, that that was all I had in my head, and that I'd never learn anything at school."

The market of bygone days also offered the picturesque spectacle of a variety of crafts and small occupations, signs of a vanished civilization. People enjoy evoking this image, but it is hard to find modern versions of such a market that actually perpetuate traditions. The region's traditional crafts—porcelain, clay pots, tanning, saddle making—have expired today, and by the early twentieth century the market was no longer an outlet for handcrafted items. As for the tooth puller that Mme. Germaine remembers—"He had a kind of red coach, a top hat and tails, and a whole blah-blah-blah for drawing people in. His assistant played the drums to drown out the patient's cries. Then he'd hold up the bloody tooth"—he now plies his grisly trade elsewhere.

Among the displays of stallholders retailing industrial products, there was the tinker who "polished your forks," the knife and scissors grinder at the Porte de Mazan, "the fellow who engraved bicycle plates," *santon* merchants,[8] boxwood sellers, dog shearers, and Senegalese shoe shiners. Gypsies rebottomed chairs, sold baskets they'd woven, repaired holes in cooking pots; Gypsy women walked by with baskets full of lace, safety pins, thread, offering to tell one's fortune, while others, on Le Quinconce, led bears: "A woman in big skirts tapped on a tambourine and the bear would dance—just like that." On the market "*aux vendanges*," coopers set up in late August to repair worn-out barrels. Wheelwrights put the finishing touches on finely worked wheelbarrows. "The craftspeople used market day to display their skill," explains Mme. Chalon. "My father-in-law was a saddler. On Fridays he got out his collars and saddles, everything he had, so people could look at it all."

Installing the "students" with their handmade bracelets, necklaces, trinkets, little wooden objects, sundials, and the like in the Passage Boyer reflects an honorable concern to "restore," but the reminder of the past is only fiction here. While the *passage* itself is of historical significance—it was constructed by workers from the Ateliers Nationaux just after the 1848 revolution[9]—it has been occupied by stallholders only since city hall's recent decision.

Surely what matters most is that regardless of deliberate commemorative moves, the Carpentras market as it is today is an occasion for many habitués to bring to mind memories of their childhood and youth. Mme. Chalon remembers Palm Sunday lotteries organized with tree branches, and others, at the peak of the hunting season, with prizes of wild game: "They drew the winners, and you would get a pheasant, a dozen birds, four thrush." She remembers the famous Valentin, a baker working in Daladier's father's *boulangerie* who made all sorts of marionettes out of dough and told stories with them. "Later—I don't remember if he was still a baker—he started telling Comtadine stories, Carpentrassian stories, they had us in stitches."

Singers peddled the most recent popular songs from one market to another. "These songs were the joy of my youth," Mme. Chalon confided to me, "especially during the war since there was nothing much to distract us. We sang war songs, we sang 'Sous les ponts de Paris,' things on Alsace and Lorraine. A man or woman sang, played the violin, the accordion, taught the song to people and everybody came in on the chorus. They passed the hat, then they sold the printed song and music for a penny or two. People don't realize it now, they've got radio and all that, but there were as many as fifty of us around those singers. A woman who worked with us at the factory would sing us songs that she bought at the market, and soon all the women would take them up. My friend Robert Sabatier recently showed me some of them.[10] He has a whole collection he bought from secondhand sellers along the Seine. And one day when he came to eat with us at the chalet, we all started singing those songs by Vincent Scotto that we had learned like that at the market[11] . . . Those were market things, Friday things."

Like the tooth puller or the bear leader, these stories, refrains, memories of all kinds attest to the close entwining of personal histories with a collective event and a weekly locus of wonder. The market is at the heart of local identity, central to the construction of a particular "we" and a particular *chez soi* precisely because of its intimate relation to the life stories of those who go to it. But the market's capacity to represent an event in memories that are being made today and will be perpetuated tomorrow is just as important as its traditional image. This is why Pascal so benevolently tolerates Gypsies scattering themselves through the market, despite the fact that they no longer repair holes in cauldrons, and why he is so concerned to judiciously place the Agen prune sellers in folklore costumes and big-draw Jacky Thevet, noisily, theatrically selling off his inexhaustible shipment of terrycloth towels made in Taiwan. Likewise Mme. Delavigne finds the young German in tails tirelessly cranking his hurdy-gurdy "splendid," and no one is surprised or displeased when, toward the end of the market day, a small brass band in the Place du Palais proffers amateurish renditions of a few old hits.

Conclusion: A Moment of Utopia

The purpose of my concern for ethnographic accuracy here has not been to represent a microculture specific to the city of Carpentras or the Comtat Venaissin. This description of the Carpentras market is meant to be valid as an example. Though I became a habitué of the place over the months I spent there, it was not my purpose to bear witness to a strictly local identity; my aim instead has been to show through detailed analysis of a particular case how a market situation generates a field of specific social relations. Market exchange as such becomes a game in which the partners think of each other as equals. This principle of formal equality may be treated socially in highly diverse ways, but all of them have in common a temporary suspension of ordinary hierarchies. Moreover, due to the particular conditions in which they unfold, exchange relations at a stallholder market induce the formation of a public space. During this firmly delimited festive time, under cover of relative anonymity, people encounter each other not only as fellow human beings but as fellow citizens.

It will be objected that Carpentras Fridays are a far cry from such markets as Cergy-Saint-Christophe or, in Paris, the Rue de la Convention. Carpentras does enjoy an undeniable symbolic advantage. Spread out through what the guidebooks refer to as the "medieval" streets of the old city, at the foot of a few history-charged edifices, the Carpentras market appears immemorial. In reality, as we have seen, the reference to the past is largely reconstructed. But it is not the point of a market (in contrast to a monument) to be historical. A market need only appear historical, and this gives us reason to have high hopes for the markets of such cities as Vancouver and the French "new city" of Saint-Quentin-en-Yvelines. Above all—and here we must be careful not to fall into eternal-Provence stereotypes—Carpentras is a small city still closely linked to the surrounding countryside; it is the active center of a microregion. As we have seen, the degree of interacquaintance in this delimited social space is relatively high. At the market, then, it is indeed a local community that manifests itself and takes on flesh, though it is of course a heterogeneous one with indistinct contours. The market is a weekly occasion in which latent networks of relations take the form of verbal exchanges and various signs of recognition. Nothing like this happens in the fifteenth arrondissement of Paris [Rue de la Convention] or other residential areas, which on the contrary bring together individuals who have no more in common than a few abstract characteristics such as living standards, socio-occupational category, and average age. The best the market can do in this type of context is to create an imitation community out of whole cloth by playing on a vague feeling of local rootedness. By instituting markets in France's new cities, moreover, municipal governments are explicitly seeking to constitute a collective identity.

I realize that it is easier to demonstrate the particular social relations generated by a market situation in a case like Carpentras than in ones where that kind of sociability is minimal, embryonic. But this should not lead us to suppose there is a difference in nature between "traditional" markets, fundamental components of an enduring local culture, and "modern" markets, instruments of deliberate policies and therefore doomed to inauthenticity. The question is not so much whether an ex nihilo or implanted custom can be perpetuated as whether the transplant "takes" and why or why not. The mode of social relations I have described as operative in Carpentras can also develop in a historically shallow urban context. The fact remains that regardless of town councilors' intentions and efforts, not all city populations feel the same "need of a market" or have the same aptitude for investing in this mode of distribution and making its accompanying social meaning work. For young people in particular, the supermarket or mall can serve as a gathering and entertainment place. Above all, every market, whether genuinely old or only recently created, "functions" traditionally by definition. In this age of supermarkets, the stallholder market distribution mode is necessarily perceived as archaic, an impression reinforced by the way it is staged. The types of social relations induced by market exchange appear to actors to bear the mark of either a premodern or an exotic world. Calmly doing one's marketing with one's shopping bag on one's arm while chatting from stall to stall with the people one chances to encounter is also playing at being of another time. The long-lasting success of markets is thus to be explained by our current world's intense consumption of the "noncurrent." A market is a collectively produced anachronism, and in this it responds to deeply contemporary logic.

From this perspective, the Carpentras market I studied as exemplary under the heading "anthropology of stallholder market exchange" also has the status of model, and this is another practical, nontheoretical way of endowing it with a certain general import. As a reputedly "typical" Provençal market, Carpentras belongs to the family of reference markets that informs the archetypal image of "the traditional market" that in turn inspires city governments, planners, and tourist guides. The daily newspaper *Libération*, for example, has touted the virtues of the market in the Place des Fêtes in Paris, above Belleville, as being of "the Provençal type"—a "quality label" guaranteeing a "picturesque" and "convivial" atmosphere.[1]

We all have more or less this model in mind when we go to a stallholder market. For a number of market customers today, behaving appropriately at a market is not a matter of "second nature" acquired in childhood through contact with the preceding generations (as it is for Rousseau or Mme. Patio). Without necessarily being conscious of it, they reproduce an image that each has pieced together on the basis of his or her experiences or memories—Carpentras for this writer, as well as Palermo and Marrakech; Figeac or Ambert for one or another of my colleagues—but also an image forcefully transmitted by French national culture: songs from the 1960s (Gilbert Bécaud's "Marchés de Provence"), repeated news reports on contemporary stars going to market in Saint-Tropez or Saint-Rémy with wicker baskets on their arms in the style of characters in Pagnol plays and films such as *Fanny* and *Manon des Sources*; regional television documentaries about the French on vacation where an interview with a token stallholder is slipped in between one with the last Mont Lure shepherd and a recipe for aioli; the summer issue of *Le Figaro Magazine* on Midi markets or a report showing the fashion designer Ungaro sniffing melons at a stall in Aix, and so forth. The Paris business executive and the doctor on vacation tend to "go overboard" at the market because they behave in keeping with an image that is both conventional to the point of being trite and overfull of "local color," thereby instantly revealing that "going to market" is not at all part of their usual activities or world.

The practices that may be observed at a stallholder market like that of Carpentras may stand as a national model in that they evoke a perhaps ill-defined
but in any case vanished world, a dominantly rural France which Carpentras,
like any small city in the Midi with its plane-tree-shaded squares and *boule* players, is living testimony of. This is of course an illusion. As we have seen, the
Friday market is not a miraculously preserved fragment of history a few minutes' drive off Highway A6. It is true, however, that people have a worshipful
attitude toward tradition in Carpentras and are concerned to preserve what remains of it. They are obsessed with survivals, as attested by old city dwellers'
endlessly reiterated accounts of the market of bygone days. This explains the
accumulation of allusive references, pseudoquotations, and carefully preserved
or restored material traces of the market, all aimed at giving today's market an
old style, an archaic coloration—everyone either does this actively or approves
of it. But the fact that "the Provençal market" is a mere *copie d'ancien* does not
preclude it from serving as a model. Reproducing the signs of it, "making like
Provençal" in the nineteenth arrondissement of Paris, amounts to producing
imitations of imitations, in much the same way people put "antique bronze"
handles on a pinewood dresser or copper saucepans in a prefab kitchen. Being
a market lover means being willing from the outset to be taken in by the charm
of these illusions without necessarily believing in them.

Despite the stereotypical vision of Provence as devoted, and doomed, to
perpetuate its traditions, in Carpentras, at the heart of a region dominated by
technically sophisticated methods for "forcing" out *primeur* vegetables, we are
in reality as far from the "natural economy" as at the market in the Avenue
Joliot-Curie in Sarcelles. At today's market, as explained, it is extremely hard
to find vestiges of a world of small farmers who come to sell off their home-
grown produce directly. Reduced after a rather complex history to little more
than professional retailers and retail selling, the Friday market is probably fairly
similar to any market in the greater Paris area.

The fact remains that in the labyrinth of crooked Carpentras streets—
though they are not far from the "slabs" of Les Amandiers and Les Eléphants—
and in the shade of the episcopal palace or the tall houses of the former ghetto,
a person at the market can still imagine himself or herself in a city from another
age more easily than they can in Saint-Quentin-en-Yvelines. Emptied of cars,
the city becomes the province of pedestrians, and it is as if the population had
suddenly begun to live out of doors. The joyous chaotic bustle, the colorful,
swarming crowd, the chance and accident that seem to reign over how mar-

236

ket and products are laid out in space, the streets groaning under mountains of merchandise of all sorts, the unloading of victuals, the displays of plucked chickens and stiff rabbits with their unsettling eyes (not even remotely related to the "Forez *cochonailles* [sausage]" stand at the entrance to the Leclerc supermarket, though it too is in deliberate disarray), the hawkers' spiels, the cries of women stallholders hailing passing visitors—everything evokes the genre scenes that everyone has a pictorial or novel-reading memory of: a page in Restif de la Bretonne or Zola, a painting by Brueghel, an engraving of Les Halles de Paris at the beginning of the twentieth century.

On Fridays, then, the city knows how to make itself rural. Though the farmers of the region are more businessmen today than peasants, the city bedecks itself in signs of country life. Though one no longer hears "the indistinct, noisy mix of barking dogs and moving carts"[2]—"In my childhood," Mme. Chalon remembers, "there were still mainly horse-drawn carriages and *jardinières*. It was marvelous! It was the market of Provence!"—one can still, with a bit of imagination, find something of the atmosphere described by Armand Lunel in the 1930s: "There was a country smell in the city air, a grassy fragrance the peasants had brought with them."[3]

No doubt texts such as André de Richaud's "Charmes de Carpentras" give a vision of the market between the two world wars in which folkloric features of the sort that now make it a vestige of a lost world were already dominant: omnipresence of the countryside, noise of carts, traditional crafts, marginal little trades. "That day, like all market days," narrates the hero of *Nicolo Peccavi ou l'Affaire Dreyfus à Carpentras*, "I was wakened by a merry din, the sound of bells and axles, neighing, cursing, snapping whips. Fresh straw was scattered on the Place aux Oies, where pottery merchants were just beginning to unload, and the rustic painted plates and bowls were already bringing back to life all the wildflowers no longer growing in the piece of thatch they were set out upon. There, against the prison wall, the blond ceramic bowls from Apt, the bronze-colored ceramic casseroles from Vallauris, sparkled in the shadows of the horse-drawn trailers, and on the other side, in front of Vallabrègue, cut-price fabric and trinket dealers were setting up fluttering bazaars that would last the space of a morning."[4] The choice of significant traits that Lunel made in 1926 recalls the one my interlocutors make today, as if the pleasure offered by the market were indissociable from a feeling of anachronism. Back home after their visit to the market, my respondents evoked not so much the mobile shops that sell jeans or pizza as the small goat cheese producers who had come down from the mountain or the vast stalls of olives of all sorts, thus inadvertently (re)constituting the "Provençal market" par excellence.

There are of course no longer any horses for sale around the fountain at Le Quinconce, each with a nosebag of hay around its neck; no silkworm cocoons for sale in the Place de la Juiverie; and on the Boulevard du Nord the live poultry market where retailers sell to a North African clientele survives only thanks to Islam. But the four or five unfortunate thrush lined up on the pavement at the "bird market," added to the numerous farm-bred and perhaps imported pheasants and partridges suspended in front of Gardiol's stand and the nearby presence of the mysterious truffle market, are there to recall the proximity of the wild: the pebbly slopes of Mont Ventoux, the *garrigues* near Venasque. Everything that evokes hunting and gathering may be used to breathe new life into the myth of a "natural" tie with nature that industrial society is believed to have broken.

Every stallholder market tries to give itself a rural touch (though it does not always succeed). In Carpentras as elsewhere, the market is a temple where "nature" is celebrated—nature as divinity of the modern world, an entity presumed immutable that we owe it to ourselves to maintain or reestablish our founding connection with by all means necessary, from the little vegetable garden we keep up at great expense to the carrot and garlic capsules we ingest in the morning with cornflakes and vacuum-packed milk. The presentation of products in bulk, untreated; sellers with peasant appearances; gritty bunches of radishes, the greens attached; eggs straight from the henhouse, their shells streaked and dirty; slugs in the salad; muddy potatoes; the pervasive, clinging odor of melon together with the "sales patter" that accompanies all this lead us to believe that the apples come from the seller's orchard, the skeins of wool from the vendor's sheep, that the feathery eggs were laid by free-ranging chickens and the pig was just slaughtered, though all of this—all these allegorical figures of country life "consumed" at stallholder markets in much the same way one takes a little farm vacation beneath the faded eye of Millet's *Semeuses*—is just as illusory (if more plausible) in Carpentras as in Sarcelles. Not to mention the fact that even Carpentras stallholders redundantly add the label "organic," as if "local strawberries" and "artichokes from Provence" no longer sufficed to signify the authentic naturalness of the product. The further the countryside is from us in time and space, the more the market becomes a place of "Nature"— smack in the center of the city and within arm's reach (though not within that of all purses). In almost every metropolis—Boulevard Raspail on Sunday mornings, Union Square in New York, Pike Market in Seattle—the "supermodern" consumer on a quest to commune with the nourishing Earth can buy a bit of genuine nature.

The figure of the stallholder seems to conserve the memory of this society from "an earlier time," as if there were some filiation between the peddler of yesteryear out in all weathers and this overequipped tradesperson regularly going the rounds of five or six markets within a tightly limited circumference. Because stallholders are associated with itinerancy and nomadism, people enjoy imagining that their life must still have an adventurous side, though when one considers Perdiguier's and Espenon's mobile shops, the figure described by Mme. Barrau of an energetic woman who "led the lineup of carts, because at the time stallholders who went from market to market stayed close together to protect themselves from thieves," seems very remote: "She was extremely well organized. Behind her at the market she had a little wood-burning stove with her *pot-au-feu* simmering on it. She set up outside as if she were at home."

Compared with a sedentary shopkeeper, the stallholder does not appear to be a real professional, especially since she herself is forever reminding us she is there by vocation, love of liberty and the outdoors. Most stallholders are in fact wise managers, attentive to their markups and careful to turn a profit, not tiny retailers just managing to survive. Even in Carpentras one no longer sees the little fruit-and-vegetable ladies once scattered throughout the city, who had bought their wares at Les Platanes that morning at what was called *le petit marché* from peasants with too much merchandise or producers whose lettuce was not pretty enough or whose fruit was too ripe to be sold to shippers. The fact remains that in Carpentras from one week to the next, in addition to the big "subscriber" stallholders, there are enough small vendors of *banons, picodons,* and other goat cheeses, enough self-declared secondhand clothing dealers, chair bottomers, leatherworkers, and other incidental handymen and repairmen, not to mention the Gypsies and their lemons, the Senegalese and their junk, and the occasional Bible seller "bringing the word of God into the street like the Apostle Paul," for the spectacle of the market, occasionally reinforced by a few exotic images, to provoke a sense of anachronism and strangeness. It is true that in Carpentras these marginal small trades owe their existence in part to the "return to sources" movement, which has readily flourished in Provence, the Cévennes, and the Ardèche. That movement has enabled all those like Martin the secondhand clothing dealer, who decided after 1968 to "live differently," to escape from the constraints of wage earning. But other causes have the same

239

effects today. Stallholder markets wherever they are function as a refuge for persons who have not been able to find a place for themselves in the labor force since the late 1980s recession.

The fact that at all such markets, next to regular stallholders, there are hawkers touting miracle spot removers, cut-rate vendors of "pure lisle" socks, stalls where a shipment of pineapples or melons gets "liquidated," and sellers of "Swiss" watches and other trinkets makes it possible to maintain the illusion that we are in a world of amateurs in which each can turn a profit according to his talents. The prize goes to the person who can find a bargain rummaging in a shipment of shirts or obtain three cauliflowers for the price of two. People feel particularly free to bargain when they don't really need the sachet of lavender or potato peeler. Every exchange takes the form of a face-to-face encounter where each partner seeks to have the last word. For the mass consumer, this alone suffices to evoke an idyllic world of patient, subtle negotiation or good deals snatched from the maw of defeat, a world that cannot be compared with the "slashed-price-of-the-day" on cans of Russian crab or vacuum-packed bags of Jacques Vabre coffee announced at the entrance to the Franprix supermarket, or in all likelihood with the serried haggling in the streets of Paris two centuries ago, as described by Arlette Farge, where "anything could happen and playing the game could mean death," since bargaining could quickly metamorphose into a nasty fight.[5] The putative bargaining option is what explains the immense success of flea markets, secondhand fairs, garage sales, and the like.

The breeziness and cordiality of the human relations established in every market situation to varying degrees evoke another society, one vaguely perceived as traditional, a world of interacquaintanceship and conviviality that modern civilization is assumed to have destroyed. There again, the "Provençal market" serves as a model, given the presumed age of Mediterranean Midi societies, closely associated with the extroverted, warm behavior of their inhabitants, at least as may be seen in Pagnol's works. But while elsewhere people think they are playing "Provençal market," in Carpentras they think they are replaying the market of bygone days. One speaks with everyone there because "that's what's done," because it is behavior specific to the market situation, but one also has the impression that it has always been done this way, that in behaving in this way one is respecting an ancestral custom—while going against all current behavior codes.

In reality, these types of social interaction were once inscribed in a very different sociological context. Quite a different use was made of the "generalized friendship" I have been describing. It was not for sheer enjoyment or amusement. As Mme. Barrau explains, the market was the great "occasion for communication." This was where important business was handled, family differences resolved, the price of the harvest negotiated, hiring done, weddings arranged. "People came to put in supplies, and there were families who only saw each other at those moments," Mme. Chalon explains. "Behavior was not free-spirited as it is today. Now it's easy for a boy to meet a girl, whereas then, my heavens, you were with papa-maman, you had gone to do the marketing. Then you'd run into friends who had a son, a daughter . . ." This did not prevent the market from being a dream spot for adulterers, especially given the escape hatch offered by the double-entrance cafés.

The function of the market has been profoundly transformed. Not only are the economic matters at stake much more modest now that the wholesale market has been moved, but there is no longer the special framework for exchanges internal to the community. Owing to more intense social diversity and mixing, the market is now a place for more heterogeneous crowds to gather; "people from here" are likely be in the minority, particularly in summer. More so than in the past this is an anonymous space where people are no longer truly *entre soi* but play at being so. The old market, influenced by today's tastes, serves as a near-mythic reference for all sorts of behavior imagined as traditional but in fact quite contemporary. This makes it possible to constitute the market as a specific social space that breaks with daily professional and family life. Though today's market is only fictively a survival, people behave at it in such a way as to produce the illusion that they are practicing a bygone type of social interaction. They thereby create, for the space of a morning, a happy enclave in a world of tension, an island of asylum where whims and fancies may be indulged, in a universe of glum rationality.

Contemporary cultural models are in fact at work both in representations of an archetypal market that one attributes to either another time or another place, and in the way people construct the market here and now. The society in which markets of this type flourished, a society vaguely, negatively defined as both preindustrial and untouched by the ills of mass consumption, appears retrospectively as an enchanted world of small, mutually supportive, harmonious communities governed by personal, near-familial relations. People have a nostalgic image of the forebears' market, an image responsive to the demands of the modern sensibility, and this is implicitly projected onto the current reality of the market.

A MOMENT OF UTOPIA

I was struck by the fact that even in Carpentras the way the market is "practiced" calls into play a set of values disseminated by the national media and imagined to be universal. These values, considered "our own" in extremely diverse social milieus, may be designated as follows: a concern for "communication," "exchange," dialogue, personal contact, that which is "relational"; a demand for energetic, multidirectional "participation"; the cult of "spontaneity," "naturalness," the "relaxed" attitude; rejection of uniformity, conventionality, constraints; return to the authentic. The subtle mix of true vestiges and pseudo-archaisms inspired by this ideology, an ideology flabby enough to be acceptable to all, makes the market not so much a locus of history as a utopia.

Most important, the market is the city as we dream it should be. Alien to the functional vision of space wherein social activities take place in distinct areas, the market is the antimodern city, a supply structure where you are just as likely to buy the superfluous as the necessary. The market is also a place to stroll, meet people, chat, gather information, be entertained. All types of logic come together and commingle there: it is all at once the "piazza," the mall, the pedestrian zone, the MJC, a "discovery park" for children, and more.[6] At the market people discover the lost city; the one you feel you could live in, not just inhabit, where there is no opposition between a hostile exterior and a reassuring inner core; the "true city" in the name of which "we denounce our modern cities as disfigured, fake, even as noncities."[7] People do their marketing in the Place des Lices in Rennes or the Boulevard Edgar Quinet in Montparnasse with *Le Nouvel Observateur* under their arm and a litany of bitterly recited criticisms of modern urban planning in their heads: the sense of despair provoked by housing developments, the terrifying silence of sprawling suburbs, the solitude of the consumer at Auchan, Carrefour, and so on, the *désertification* of city centers.[8] Every Friday they offer themselves the pleasure of a human-scale city with its welcoming streets and pleasantly crowded little squares, where disorder is not bothersome but joyous, the crowd does not engender violence, tight physical proximity gives rise to warm relations, standing elbow to elbow with strangers induces a feeling of amicable solidarity.

Presumed a vestige of the lost city, the market is a utopian social world. In place of today's retreat into the self or a world dominated by the "tyrannies of intimacy,"[9] the market reactualizes the virtues of the agora, where each person becomes an actor in his or her polis. For the space of a morning, people give themselves the illusion of living in and belonging to a transparent society (which none would enjoy in reality), where the private opens onto the public, where it is good to be "implicated" and "express oneself," show one's feelings to one's neighbor, utter to whomever one happens to meet what one really thinks. Like neighborhoods where certain social strata work to make their part of the big city a foundation for more communitarian life,[10] the market stages the pleasure of coming together "among ourselves" that is understood to be characteristic of traditional societies. At the market people enjoy both anonymity and interacquaintanceship, relations that come apart almost as soon as they are initiated, the freedom of going incognito and of encounters that do not imply commitment. Instead of being drowned in the mass one moment, prisoner of one's narrow world the next, one is alone without being lonely. As in other places—beaches, cafés, vacation clubs—people not quite innocently activate a utopian model of the social tie, a daily experienced democratic ideal: a pleasure and happiness all the more appreciated in that one need not fear the ideal will last. Social barriers are lowered at the market; the struggle for recognition takes a breather. What we are treated to around noon is the improbable spectacle of a society from which no one is excluded, in which the other is treated as a fellow. While combining the useful with the pleasant, everyone nearly everywhere and for nearly nothing can enjoy the fleeting, thrilling sensation of equality to be had in Carpentras on Friday mornings.

243

Notes

Introduction

1. Financial assistance for this study, in which I was aided in part by Guy-Patrick Azémar, was generously provided by the Délégation Générale à la Recherche Scientifique et Technique in the framework of a research contract for the "Urbanisme commercial" section, and by the French Ministry of Research as part of its "Sciences sociales et aménagement" [Social sciences and development] program.

2. Cf. Karl Polanyi, *The Great Transformation: The Political and Economic Origin of Our Time* (Boston: Beacon Press, 1944).

3. Cf. Karl Polanyi and Conrad Arensburg, eds., *Trade and Markets in the Early Empires* (New York: Free Press, 1957).

4. Cf. Jacqueline Matras-Guin, "Vente aux enchères et tirage au sort dans les criées en gros du poisson," in *Ethnologie française* 17, 2–3 (1987): 227–34.

5. [*Petit blanc*: small glass of white wine, usually served at the café counter.]

6. Mainly studies of rural markets; cf. those collected on Isac Chiva's initiative in *Foires et marchés ruraux en France, Etudes rurales*, special combined issue, 78, 79, 80 (Apr.–Dec. 1980).

7. Jacqueline Beaujeu-Garnier, "Mutations commerciales et études géographiques," in *Le commerce urbain français* (Paris: Presses Universitaires de France, 1984), 10.

8. Michel de Certeau, *The Practice of Everyday Life*, trans. Steven Rendall (Berkeley: University of California Press, 1984), xii. Originally published as *L'invention du quotidien*, vol. 1: *Arts de faire* (Paris: Union Générale des Editions, 1980), 10.

9. The expression is Roger Chartier's in "L'histoire ou le savoir de l'autre,' in *Michel de Certeau*, ed. Luce Giard (Paris: Centre Georges Pompidou, 1987), 164.

10. Max Weber, *Economy and Society*, ed. Guenther Roth and Claus Wittich, trans. Wright Mills, Talcott Parsons, Edward Shils, et al., vol. 1 (Berkeley: University of

California Press, 1978), 636. See also Georg Simmel: "It is not that it is this *or* that trait that makes a unique personality of man, but that he is this *and* that trait. . . . Such a personality is almost completely destroyed under the conditions of a money economy. The delivery man, the money-lender, the worker . . . do not operate as personalities, because they enter into a relationship only by virtue of a single activity such as the delivery of goods, the lending of money, and because their other qualities, which alone would give them a personality, are missing." *The Philosophy of Money,* ed. David Frisby; trans. Tom Bottomore and David Frisby from a first draft by Kaethe Mengelberg (London: Routledge, 1990), 296.

11. Marshall Sahlins, *Stone Age Economics* (London: Routledge, 2004 [1972]).

12. Because it presupposes "independent" partners, "the exchange of commodities begins where communities have their boundaries, at their points of contact with other communities." Karl Marx, *Capital* (London: Penguin Books, 1990), 1: 182.

13. Montesquieu, *The Spirit of the Laws,* trans. and ed. Anne M. Cohler, Basia Carolyn Miller, and Harold Samuel Stone (Cambridge: Cambridge University Press, 1989), 53 (bk. 5, chap. 8).

14. Françoise Raison, "Le travail et l'échange dans les discours d'Andrianampoiniamerina, Madagascar, XVIIIe siècle," in *Le travail et ses représentations,* ed. Michel Cartier (Paris: Editions des Archives Contemporains, 1984), 248.

15. Marx, *Capital,* 1:178–79.

16. [*Cabanon*: rustic drystone shelter in the fields of Provence used to store farming implements but also for family picnics and relaxation.]

17. [Sarcelles: suburb just north of Paris with a high number of 1950s and '60s apartment slabs; the name has become a symbol in France of this type of housing development.]

18. Antoine Denoves, ms. 1189, Bibliothèque Inguimbertine. The Carpentras market is "the finest that exists in France," wrote the Abbé de Pazzis in a report commissioned by the prefect of the Vaucluse shortly after the Comtat was reincorporated into France. Even stripped of its papal privilege, then, it remained incomparable. Cf. *Mémoire statistique sur le département de Vaucluse* (Carpentras: Imprimerie Quenin, 1808).

19. This name, wrote Robert Caillet, former director of the Bibliothèque Inguimbertine, "is the sole reminder of the market of the time" (*Foires et marchés de Carpentras du Moyen Age au début du dix-neuvième siècle* [Carpentras: Imprimerie Batailler, 1953], 19). In fact the term *forum* does not necessarily imply the presence of a market.

20. Caillet mentions a register of church documents for the bishopric dated 1309, in which the bishop sets about barring merchants from using the space adjacent to the church, the cemetery, and the Place de la Fusterie. In self-defense the merchants cite a long tradition of trading in those spots (ibid., 20).

21. The market at Arles also has its dissertation, for the fifteenth century; see Louis Stouff, *Ravitaillement et alimentation en Provence aux XIVe et XVe siècles* (Paris: Mouton, 1970).

22. Georges Bataille was appointed director of the Bibliothèque Inguimbertine in 1951.

23. Strange sculpture of a sphere with rats scurrying over it. The meaning has never been elucidated.

24. A horse's bit [*mors*] believed to have been forged out of two nails from the Cross and known for its exorcising power; also called *le Saint Clou* [the holy nail]. Pope Clement VII solemnly declared that the bit cast evil spirits out of the human body. It also had the power of holding plague and cholera at bay, and was carried in processions through the city streets when epidemics broke out.

25. The last remaining vestige of the city's Roman past. Dates from the century of Augustus and represents captured Gauls chained to a trophy. Prosper Mérimée, *Notes d'un voyage dans le midi de la France* (Paris: Adam Biro, 1989 [1835]), 126.

26. André de Richaud, "Charmes de Carpentras,' in *Quarante-quatre textes retrouvés ou inédits* (Cognac: Le temps qu'il fait, 1985), 12. Originally published in the review *Le Feu*, Aix-en-Provence, 1927. [*Berlingot*: hard, bright-colored candy in the shape of a plump cushion, specialty of Carpentras.]

27. The "Comté" [county] Venaissin is named after Venasque, a craggy hill town a dozen kilometers southeast of Carpentras. After the crusade against the Albigensians and the defeat of the counts of Toulouse, Louis VIII granted the Comtat to the Holy See. The monarchy made three vain attempts to annex it, and after multiple political and military disputes, it was finally integrated into French national territory on September 14, 1791, in mid-Revolution. In 1793 it became part of the newly created *département* of the Vaucluse.

28. After days of intrigue and brawls, the twenty-three cardinals reemerged without having elected a successor to Clement V.

29. The city's water was apparently so bad that Clement V is said to have had an aqueduct constructed to bring his personal supply in from an Alpine spring purchased from one Barral de Baux, lord of Barroux and Caromb.

30. [Parti Radical: political party of republican, anticlerical origins, Dreyfusard, later defining itself as more moderate than the socialists; considered representative of the opinions and aspirations of "the average Frenchman."]

31. The invention of alizarin, an artificial dye, at the end of the nineteenth century put an end to cultivation of the madder plant.

32. *Rabasse* is the Provençal name for the black truffle commonly known as Périgord.

33. Marc Augé, *Domaines et châteaux* (Paris: Le Seuil, 1989), 178.

247

Chapter One. City Tour

1. For the most part, I will be describing the city as it was when I conducted this study in the 1980s, occasionally mentioning changes that have occurred since then.

2. Malachi d'Inguimbert, a native of Carpentras, bishop of the city from 1735 to 1757. As confidant to Pope Clement XII he accumulated great cultural treasures and made them available to the city. Particularly significant was his gift of four thousand books to the library that bears his name.

3. [BHV: Bazar de l'Hôtel de Ville, large department store in the center of Paris. The basement is occupied by a vast selection of hardware, gardening, and do-it-yourself items.]

4. [*Posticheur*: hawker; *postiche*: toupée, something fake or added on.]
5. [*Halle*: a produce and food market, originally wholesale.]
6. [*Gitans*: Gypsies, name for Romany of Spain and France.]

Chapter Two. Well-Ordered Chaos

1. Cf. Gérard Althabe, "Ethnologie du contemporain et enquête de terrain," *Terrain* 14 (Mar. 1990).
2. People in Carpentras are generally designated by their family name, which may or may not be preceded by Monsieur or Madame, while first names are rarely used. I have tended to follow this custom, in some instances concealing the names of my interlocutors to protect their anonymity.
3. Magnificent ramparts, including thirty-two round towers and four gates [*portes*], were constructed to replace the Roman walls (see Caillet, *Foires et marchés de Carpentras*, 21).
4. The Porte d'Orange is all that remains of the medieval walls, though drawings by J. B. Laurens and D. Bonnet have preserved the memory of the others (ibid., 23).

5. "Leis embarras dou marca de Carpentras," in *Recueil de Poésies de divers auteurs vauclusiens copiées par le docteur Barjavel*, ms. 976, Bibliothèque Inguimbertine, Carpentras.
6. See studies conducted by the chamber of commerce and industry of Avignon and the Vaucluse. Supermarkets near city entrances create an influx of consumers that is generally good for the city center, and the Auchan supermarket, which opened its doors in 1976 and appears very much a part of Carpentrassians' daily lives, seems to have been more damaging to local supermarkets than to city center shops.
7. Since my study, the center of the old city has become a pedestrian zone. The market has tended to develop on the outskirts.
8. [RPR: Rassemblement pour la République, former name of the Gaullist political party founded by French president Jacques Chirac.]
9. These are nearly identical to the ones explained in professional organization documents (Syndicat des Commerçants Non Sédentaires and the Centre d'Etudes de la Commercialisation et de la Distribution, headed by the chambers of commerce).
10. [France's finest prunes are reputed to be from Agen; the fruit and the place-name are linked in French minds.]

Part Two. An Economy of Enticement

1. [*Baccalauréat*: national high school leaving exam and degree; passing the *bac*, that is, obtaining the diploma, is a capital event in a French life.]
2. See Roger Caillois, *Man, Play, and Games*, trans. Meyer Barash (Urbana: University of Illinois Press, 2001). Originally published as *Les jeux et les hommes* (Paris: Gallimard, 1967).

Chapter Three. The Art of Taking One's Time

1. See in particular Bernard Chevallier, *Les fonctions du centre de Carpentras*, Chambres du Commerce et de l'Industrie d'Avignon et du Vaucluse, 1982.
2. ["Market" here refers to one in the series of recurring Friday events at Carpentras. A "big market" is a market morning with a high number of stallholders and customers.]
3. It is traditional in Carpentras to assimilate the fair with what continue to be called "grands vendredis" [big Fridays]. A municipal decree of 9 Frimaire, Year XIV, specified there could be three such days per year: the Fridays before Jeudi Gras and Easter week and the penultimate pre-Christmas Friday. "[*Grands vendredis*] are remarkable for the number of foreigners—they come from twenty-five leagues around. Carpentras is like a fair; people come from Nice, Antibes, Barcelonnette, Narbonne, Mende, Puy-en-Velay, Clermont-en-Auvergne, Vienne-en-Dauphiné, Voiron, Gap, the Lyonnais, the Forez, Lorraine, Alsace, Paris . . ." (Doctor Barjavel, quoted in Caillet, *Foires et marchés de Carpentras*, 95, 96).
4. On two arbitrarily chosen market days, one in August, the other in December, I observed that the number of stalls selling such products varied more than for food, clothing, hardware, and household supplies.
5. Octave Mannoni, *Clefs pour l'imaginaire ou l'Autre Scène* (Paris: Le Seuil, 1969), 109–10.
6. [French supermarkets also often sell clothes, cosmetics, and a wide selection of household appliances.]
7. Cf. Jacques Ion's analyses of customer behavior in supermarkets in "De l'échoppe à l'hyper: évolution des manières de consommer," mimeograph, Centre de Recherche et d'Etudes Sociologiques Appliquées de la Loire, 1978.
8. Philippe Sollers, *Portrait du joueur* (Paris: Gallimard, 1985), 24.
9. Colette Pétonnet, "L'anonymat ou la pellicule protectrice," in "La ville inquiète," *Le temps de la réflexion* 8 (Paris: Gallimard, 1987): 259.

Chapter Four. Familiar Strangers

1. The Ministry of Commerce lists three categories of nonsedentary tradespeople, of whom there are between 100,000 and 130,000: itinerants, living in a fixed place of residence for more than six months and registered with the department of commerce; stallholders without a fixed place of residence but registered with the department of commerce; small vendors who, though not registered, have permission to sell on the public right of way. In reality, this set of categories covers extremely different situations (see "Les aspects techniques du commerce non-sédentaire," Centre d'Etude du Commerce et de la Distribution [CECOD], 1983).
2. Chiva, "Les places marchandes et le monde rural," in *Foires et marchés ruraux en France*, 10.
3. D. Margairaz, "La formation du réseau des foires et des marchés: stratégies, pratiques and idéologies," *Annales ESC* 6, *Espace et histoire: hommage à Fernand Braudel*

(1986). By the same author see *Foires et marchés dans la France préindustrielle* (Paris: Editions de l'Ecole des Hautes Etudes en Sciences Sociales, 1988).

4. [*Bouchée à la reine*: cylindrical puff pastry filled with chicken, veal, and mushrooms in a bechamel sauce.]

5. ["*Pieds noirs*": Europeans who left Algeria for France after the colony became independent in 1962.]

6. [MIN: Marché d'Intérêt National, component of the national, state-regulated system of wholesale farm-produce markets.]

Chapter Five. Delights of Free Trade

1. In addition to registration with the board of commerce, a formality required of all tradespeople, market stallholders have to carry a professional "itinerant merchant" card issued by the prefecture or subprefecture of the *département* they reside in.

2. [Félix Guattari (1930–92): French intellectual, psychoanalyst, and leftist militant; coauthor with Gilles Deleuze of *Anti-OEdipe: Capitalisme et schizophrénie*, among other works (see n. 5). Jean Baudrillard: French intellectual renowned for his critical analyses of consumer society.]

3. [*Jardinière*: light two- or four-wheeled horse-drawn vehicle used especially by market farmers.]

4. [*Broderie anglaise*: embroidered fabric, usually white cotton, in which holes are cut in patterns and oversewn, often to decorate lingerie, shirts, and skirts.]

5. [Clinique La Borde: renowned French private psychiatric institution founded after World War II where a new approach to treating psychosis was applied. Félix Guattari (see n. 2) played an active role in the life of the clinic, particularly in the 1960s and '70s. David Cooper: initiator and theorist, with R. D. Laing, of the antipsychiatry movement.]

6. See Jacqueline Lindenfeld, "Etudes des pratiques discursives sur les marchés urbains," *Modèles linguistiques*, vol. 4, pt. 1, 1982.

7. In *Le culte de la performance* (Paris: Calmann-Lévy, 1991), Alain Ehrenberg shows how the tactic of effacing all signs of work is used by the GOs [*gentils organisateurs:* nice organizers] of the Club Méditerranée vacation agency.

Chapter Seven. "Pumpkins are rounder at the market"

1. [See chap. 4, n. 6.]

2. Roland Barthes, *Empire of Signs*, trans. Richard Howard (New York: Hill and Wang, 1982), 19. Originally published as *L'empire des signes* (Geneva: Skira, 1970), 29.

3. [*Daube:* any meat stew (beef, mutton, rabbit, turkey, and so on) with aromatic herbs, vegetables, often a wine sauce, e.g., *daube de boeuf à la provençale*.]

4. [Aleksandr Chayanov: Russian rural sociologist who did pioneering work on peasant economies.]

5. [*Raton laveur*: raccoon. Reference is to the recurring item in Jacques Prévert's re-nowned song "Inventaire": "une triperie deux pierres trois fleurs un oiseau vingt-deux fossoyeurs un amour le raton laveur . . ."]

Chapter Eight. "Let me have some pâté, but *your* pâté"

1. [*Faucon*: hawk; *grange*: barn; *campagne*: countryside.]
2. [*Salaisons*: once referred to salt-cured meats, but now often designates all products that don't require a cold room.]
3. [*Boudin (noir)*: blood sausage; *boudin à la viande*: white-meat sausage—veal, chicken, and/or rabbit—in fine intestine casing like *boudin noir*.]

Chapter Nine. "I sell Provence"

1. *Caillette*: large ball of ground pork and pork liver mixed with chopped Swiss chard, spinach, and spices and wrapped in caul fat. [*Panisse*: smooth batter of chickpea flour and water, thickened over the heat, cooled, cut into squares, and fried in olive oil like polenta.] *Tapenade*: spread made of crushed black olives, anchovies, pine nuts, and olive oil; some recipes call for capers. [*Fougasse*: hard-crust oven- or cinder-baked bread usually made with olive oil.]
2. [*Parler pointu*: speak French with what in the Midi is heard as a "northern" or Parisian accent.]
3. [*Pan bagnat*: open roll daubed with olive oil and topped with tomato and onion slices, tuna, hard-boiled egg.]
4. [*Tian*: Provençal earthenware baking dish and, by extension, what's cooked in it, often fish and vegetable dishes au gratin.]
5. [Reference is to the French tennis champion Yannick Noah.]

Chapter Ten. Ordinary Authenticity

1. [Ain: name of the *département*.]
2. [*Images d'Epinal*: widely diffused, nineteenth-century colored prints made in the eastern, paper-producing city of Epinal and featuring a vast variety of popular sub-jects (fables of La Fontaine, Napoleon's campaigns, peasants working in the fields); the term connotes images of national history and culture familiar to every French person.]
3. Fernand Braudel, *Civilization and Capitalism, Fifteenth to Eighteenth Century*, vol. 2: *The Wheels of Commerce*, trans. Siân Reynolds (New York: Harper and Row, 1982–84), 55. Originally published as *Civilisation matérielle, economie et capitalisme, XVe au XVIIIe siècle*, vol. 2: *Les jeux de l'échange* (Paris: Armand-Colin, 1979), 42.
4. Jean Baudrillard, *Le système des objets* (Paris: Denoël-Gonthier, 1972), 196–97.

Chapter Eleven. The Truffle Circle

1. A *lot* is a land parcel leased out to a truffle hunter for five-year periods during which he or she has exclusive rights to *caver*, excavate truffles. Also designates the batch of truffles a *rabassier* brings to market on any given day.

2. There are approximately thirty varieties of truffle. A few may be found in the Vaucluse, among them the summer truffle (*Tuber aestivum*), black on the outside with whitish flesh; the *brumale*, which resembles the melanosporum but with slightly looser mottling, the *nez de chien* [dog's nose] (*Tuber rufum*), which ranges from gray to rust in color and is not of great gastronomical value. On the Carpentras market the only truffle officially traded is the finest, i.e., the black Périgord, characterized by powder-grain black and white marbled flesh called gleba.

3. On the botanical properties of truffles, see Jean Rebière, *La truffe du Périgord* (Périgueux: Editions Pierre Fanlac, 1981). See also Jean-Marie Rocchia, *Truffles, the Black Diamond and Other Kinds*, trans. Josephine Bacon (Avignon: Editions A. Barthélemy, 1995). Originally published as *Des truffes en général et de la rabaisse en particulier* (Avignon: Editions Barthélemy, 1992).

4. In 1970, on the initiative of two researchers, Grente and Delmas, the Institut National de la Recherche Agronomique (INRA) requested permission to "sow" black truffles by planting species that foster the symbiotic relation required by these fungi. In 1972, a mycorrhized seedling was developed and patented by ANVAR (Association Nationale pour la Valorisation et l'Avancement de la Recherche [national association for promotion and advancement of research]). These plants, called INRA-ANVAR, are sold today by the Agri-Truffe company. The term *truffière* designates any spot where truffles are likely to be found. There are natural ones (the foot of this or that individual tree) and "artificial" ones, that is, places where truffle-producing trees have been systematically planted. For many centuries the truffle was gathered exclusively in the wild. Domestication was attempted only in the nineteenth century.

5. Truffle excavation begins only in mid-November. The market is particularly active during the winter holiday season, though the best truffles are not to be found before January. Truffle gathering generally ceases after mid- or late March. The cycle of nature thus knits up with liturgical and festive time and the economic calendar to determine activity peaks and declines.

6. *Picholon* or *piochon*: tool used to excavate truffles; *biasse*: truffle-gathering sack; *banaste*: large basket in the shape of a barrel once used by peasants for transporting vegetables to market.

7. This is where the event took place at the time of my study. The Bar du Théâtre has since closed and the truffle market is held in front of the Hôtel de l'Univers café, on the other side of the Place Aristide-Briand.

8. A "musky" truffle has an intense black peridium difficult to distinguish from that of the melanosporum, while the inner marbling appears less tight. Above all, it is foul smelling and tasting. Regulations specify that it must be sold separately from the

other types, along with broken truffles and truffles weighing under five grams (cf. *Journal Officiel*, Nov. 5, 1960).

9. Cf. Michèle de La Pradelle, "Il tartufo, lo se scambia un po religiosamente," in *La Ricerca folklorica* 20 (1990).

10. Annual French production of *Tuber melanosporum* has fallen continuously in the last century. From the late nineteenth century to the present, the fall was from 800–1,000 metric tons annually (2,000 tons according to A. D. Chardin in *La Truffe* [Paris: Baillière, 1992]) to between 20 and 30. In the catastrophic "campaign" of 1989–1990 it plummeted to 10 tons. The truffle's rarefaction is linked to changes in farming—decrease in small hillside farms and increased planting of conifers—neglect, and lack of interest in a product requiring so much patience at a time when farmers are increasingly forced to consider immediate profit.

11. Pierre Bourdieu, *Outline of a Theory of Practice*, trans. Richard Nice (London: Cambridge University Press, 1977), 173. Originally published as *Esquisse d'une théorie de la pratique* (Geneva: Droz, 1972).

Part Four. Pleasure of the Agora

1. As Richard Sennett points out in *The Fall of Public Man* (Cambridge: Cambridge University Press, 1974), an open space is merely a void in which people may move; being open is not what makes a space public.

Chapter Twelve. Equality of Opportunity

1. In Carpentras, as explained, those tasks are carried out by Nicolas's office at the *marché-gare* and fall under the authority of the market commission. This was not always the case. In the nineteenth century, when stallholder selling was mixed in with the various specialized, wholesale producer-markets in one vast space, the resulting complexity required the services of numerous, diversified city hall personnel: employees to collect city entrance and usage fees as well as customs and weighing fees; weighers; circulation monitors and security guards. For specialized markets, management rights and spot-fee collection were granted by adjudication. This system was gradually abandoned after 1850, when the municipality again took exclusive control of its market space.

2. In cities with long stallholder waiting or "call back" lists, spots left open by "subscribers" who have notified the *placier* of their absence on a given day are sometimes reserved for these stallholders. As he proceeds through the city, the *placier* determines which candidate to attribute a vacant spot to by position on the list. On markets in Mâcon and Lyon, see Danièle Bonniel, "Ethnographie d'un milieu urbain: les marchés forains," in *Cahiers de Recherche* 4, Université de Lyon II, ERA 631 (1983);

on the market in Tarbes see Rolande Bonnain, "Le système des places marchandes des Hautes-Pyrénées," in *Etudes rurales* (Apr.–Dec. 1980): 231–46.

3. [*Gauche populaire*: fraction of the left whose stated priority was traditional social welfare goals, as opposed to the *"Deuxième gauche,"* more open to addressing issues of management efficiency.]

4. [Rungis: the vast wholesale food market just south of the capital that supplies the greater Paris area; built after the 1970s demolition of the centrally located Les Halles market, "the belly of Paris."]

5. Karl Marx, *A Contribution to the Critique of Political Economy*. http://www.marxists. org/archive/marx/works/1859/critique-pol-economy. [*Cours des Halles* refers to both the rates or prices (*cours*) determined at the main wholesale food market and the site of that market.]

Chapter Thirteen. All at the Market, All in the Same Boat

1. This condition is not met equally on all markets. At a rural market like the one in Monteux, for example, most people are in fact acquainted with each other.

2. Cf. Alain Metton, "Contribution à l'étude géographique du commerce en banlieue parisienne" (doctoral thesis, Université de Paris I–Sorbonne, 1978), and Christina Nordin, *Marchés, commerçants, clientèle: Le commerce non sédentaire de la région parisienne* (Göteborg: Cinor, 1983).

3. In 1985 the service sector accounted for 47 percent of occupied persons.

4. [*Bastide:* typical Provençal villa.]

5. Elias Canetti, *Crowds and Power*, trans. from the German by Carol Stewart (New York: Seabury, 1978), 29

6. Cf. "La résidence comme enjeu," in *Urbanisations et enjeux quotidiens*, ed. Gérard Althabe, C. Marcadet, Michèle de la Pradelle, and Monique Sélim (Paris: Editions Anthropos, 1985); also Monique Sélim, "Rapports sociaux dans une cité HLM de la banlieue nord de la région parisienne" (doctoral diss., Ecoles des Hautes Etudes en Sciences Sociale, 1979), and Jean-Louis Siran, "Les nouveaux villages de la région parisienne" (doctoral diss., Université de Paris V, 1980).

7. Sennett, *Fall of Public Man*, 81.

8. See Françoise Kerleroux, "Le marché, une routine commerciale transformée par le jeu," in *Langage et société* 15 (1981): 58. Also Jacqueline Lindenfeld's analyses, which mention "the somewhat aggressive nature of relations between customers and sellers" ("Le marché dans la ville," *Langage et société* 33 [1985]: 26). Most studies of markets make similar assertions. Danielle Bonniel, for example, who studied the Lyon market, sees this way of roughing up the customer as a sign of the "tension" inherent in any business exchange situation because of the opposed interests of the two partners, a tension said to be particularly sharp in the "immediate competition" characterizing the market, and reduced by recourse to banter. These views have much in common with Ulf Hannerz's, for whom "relationships of provisioning" are "asym-

metrical" by definition, with the merchant "coercing" the customer (*Exploring the City: Inquiries toward an Urban Anthropology* [New York: Columbia University Press, 1980], 103).

Chapter Fourteen. In Full View

1. [*Gare Saint-Lazare*: one of Paris's biggest, busiest rail and public transport stations.]
2. Hannerz, *Exploring the City*, 105–6 (internal quotation is from Erving Goffman).
3. Ibid., 219.
4. "His movement is quick and forward, a little too precise, a little too rapid; he comes toward the patrons with a step a little too quick, he bends forward a little too eagerly. . . . All his behavior seems to us a game. . . . But what is he playing? We need not watch long before we can explain it: he is playing at *being* a waiter in a café . . . the waiter in the café plays with his condition in order to *realize* it." Jean-Paul Sartre, *Being and Nothingness*, trans. Hazel E. Barnes (New York: Washington Square Press, 1992 [1956]), 101–2.
5. Erving Goffman, *The Presentation of Self in Everyday Life*, vol. 2: *Relations in Public*: *Microstudies of the Public Order* (New York: Basic Books, 1971), 146.
6. [*Tomme:* generally unripened, low-fat farm cheese.]
7. ["La Famille Fenouillard": film based on a well-known late-nineteenth- and early-twentieth-century picture book series about a happy, discombobulated family and their travel misadventures.]

Chapter Fifteen. Generalized Friendship

1. "The Provençal temperament has a unity to it whose principal component is sociability," wrote Fernand Benoît. "The community framework in which Provençal people live and move, grouped together in villages or towns, has created points of contact that we would seek in vain in regions where settlement is sparse and the social cell is the household." *La Provence et le Comtat Venaissin* (Paris: Gallimard, 1949), 25.
2. [*Tabacs*: state-franchised tobacconist shops that also sell stamps and usually double as cafés.]
3. Not to mention Masonic lodges and the three confraternities of penitents, black, gray, and white, founded as charity associations, though at the end of the century they were active above all in the battle against anticlerical republicans.
4. In *The Republic in the Village: The People of the Var from the French Revolution to the Second Republic*, trans. Janet Lloyd (New York: Cambridge University Press, Editions de la Maison des Sciences de l'Homme, 1982), Maurice Agulhon notes the importance of such forms of organized sociability in Provence at that time. Originally published as *La République au village* (Paris: Plon, 1970),
5. [Aurès mountains, Algeria, where many French soldiers were assigned to duty during the Algerian war of 1956–62.]

255

6. I do not mean that these are "optional" verbal exchanges with "the status of orna-
ments in a vocal piece" as opposed to the "utilitarian communication" required by the
transaction. This distinction, used by sociolinguists such as Kerleroux ("Le marché")
and Jacqueline Lindenfeld ("Etude des pratiques discursives sur les marchés urbains," *Modèles linguistiques,* vol. 4, pt. 1, 1982), seem to me to miss what makes
the market situation specific.

7. Georg Simmel, "Soziologie des Geselligkeit," opening speech at the first congress of
the German Sociology Society (Oct. 9–12, 1910). English trans. Everest C. Hughes,
in *American Journal of Sociology* 55 (Nov. 1949): 259.

8. [*Grandes écoles*: the most rigorous, prestigious higher learning institutions in France;
in contrast to the university system, admission to the limited number of places in the
grandes écoles is by nationwide competitive exams called *concours*; these schools are
commonly understood to train "the elite of the nation."]

Chapter Sixteen. "Do you still make those little *caillettes* of yours?"

1. [Reference is to the late-nineteenth-century cookbook by Jean-Baptiste Reboul, *La
Cuisinière Provençale.*]

Chapter Seventeen. In the Forebears' Footsteps

1. "I, Raymond, Count of Toulouse, hereby recognize . . . that the fair [*forum*] that has
existed since ancient times in the city of Carpentras, together with all the revenues
deriving therefrom, belong to the bishop. I further agree that in no place between the
Ouvèze and the Sorgue shall any fair be established but in Carpentras" (Charter of
1155).

2. *Mémoire statistique sur le département de Vaucluse* (Carpentras: Imprimerie Quenin,
1808). [Myriametre = 10 km.]

3. "Leis embarras dou marca de Carpentras."

4. R. Fayot and C. Tiran, *Mazan, histoire et vie quotidienne d'un village vauclusien* (Carpentras: Editions du Nombre d'Or, 1979), 168.

5. The city was afflicted by three scourges in the space of twenty years: the discovery
of an artificial dye, alizarin, which ruined the madder plant (*garance*) industry; the
diseases that ravaged silkworm farms; phylloxera, which devastated the vineyards.

6. [*Chasse au poste*: hunting from a fixed position to which game are driven or birds
drawn.]

7. See for example the municipal decree of March 13, 1878, in which it is declared that
"the market for edible oils held in this city for many years is taking up more space
every year and not being contained in the squares and streets designated to that effect. . . . This overflow undermines the ease and comfort of transactions. Conse-

quently there is reason to allocate a locale to this market which shall be for sellers and buyers a meeting place known to all, easily reached, and at the center of all commercial transactions."

8. [*Santons:* traditional painted clay figurines representing nativity scene figures in Provençal attire.]

9. [Ateliers Nationaux: construction sites and factories created by the short-lived Second Republic to provide employment.]

10. [Robert Sabatier: prolific French novelist.]

11. [Vincent Scotto (1876–1952): prolific Marseille composer of operettas and popular songs; "Sous les ponts de Paris" is one of the best known.]

Conclusion. A Moment of Utopia

1. "Sept marchés découverts aux quatre coins de Paris," *Libération*, Oct. 22–23, 1994.

2. Armand Lunel, *Jérusalem à Carpentras* (Paris: Gallimard, 1937), 66.

3. Ibid.

4. Armand Lunel, *Nicolo Peccavi ou l'Affaire Dreyfus à Carpentras* (Paris: Gallimard, 1926), 124.

5. Arlette Farge, ed., *Vivre dans la rue à Paris au XVIIIe siècle* (Paris: Gallimard, 1979).

6. [MJC: Maison des Jeunes et de la Culture, local youth and community activity centers and associations throughout France.]

7. Introduction to "La ville inquiète," *Le temps de la réflexion* 8 (Paris: Gallimard, 1987): 9.

8. [*Le Nouvel Observateur:* left-leaning weekly magazine with critical analyses of contemporary society.] At the time of this study, many middle-class inhabitants of medium-sized French cities were leaving the city center and moving into houses with gardens close by.

9. ["Les tyrannies de l'intimité," French title of Richard Sennett's *Fall of Public Man* .]

10. See Sabine Chalvon-Demersay's analysis of the fourteenth arrondissement in Paris in *Le triangle du XIVe* (Paris: Editions de la Maison des Sciences de l'Homme, 1984).

257

Index

Cathy (jewelry maker), 78–79
caver, 139, 142, 145, 252n1
caveur, 143
Cérès, Thérèse, 79
Ceret, Annick, 32, 95–96, 198
Cergy-Saint-Christophe, 233
Certeau, Michel de, 5
Chalon, Mme., 187–88, 227, 228, 230, 231, 237, 241
charcuterie, 43, Photo gallery
charcutiers, 32, 119
Chardon (wine-grower), 16
Charretier, Maurice, 40
Charvet, Henri, 133, 136
Chavance, Mme., 182–83
Chayanov, Aleksandr, 114, 250n4
city centers, *désertification*, 242
Clement V, Pope, 14, 247n29
Comtat Venaissin, 13–14, 115
Concarneau fish market, 3
la confection, 25, 32
"cornering," 97–98
Coste, Mme., 57–58, 61, 110, 112, 127, 216
"country pâté," 120, 125
Cours des Halles, 254n5
crafts, 26, 32, 34
craftspeople, 78–79, 118

Daspas (shoes), 189
daube, 107, 250n3
David (shoes), 101, 103
Delavigne, Mme., 63, 101, 136, 171, 209, 214, 231
Deleuze, Gilles, 250n2
Delvaux *(charcutier)*: on discounting, 170; on "homemade" products, 119, 121; on joking, 180, 181–82; on "local" products, 125, 129; on market ethnography, 75–76; on price slashing, 106–7; Provençal accent, 126; on stallholder aggressiveness, 183; on stallholder business requirements, 82, 84; on stall spots, 49

"Dentelles," 30
Deredjan (clothing), 75
d'Inguimbert, Malachi, 247n2
discounters, 164
display windows, 65
"distanced communication," 209
division of labor, 43
Ducros herb and spice company, 15
"dumping," 105
Duval, Jean-Michel, 217–19

economic anthropology, 2
economism, 2, 5
Editions du Nombre d'Or, 12
"embarras" (traffic jams), 41
episcopal palace, 28
Espenon (hardware): appearance as expert, 96; on Auchan, 67; on "catching" customers, 68; on demonstrativeness of market relations, 204, 205; on going to market as a child, 213–14; market circuit, 73, 74–75, 76; pricing, 105, 167; on product display, 66, 132; on suppliers, 103; on truffle market, 149–50
Estève (fairs and markets commission), 40, 44, 48
ethnic stereotypes, 192
exceptional-purchase goods, 75

fabric stalls, 28
"fairs and markets" commission, 40
Farge, Arlette, 240
Favier, M., 166–67
Favier, Mme., 127, 133–34, 167, 168, 189
Field, Jean-François, 41, 226
filoche, 146
fish stalls, 30
flâner, 155
Flunch cafeteria, 154
Fontaine de l'Ange, 29
Forum Neronis, 11
Forum novum, 41
Fouvot (herbs and spices), 29

261

Macaire (olives, nuts, dried fruit), 75
madder plant *(garance)*, 14, 247n31, 256n5
Mallarmé, Stéphane, 64
malls. *See* Auchan mall
Mannoni, Octave, 64
Manu (peanut seller), 165
"Marché aux vendanges," 228
marché forain (itinerant stallholder street market), 7
marché-gare, 3, 58, Photo gallery; café, 4; Château, 39; history, 14–15; *le petit marché*, 115; as a place of serious business, 17–19, 54; price-setting, 173; specific social fields developed around exchange, 19–20; wine grapes, 31
"Marchés de Provence," 235
Margairaz, Dominique, 73
market: ambiance, 102, 201; demand for, 1; as distinct and separate world, 153; "entertainment" function, 4; for geographers, 4; occasion to stage a representation of a shared local identity, 156; physical parameters, 26; "the Provençal market" model, 236, 240; as a utopian social world, 242–43. *See also* Carpentras market; market products; market relations; stallholders
market circuit, 73, 74–75, 82
market economy, and presumed irrelevancy of marketplaces, 1–3, 234–35
market gardening, 227, 228
"market men" *(sans domicile fixe)*, 73, 160
market prices, 105–7, 167, 172
market products, 102–3; assumed to be local, 123–30; "homemade" illusion, 117–21; myth of "freshness," 109–11; ordinary products, 132–37; reputed to be cheaper, 105; stall arrangement, 111–15
market relations: constructed on the model of the game, 53–54; crowd internal to, 190–91; effusiveness, 204, 205–6; equivalency of all players, 5,

20, 159–60, 233; freedom of, 71–72, 81–82; generalized friendship, 156, 201–10; illusion of practicing a bygone type of social interaction, 241; induce formation of a public space, 233; intervention of circumstantial identity, 196–99; "market utterances," 190; microsocieties around each stall, 201; observation activity, 192–93; pseudoconfidences, 208–10; self-identification tactics, 215–20; as social relations, 5–6, 7, 71, 80, 180, 201, 212; stallholder and buyer exchanges (*See* stallholders)
Martigues market, 163
Martinez, Mme., 44, 154, 202, 216
Martin *(fripier)*, 83, 85, 90–93, 98–100, 135–36, 168–69, 239
Marx, Karl, 6, 7, 254n5
meddling, 193
Meminians, 11
Midi societies, 240
MIN: Marché d'Intérêt National, 250n6
Mistral (olives), 29, 96, 140
money economy, 245n10
Montesquieu, Baron de, 6
Mont Ventoux, 8, 9, 30
Morin family, 29, 133
Muslim women, 176
mycelia, 141
mycorrhiza, 141, 252n4

Neboit, Suzanne (socks), 133
"negative reciprocity," 6
"neighborhood" markets, 74
Nicolas (director of *marché-gare*), 39, 49, 61, 173, 253n1
Nicolo Peccavi ou l'Affaire Dreyfus à Carpentras (Lunel), 237
Nîmes market, 163
Noah, Yannick, 251n5
noblet *(salaisons)*, 129
nonsedentary tradespeople, 249n1

263

Ricci (smocks), 29

Richaud, André de: "Charmes de Carpentras," 13, 237

Rodriguez *(viennoiseries)*, 75

Rousseau: on buyers, 131, 189; on buying as secondary activity for locals, 59–60; on freedom of market exchange, 71–72; market as opportunity to run into produce brokers, 206; on Provençal sociability, 202; sense of the market as traditional institution, 221–24; on social aspect of market, 201, 212

rural authenticity, 119–21, 134

Sabatier, Robert, 231

Sahlins, Marshall, 6

le Saint Clou (the holy nail), 247n24

Saint-Didier market, 3

Saint-Quentin-en-Yvelines, 234

Saint-Siffrein cathedral, 28

Saint Siffrein's Day festival, 32, 40, 60–61, 77, 144

sales techniques, 65, 67, 93–95, 96–97, 192

"Santa Claus logic," 135

Sartre, Jean-Paul, 255n4

Saulnier *(rabassier)*, 142

secondhand shop, 66

selling arrangements, 111–15

Semeuses (Millet), 238

Senegalese, 79, 164, 169

Sennett, Richard, 178–79

Simmel, Georg, 207–8, 245n10

"slave market," 31–32

Sollers, Philippe, 68

Spinelli, Jojo, 80, 188

spot drawing, 78, 160–65

staging: of freedom, 81–100; of ordinary products, 125, 132–37

stallholders: aggressiveness, 183; appropriate "look," 125–26; associated with itinerancy and nomadism, 239; attitude toward supermarkets, 105; business requirements, 82, 84; call-outs, 95, 179, 180, 181; concern about their "spot," 49–50, 82–83; creation of meaning, 124–25; discounting, 170; distanced relation to work, 92–93; encounters with customers, 85, 96–100; as "entertainment" specialists, 94–95, 191–92; faked aggressiveness, 182–84; "homeless," 77; impression as people who love their art, 96; impression of as "people from elsewhere," 72, 77–78; intimate knowledge of merchandise, 120; "itinerant merchant" card, 250n1; joking, 180–82; market as phase on the way to having their own shop, 86; narrow-range trade, 112–15; North African, 176, 182; pragmatic intuition, 49; pricing, 105–6, 167, 172; "regional" costumes, 129–30; "rounds," 73–76; sales techniques, 65, 67, 93–95, 96–97, 192; selling arrangements, 111–15; selling technique, 64–68; specialization, 132–33; spot drawing, 78, 160–65; stage-managing, 63–64, 194–96; staging of own freedom, 81–100; staging the "typical product," 125; two competing representations of nature, 111–15

stereotypes, 134

supermarkets, 44, 60, 67, 105. *See also* Auchan supermarket

Syndicat des Commerçants Non-Sédentaires, 90

terroir, 149

Thevet, Jacky, 27, 48, 53, 63

Tiberius Nero, 11

toilettes, 139

trufficulteurs union, 149

trufficulture, 141–42

truffière (truffle ground), 142, 252n4

truffle market, 143–51; archaic, authentic market, 15, 16, 238; delimited area, 17; demand always greater than supply, 19; professionals-only, 144; as a reference

265

truffle market (*continued*)
   point, 24–25; ritual formalism, 147–51;
   specific social fields developed around
   exchange, 19–20, 151; truffle broker,
   Photo gallery; truffle buyers, 144; truffle
   circle, Photo gallery; truffle *placier,* 145
truffles: major subject of Carpentras
   conversation, 144; mediating role, 151;
   "musky," 252n8; "natural product"
   par excellence, 139–41, 143; relation
   to weather, 141; scarcity, 141, 148;
   symbiotic fungus, 141; varieties
   of, 252n2; weighing a *lot,* Photo
   gallery
truffling, 142–43, 252n5

Tuber melanosporum, 140, 253n10

Valérie (bread), 85
vernissage ceremony, 150
Vieini (cheese man), 120
viennoiserie, 30, 75
"Ville moyenne" agreement, 30
"voyager" market, 77
voyageurs, 73

Wall Street stock exchange, 3
Weber, Max, 6
wholesale markets, 48
Wittgenstein, Ludwig, 54
wood and grapevine market, 58